MENTORING GOD'S WAY

Fulfilling the Great Commission

Tomas W. Schafer

S.MB
Sunrise Mountain Books
Boise, Idaho

Case Studies examples herein should not be construed to be any specific person or event. They are compilations of a variety of observations and experiences common to challenges, persons, reactions, and circumstances.

This book is available for bulk purchase from the publisher. Contact Sunrise Mountain Books, (208) 938-8338, or email the publisher at publish@sunrisemountainbooks.com

ISBN 978-1-940728-05-6

Published by Sunrise Mountain Books
13347 W. Tapatio Drive
Boise, ID 83713
www.sunrisemountainbooks.com

Printed in the United States of America
2016 First edition

Contents

INTRODUCTION

Mentoring is not accomplished by formula or pre-set rules. Mentoring is heart-based with many twists and turns that can defy traditional thinking. With this in mind, this book may be referred to as a guidebook that contains information that serves to give direction and advice without stifling the interaction.

The first section of this guidebook establishes the *who, what, when, where,* and *why* about mentoring, mentors, and mentees. The middle section is devoted to case studies of actual people and events of mentoring. They deal with issues that mentors face during their tenure. This section also contains a core element to mentoring—identifying and dealing with spiritual warfare. The third part of this section is the case study analysis of what actually happened. The last portion deals with important aspects to mentoring.

This guidebook can be studied and meditated on individually or as part of a group discussion between two or more individuals who feel led by God to be His servant mentors. Either way, personal, emotional, and spiritual growth can result from study and meditation of principles offered in this guidebook. It is highly recommended that prior to reading and meditating on the contents of this guidebook, the reader should go to God's Word, specifically in two books of the New Testament, 1 Corinthians 8 and 10, and 1 Timothy (especially chapter 1).

In 1 Corinthians 8, the Apostle Paul gives four main principles as guides for making good personal decisions about questionable areas of living a life Christ wants us to live. Mentors frequently encounter questionable areas with which they may not have previous personal experience; therefore, sound guidelines are in order to ensure the mentoring is done God's way. The four principles established by Paul are centered on the word *balance,* avoiding extremes that too often occur in ministry.

First, is to balance knowledge with love. Knowledge is a two-sided sword; it either becomes a weapon of destruction (e.g., Pharisees and legalism, the ways of the world), or it becomes a tool that builds, as in the case of mentoring and assisting mentees in building their relationship with Christ. A person can become "book smart," yet be clueless in performing even simple tasks. Much the same is true in ministry and especially mentoring. It's one thing to know *about* God, and quite another to *experience* God by seeking His Face through a personal relationship with Him and carrying out His will, plan, and purpose in the works He wants us to do. Acquiring knowledge alone should never be seen as more important than growing in God's grace.

Second, Paul states that authority must be balanced by discipline. Just because a person can do something doesn't mean they should or that God wants them to free-wheel as His servant.

Third, Paul exhorts followers of Christ to balance their experience with caution (Chapter 10). At the beginning of this chapter, Paul admonishes the Corinthians not to grow overconfident and fall into the clutches of pride, arrogance, and control, all of which are fueled by deception and temptation. In verses 1-22 of this chapter, Paul warns that privileges are no guarantee of success; that good beginnings do not equate to good endings; and finally, that only by following God's Holy Spirit can His chosen servant overcome deception and temptation. We will benefit from remembering that sins of pride, arrogance, and control resulted in Satan being forever banished from heaven and relationship with the Godhead.

Fourth, Paul's admonishment is found in verses 23-33 of chapter 10 where he exclaims that freedom must be balanced by responsibility. Without responsibility, freedom degrades into anarchy and lawlessness. This was exemplified by the number of false teachers who attempted to permeate the Corinthian church and undermine the followers of Christ. When God gives His elected minister the privilege of ministry, the responsibility of the minister is to build up weaker believers in Christ so that their faith becomes strong, and they are able to bear fruit. We are all called to be God's servant ministers, yet few follow through on this, His commandment.

Timothy was Paul's protégé, or mentee, and in his first letter to Timothy, Paul addresses the issue most affecting the young minister—the lack of encouragement. Timothy was stationed in a hotbed of immorality, the city of Ephesus. In addition to facing opposition from the heathen citizenry, Timothy did not have the respect of the early church members because of his young age. In the first chapter of this personal letter to his mentee, Paul exhorts Timothy to remain steadfast by teaching sound doctrine, proclaiming the Gospel, and defending the faith. In so doing, Timothy would remain on solid spiritual ground, capable of withstanding the storms that confronted him in that pagan city. Paul's advice to Timothy remains true for our modern day disciples, ministers, and followers of Christ.

As you read and meditate on these teachings by Paul, you can reflect on these truths and apply these principles to the case studies and determine how or if these principles were followed. Hopefully, after reading and meditating on the biblical principles in this guidebook, the Holy Spirit will guide you to many other readings in the Bible that can be applied to the true ministry that God has chosen you to do, so that He can proclaim you His "good and faithful servant."

ॐ

CHAPTER 1: **EARLY MODELS OF MENTORING**

First, we should establish a common background and vocabulary that will be referred to in Chapters Two, Three, and Four. This will help us as we deal with the contemporary mentoring challenges in the case studies presented later in the book. Ready? Let the curtain rise on this first century scene which gives an early model for elements of mentoring.

ॐॐॐ

In the cool early morning, Marius stood leaning on the balcony of his spacious villa looking down at the courtyard where his son Flavius was practicing swordsmanship with his instructor. His lowered head was anchored by massive shoulders. His long, strong arms created ample support for his muscular frame to watch the movements taking place below him. The soft morning light, combined with the dust from the movements of the two participants, created a shroud, making it difficult for Marius to identify Flavius. The fifteen-year-old youth was in his second year of training and had already proven to be an eager student.

Marius proudly followed the footsteps, lunges, and sword thrusts by Flavius. He was pleased to see the progress his son was making in learning techniques of swordsmanship and hand-to-hand combat that he, too, had been taught years before. Marius was confident that his son Flavius would progress with his weaponry training, and would qualify within ten years to become a centurion similar to what his father had accomplished. As the oldest son of his military commander father, Flavius was expected to join the ranks of the great Roman army. His performance and courage would determine his future role as a leader in the military or other service in the Roman government. He was exhibiting talent, intelligence, courage, and an eagerness to follow his father's chosen path. Seeing this, Marius was more determined than ever to make sure that Flavius would get all the necessary knowledge and training to ensure his success.

The clanging of the swords and the grunts of the combatants in the courtyard were interrupted by a slave servant who approached Marius, announcing the arrival of his special guest. Marius nodded his acknowledgement, thanking the servant, and turned to greet his special friend. Marius extended his arms to greet this man whom he loved like a father. His broad smile was followed by a hearty welcome to Cato as he led him to a comfortable seat awash in the early morning light. After their friendly exclamations, they settled into the soft lounges. The slave servant reappeared with a tray and stood by, awaiting the approval of his master. Marius was pleased with the tray of food and drink, wanting to provide the best for his long-time friend whom he deeply loved and respected. He dismissed the servant with an approving nod, and the servant discreetly disappeared from the room, leaving the two men to their discussion.

Marius savored the company of his loyal friend and was in no hurry to address his real purpose for their meeting. He listened intently as Cato relayed events that had taken place in his life since their last meeting so many years earlier. Cato was soft-spoken, direct, and riveting as he told his tales. Marius enjoyed visualizing how Cato's challenges and decisions had taken place. He always admired Cato's uncanny ability to describe events in such a way that Marius felt he had actually been there with him. He appreciated Cato's careful and colorful descriptions and, as always, he vicariously participated in his friend's experiences, temporarily forgetting his present surroundings, focusing only on Cato's stories.

Cato indeed had a plethora of experiences that spanned the twenty years since he had last been involved with Marius. For a brief period of time, Cato had tutored Caesar's middle son in matters of government and diplomacy; but this assignment had terminated when the youth rebelled and failed to do the required lessons imposed by Cato. Cato had also served as a mentor for two young leaders of a conquered tribe of nomads, teaching them about the Roman culture, legal system, and various gods that the Romans venerated. He confided to Marius that this assignment had been extremely rewarding, for he had learned much about some perplexing aspects of the nomadic tribe's culture and belief system.

Cato felt gratified to have helped these young men become strong leaders to their people as they adapted to the Roman culture. He went on to tell Marius about his most recent experience of three years during which time Cato counseled a diplomat who had been assigned to a conquered region inhabited by a peculiar people known as Jews. Cato's knowledge of the Jewish religious beliefs and cultural mores were valued by the diplomat who was about to become a governor over these conquered people. Providentially, Cato had earlier acquired this knowledge from a Jewish slave who had been purchased by Caesar during the time Cato was attempting to instruct Caesar's rebellious son.

Marius marveled at the diverse talents and skills of his friend Cato, and his willingness to be of service to the Roman government. What Marius especially admired about Cato was that he had once been a slave and had impressed his master with his wealth of knowledge and experience. Because the master had benefited greatly from Cato's background, the master responded, as was the custom of the time, and paid for Cato's freedom and his Roman citizenship. Along with this new freedom, his master had arranged for a name change for him, as well. He dropped his birth name in favor of the name his master felt was truly appropriate for him--Cato, meaning "wise one." It was appropriate, reflecting his maturity, perception, and ability to control his emotions and actions during times of duress.

Cato humbly accepted the freedom and his new name, and soon afterward, based on plaudits and referrals from his former master, Cato was sought out by prominent Roman politicians, military leaders, and businessmen to assist their various needs. Cato had quickly achieved a reputation that extended well into the expansive reaches of the Roman Empire. Along with his reputation came a comfortable new lifestyle.

Cato's honesty, character, deep sense of fairness, and refusal to gossip or disclose intimate information concerning his clients were valuable traits. These traits propelled him beyond typical political or religious limitations. Cato valued his Roman citizenship, yet he was bold in disagreeing with those in authority, often pointing out their limited thinking or errors in their point of view. Despite expressing opposing views, Cato never lost his temper, always being mindful that his suggestions might not be acted upon and that his client might even vehemently disagree. Because Cato was non-political, politicians trusted him and were more easily influenced by his advice. Roman politics of the first century were filled with intrigue, power alignments, and betrayal.

Therefore, a man of Cato's reputation was valued by all who knew him—even politicians.

After Cato ceased sharing his latest experiences with his long-time friend, the two stopped to enjoy the bountiful food on the tray. As they ate, topics of discussion were widespread, based on the many interests they had in common. Marius told Cato about an experience that occurred with Flavius, and they laughed about how similar it was to what the two old friends had shared years earlier. Cato was fifteen years older than Marius, and their relationship was similar to a close father and son relationship. When the friends locked eyes there was an unwritten understanding and communication that went directly to the other's heart. Their father-son-like relationship was special, built on a strong bond of trust, mutual respect, and willingness to listen.

Soon after their shared meal and laughter over life's twists and turns, they settled back into the softness of the lounges. Marius moved slightly in the direction of Cato. He began to speak earnestly to his friend, "Cato, you have been and continue to be a big part of my life, and I'm so grateful for all that you've done for me, helping me through great difficulties. You taught me many valuable lessons. Without you, I know I wouldn't be in the position I am in or have the relationship with Flavius and my other children that I do." Marius paused as he looked steadily into his friend's eyes. He sighed deeply and continued, "I've received orders from Caesar to go north into the land inhabited by the Turks and assist the governor there in controlling the people. The governor is weak and Caesar is training a replacement. He wants me to provide stability to the region until the new governor arrives." Marius paused again, letting Cato absorb this news. Then he added, "The current governor knows nothing about his replacement. He knows only that I am becoming his military commandant. He welcomes my presence and the fact that Caesar has answered his request for a military leader."

Again Marius stopped, and Cato nodded his head in silent understanding. Then he sat upright and leaned forward. Bringing his hands together, Cato paused to gaze silently into his friend's eyes, searching for the emotions that Marius was containing. He took a deep breath, slowly exhaled, and said, "Marius, this is a great honor that Caesar is entrusting to you. It reflects the confidence he has in your ability to serve Rome—especially your ability to keep a difficult situation from becoming an open rebellion. I am very happy for you and know that you will not fail in your assignment." At this, Cato detected relief in Marius' facial expression, so he continued, "You are well prepared for this assignment—but tell me, my friend, what is it that you desire of me?"

Hearing these words, Marius was quick to reply. "I must leave within the next twenty days. Caesar prefers that I depart for the north next week, but I requested time to make arrangements for Flavius. It will not be possible for him to accompany me initially because of the uncertainty. Once the new governor is established and the transition complete, he can join me for the duration of my assignment there. We have discussed this, and Flavius is disappointed over not being able to come with me. He believes he's ready to be my assistant."

Both Cato and Marius chuckled at Flavius's eagerness and his impetuous assertion that he was ready to deal with situations involving grown men. Marius sighed and continued, "Flavius is very dear to me and knows my deep love for him. He is mature enough to handle this separation. We do not wish that it to be this way, but look forward to that time when we can be reunited. His young brother Darius and sister Penelope are taken care of by relatives and will be in good hands, but it is Flavius who needs guidance."

Cato, anticipating Marius' request, momentarily closed his eyes, then quietly urged, "My dear friend, my heart goes out to you and to Flavius, so please make your request known to me."

Marius dropped his head, nodding thoughtfully, and his shoulders relaxed as he considered his next words. Then he raised his head, smiled, and looked earnestly into Cato's eyes. "It is my sincere desire that you would do for Flavius what you did earlier in my life with me. Be a substitute for me and mentor my son, my blood, and prepare him the way you prepared me to be a worthy servant to Rome. Flavius is training to be in the Roman army and wants to become a centurion, following in my footsteps."

Cato reached across the short expanse separating the two men and firmly grasped Marius' hands. Leaning forward and returning Marius's smile, he said, "It would indeed be a privilege and an honor to do this for you, but we both know the decision isn't mine, it's that of Flavius. He must be in full agreement for this arrangement, otherwise it won't succeed."

At that moment, the sound of a warrior's heavy sandals striking the tile floor interrupted the exchange between Cato and Marius. The cadence of the footsteps grew louder as the warrior approached from the rear of the room. Peering over Cato's shoulder, Marius began to see the image coming out of the shadows. Cato followed Marius' eyes and turned toward the sound of the footsteps.

The light entering the room from the nearby balcony glistened on the metal of the warrior's breastplate, his sheathed sword handle, and the helmet he held in his hand. The young warrior strode purposefully toward the seated men who had turned to face him. Standing erect, the warrior looked towards Marius and said, "My father, I have silently listened to your conversation and I thank you for your love and desire of wanting the best for me."

Flavius turned towards Cato and bowed respectfully. Straightening, he looked him in the eye and stated, "Cato, it would be my privilege and honor to receive your wisdom, that I may bring honor to my father and continue our family tradition." Gazing intently into Flavius' eyes, Cato deliberately nodded. Flavius then added, "My hope and prayer is that you will find me worthy." At that, Cato unhesitatingly affirmed his willingness to mentor Flavius. Marius stood and embraced his son tightly. He then motioned for Flavius to sit between himself and Cato, and the three men began to discuss what was to lie ahead.

❧❧❧❧❧❧❧❧❧❧

The ending of this brief narrative is the beginning of a shared journey of discovery by three close-knit people into the uncharted waters of mentoring. Each participant on this journey has a certain idea of where the winds of hope, knowledge, and experience will carry their vessel. But there are also unknown aspects that each man will contend with and personally address throughout the entire journey.

Similar to any journey, theirs will start out on calm, tranquil waters; but shortly after leaving the harbor, they will encounter turbulence that requires skill, sound decision-making, and adjustments to the elements. If the turbulence is not adequately addressed, their vessel will flounder and sink into the dark abyss. The single certainty of this journey, as in all journeys, is that where the three men begin is not where they will end. Journeys are a process and not a destination. Mentoring is also a process, not a destination.

Our three travelers are embarking on the journey of mentoring from the perspective of three different roles: Cato being the mentor, Flavius the mentee, and Marius the parent/mentor, delegating his responsibilities to one trusted, wise, and knowledgeable. Flavius states the purpose of his journey is to learn all that would be necessary for him to follow in his father's footsteps of becoming a man, continuing their family tradition of military service, and being a responsible Roman citizen.

Cato's purpose is to make sure Flavius reaches his goals, and fulfills his purpose successfully. Marius, father and esteemed Roman commander, knows his responsibility as a parent requires him to do what is necessary to ensure there is no gap in this important learning process of his son. What Marius had initiated with Flavius in his younger years is about to suddenly face a major interruption that potentially could hinder or destroy the vital teaching he has been giving his son.

Marius realized he needed a surrogate, but did not want to turn his responsibility over to just anyone. Therefore, he enlisted the services of his former mentor, Cato, who was genuine, trusted, and credible. Marius knew that while he was away, his son Flavius would obtain the best possible mentoring available, freeing Marius to concentrate on his assigned duties as Roman commander. Cato's character qualities are the same for today's mentors, whether secular or Christ-centered.

Each person's stated purpose on his journey is sufficient for our more detailed examination in the upcoming chapters about what mentoring is; who is a mentor; why the need for mentoring; how mentoring is conducted; and when and where mentoring takes place.

Our brief narrative of first century mentoring coincides with earlier Greek mentoring and is the basis for mentoring today, thousands of years later. The Greeks and the Romans understood the value of mentoring and fostered its involvement as part of the education process of their citizens, military commanders, government, and business leaders. Christ Jesus mentored His twelve chosen apostles during His three-year involvement with them. This brings to the surface a fact concerning mentoring—some basic principles are the same for secular as well as spiritual involvement. The attributes of Cato are also needed in a Christ-centered mentor. The desire and willingness of Flavius as a mentee are also requirements for those seeking a deeper relationship with Christ Jesus. Mentoring goals are the same--emotional strength and increased ability to deal with life situations. There is one notable difference, though. Secular mentoring serves a government or an organization, but Christ-centered mentoring serves a greater calling. It fulfills the Great Commission of Christ, who commanded His followers to make disciples.

჻

CHAPTER 2: **WHAT IS MENTORING?**

Mentoring is the process of imparting wise teaching/counseling by means of relational interaction to an individual who is receptive to the process.

This definition is inclusive for the two distinct forms of mentoring--secular and Christ-centered. Mentoring is significantly different than just teaching, tutoring, and counseling. This difference lies in the fact that true mentoring is relational; the mentor makes a concerted effort to know the mentee's feelings, emotions, and mindset, and how different stimuli impact the mentee, either positively or negatively. The relational aspect comes when the mentor reciprocates and shares his feelings, emotions, and mindset as well. Should the mentor or the mentee not be willing to share and relate inner feelings, then the interaction between the two would not be mentoring. It would be merely an impersonal exchange of information.

Because mentoring is relational, it is a process based on a series of interactions to reach a desired accomplishment, and therefore is not limited to a single event. The relational aspect of mentoring means that both the mentor and the mentee share details concerning themselves. This creates a bond of trust and connectedness that is essential to achieving the desired goals.

Secular mentoring is fundamentally centered on the mentee's goals. In our beginning narrative, Flavius openly stated his goals that paralleled his father's. His statement becomes the foundation upon which Cato can begin the mentoring process. Willingness to accept mentoring is crucial to the mentoring relationship. Having the mentee state his goals and purpose allows the mentor initial insight into the mindset of the mentee. The mentor then has a beginning point of reference for what is needed in the form of teaching and counseling to assist the mentee in his journey on the waters of self-discovery and growth.

During the mentoring period, the mentor will compare what the mentee says to what he is actually doing, and make suggestions when the desired purpose does not align with the actual implementation. Cato knew that Flavius' goals must also align with the duties and responsibilities of being a Roman citizen as defined by Roman law, tradition, and culture. Cato's mentoring had to adhere to the higher Roman authority; otherwise, both he and Flavius would be punished. In our narrative, Cato would be engaging Flavius in the secular form of mentoring. Cato, the mentor, would be assisting Flavius in government, developing character through honesty, ethics, leadership, and continuation of family tradition.

Cato would not be mentoring Flavius in military components of weapons or strategy despite the fact that Marius was a Roman commander and Flavius sought to continue the family tradition. Instead, Flavius would be instructed in military matters by someone other than Cato. Learning the military procedures would come from an instructor experienced in battlefield warfare. This person would be highly skilled in military matters and an instructor, but he would not be a *mentor.*

Because the Roman culture of the first century was polytheistic, Cato would spend time integrating the culture's polytheism with his studies of government, citizenship, and character development. Cato would stay within the boundaries of his knowledge and experience. He wasn't a diplomat, lawmaker, businessman, or spiritual leader; however his in-depth knowledge about these disciplines would allow him to teach them to Flavius in an instructional format.

In modern day mentoring, mentees may obtain assistance in specific areas from a variety of sources. One mentor may not be qualified to assist the mentee in all his desired areas. In today's complex society a mentee may receive assistance and guidance from specialists who help, but who are not actually mentors. These individuals are instructors or tutors focused primarily on the subject matter and less so on the mentee. There is little in the way of real relationship with an instructor. In contrast, a true mentor assists the mentee in taking the various puzzle pieces of instruction and helps put them together for the mentee's bigger picture and better understanding of life.

CHRIST-CENTERED SPIRITUAL MENTORING

Spiritual mentoring in many ways parallels secular mentoring. The big difference is that spiritual mentoring should be founded on obeying Christ's commandment stated in Matthew 28:18-20, known as the Great Commission to go into all nations, making disciples—followers of Christ Jesus. Spiritual mentoring, making disciples, must focus on how the mentee develops a growing relationship with Christ. Spiritual mentoring should never attempt to get the mentee to *blend* the worldly culture, morals and perspective with the mentee's relationship with Christ. Spiritual mentoring establishes the *difference* between following the ways of the worldly culture to the ways established in God's Word, the Bible. Spiritual mentoring does not include training or indoctrinating the mentee into any religion, denomination, or organization. Spiritual mentoring is not evangelizing. Evangelism is a complete and separate ministry.

A spiritual mentor must never espouse ritualism or denominational doctrines to a mentee with the purpose of converting that person to their particular preferences or persuasion. Spiritual mentors must never attempt to change a mentee to the mentor's personal viewpoint on politics, denominations, or their interpretation of how to have a personal relationship with the Godhead. This is the role of the Holy Spirit and the mentor must allow the Holy Spirit to do His work. (Read the book of John and Acts 1-3.) Spiritual mentoring should steadfastly rely on God's Word, the Bible, which is the only truth. It should not be tainted with ritualism, denominationalism, or religion. This is why it is imperative to know, understand, and follow Christ Jesus' example of mentoring that is modeled in the New Testament by Christ, and later, Paul, as they mentored and ministered to their disciples.

Nowhere in Christ's teaching or Paul's is there any reference that indicates ritualism or religion is the foundation for relationship with God, or will lead to eternal salvation. In fact, Christ rebuked the Pharisees for putting religion, tradition, and ritualism above following Him. Relationship with Christ is the essence of the Great Commission and the foundation of spiritual mentoring. Throughout his epistles, Paul admonished the various churches for combining Gnosticism and Judaism in their faith. The Gnostics and Judaizers were rebuked for their deviance from Christ's commandment when they attempted to include religion and ritualism in the making of disciples.

Paul's epistles repeatedly address this problem, especially in 1 and 2 Corinthians. The Book of Hebrews and the Epistle of James clearly address the how and the why of being a true follower of Christ, not merely a convert from one religion to another. Being a true spiritual mentor is predicated on following Christ Jesus only, and staying within the confines of His Word. In spiritual mentoring, the mentor always surrenders to the guidance, direction, and admonishment of the Holy Spirit. In essence, the mentor is a conduit the Godhead can work through to help His people grow in their faith.

WHO IS A MENTOR?

In our narrative, Cato was knowledgeable not only about Roman culture and law, but also about a variety of cultures and subject matter. Cato was also experienced, beginning with his tenure as a slave to his master, tending to his master's needs and desires, and later to the mighty Caesar. Cato exhibited fusing knowledge with experience. He was able to impart his worldly knowledge to his mentees so that they were able to understand and use their understanding. Mentees learned how to effectively adapt to their culture and to serve the authority governing their culture. This was the purpose of ancient mentoring and continues today. In spiritual mentoring, the mentee learns how to become a Follower of Christ Jesus as His servant, and how to turn away from the deception of the devil's usage of the flesh and the worldly culture. Cato's inner desire and thirst for knowledge were big factors in developing the breadth of his subject matter. His continued learning made him more valuable to a variety of people.

The descriptions of Cato revealed he was mature, direct, discreet, of strong character and ethics, an eager learner, and astute in dealing with people of strong opinions, even those who were heavily influenced by their emotions and feelings. Cato retained credibility by remaining neutral and in control of his own feelings and emotions. Cato was humble, a student of diverse cultures and personalities. He knew he could learn and benefit from interaction with different people. These same attributes are necessary for a spiritual mentor in today's fallen world that is continuing to spiral down. In spiritual mentoring, the mentor learns about different cultures and the ways of the world, but never embraces them or makes them foundational to his mentoring.

Cato's versatility was necessary to his effective mentoring, as opposed to merely teaching, tutoring, or counseling a mentee. Teaching, tutoring, and counseling are stand-alone entities, but are also component parts of the greater entity, mentoring. A mentee's needs and desires are such that a good mentor has both knowledge and understanding of diverse subject matter. This does not mean the mentor is an expert in each subject matter, but that the mentor can create the desire within the mentee to pursue further study on his or her own. Experience is a key component in both secular and Christ-centered mentoring.

It is important that an effective mentor realizes his weaknesses and limitations, is honest about them, and doesn't attempt to diffuse or hide them from the mentee. This sustains the relational aspect of mentoring. An effective mentor does not try to portray himself as an "expert." An effective mentor stays within his limits. It has been said the definition of an "expert" is a fool waiting to be exposed. "Experts" may be quick to boast of their accomplishments, degrees, and opinions; yet are not willing to continue learning or to admit their shortcomings. "Experts" are prideful of their status. The ancient Pharisees were "experts," exposed by Christ and His disciples. Mentors should never become "experts."

It is important to distinguish mentors from teachers, tutors, and instructors. Teaching, tutoring, and instructing are not the same as mentoring.

In tutoring and instructing, the emphasis is on imparting knowledge more than on developing relationships. In teaching, instructing, and tutoring, interaction with a student usually does not include relational aspects, due to the limited time spent on a subject matter and to the number of students in a class. Time restraints in modern day learning environments severely limit the potential for relational mentoring to flourish.

An instructor typically limits his participation with the student to a particular specialty and does not expand into other areas that require in-depth knowledge.

An example of a tutor is often found in professional athletics when a veteran player takes a rookie under his wing and refines his skill level at a particular position until the rookie can effectively compete at the high level associated with the sport. The tutor is often referred to as a mentor, but usually this is not the case. It's a misuse of the term, and an inaccurate meaning of mentor.

What adds to the confusion between these terms is how they are often erroneously used within the American culture. Even the dictionary defines each term by incorporating the other terms in its definition.

The point here is to show that tutoring, instructing, and teaching are component parts of mentoring but, individually, do not define mentoring. The purpose of Christ-centered mentoring is to help the mentees to seek a deeper relationship with the Godhead and to wean themselves from the ways of the world. Christ spent three years mentoring His apostles. Afterwards, the Holy Spirit continued with individual personal mentoring as He does today.

To facilitate real mentoring, mentees of the first century often would live with their mentors in the mentor's home. On some occasions the mentor would live with a young mentee in his parents' home. These two formats were prevalent during the Roman and the Greek empires and are documented in writings by both Plato and Socrates. Many renowned artists including Rembrandt, Picasso, and Salvador Dali began their careers living with mentors. A mentor's value was maturity and the ability to integrate subject matter with passion and experience and to spark that same passion within the mentee, and to become absorbed in their shared subject matter. Ancient mentors provided perspective to the mentee on how seemingly different areas of subject matter were part of a bigger whole.

Today, many churches, denominations, and organizations use tutoring as a prototype for spiritual mentoring. Their "mentors" must qualify according to their criteria, including, first and foremost, being a member of that particular church, denomination, or organization. The majority of these organizations do not adequately address the core issue of the mentor being spiritually mature and chosen by Christ. Unfortunately, too many churches today equate teaching a Sunday school class or a Bible study as being mentoring, and this simply is not the case. Spiritual mentoring is meant to take God's Word and show how to apply it to everyday life. Mere Bible studies may never go beyond the talk stage about God's Word. If there is little or no guidance on how to apply it to specific situations one encounters along life's journey, or how to use these encounters to glorify God and carry out His purpose, this lack becomes academic teaching, alone, not mentoring.

A true spiritual mentor must first have accepted Christ as personal Savior, then be spiritually and emotionally stable in Christ Jesus. They must receive His authorization to become His vessel in fulfilling the

Great Commission to make disciples of all peoples and nations. Authorized spiritual mentors are appointed and anointed by Christ through the Holy Spirit. In studying Matthew 28:18-20, it is learned that making disciples is mentoring and exampled by Christ's mentoring to His Apostles and later to Paul and in turn Paul to Timothy. Ancient spiritual mentors guided mentees in how to separate from the culture and from religion to become a true follower of Christ.

Paul's epistles reveal how time-consuming the making of disciples was and the various obstacles and dangers that needed to be overcome during this process. Christ and His Apostles were exposing the fallacies of religion and replacing it with a personal relationship with Christ. Personal relationship with Christ trumps religion and its various sub-forms. Religion in reality is an effective tool the devil uses to keep people from experiencing Christ through personal relationship with Him.

CHRIST-CENTERED SPIRITUAL MENTORING IS IMPERATIVE

Since making disciples is a divine commandment and not an option, it becomes our divine ministry to carry out God's plan and purpose. There are true ministries established by the Godhead, and it is the Godhead who chooses and equips the chosen one to carry out that particular ministry. It is not man or any of man's institutions or organizations. God lights the fire within the heart of His chosen vessel by means of His Holy Spirit Who then guides His chosen vessel in the direction He wants. Such is the case with mentoring. God, through His Holy Spirit, makes it known in the heart of the chosen one that He has an assignment for that person, be it mentoring or evangelizing, or something else. The foundation for being chosen is to have a vibrant, growing relationship with Christ; a willingness to follow Christ alone in all situations; and obedience in carrying out His plan and purpose. Simply put, it's a matter of heart that takes precedence over one's intellect, emotions, or preferences.

Relationship with Christ begins with accepting His eternal salvation and asking Him into one's heart. After receiving Christ's eternal salvation, that person then has the option (choice, free will) of merely believing in Christ or surrendering one's life to Christ by forsaking the worldly culture and its temporal, carnal, sinful pleasures. After the initial step of surrender, the process of building a vibrant relationship with

Christ ensues. This is a wonderful lifelong process, a journey. Through a series of tests and trials, Christ, through the Holy Spirit, is able to impart discernment and wisdom as well as humility and obedience into His follower, leading to His authorization for becoming a mentor. Should a person who is not spiritually mature in the ways of the Lord attempt to assume the role of disciple-mentor, it won't last. Christ will intervene and stop the efforts of this individual who is subject to His admonishment and rebuke. Very often this takes place through the mentee refusing to continue with the mentor. The Holy Spirit guides the mentee elsewhere.

In 1 Kings 19:16, God directs Elijah to go and minister to Elisha whom God chose to replace Elijah. This verse is important to understand that mentoring is directed by God and therefore is a ministry. After receiving God's directive, Elijah found Elisha. God had spoken to Elisha's heart earlier, preparing him to become a mentee of Elijah. By the time Elijah encountered Elisha plowing in his field, Elisha was mentally, emotionally, and spiritually ready to heed God's calling. The two men had no previous meetings with each other and each was on a separate path that would not have included interaction with each other. God had other plans and orchestrated their meeting and subsequent mentoring. Referring to this particular passage is a good reminder that mentoring is a ministry from God for whom He chooses, in His perfect timing. Ministry is carrying out God's plan and purpose as His servant, and not imposing our beliefs and opinions on others.

MENTORING IS NOT GENDER BIASED

In reading about Elijah, it is easily understood he was in a growing, close relationship with God, and blessed with spiritual maturity, discernment, and wisdom. These are key components to being qualified as a mentor. Also in the Old Testament it is revealed that being a mentor is not limited to the male gender. Read about Ruth and Naomi, a powerful depiction of mentoring. First, there was the agape love between the two women, that special love God wants us to have with our fellow members of His family. The more the two women interacted and had shared experiences this agape love created a deep affection that distinguished their relationship. An important aspect of the mentoring by Naomi to Ruth and Elijah to Elisha is *shared experience.* Shared experience becomes a foundation for connection between a mentor and mentee. This type of love is Christ-centered, focused, and resolved to be His servant.

A shared experience does not necessarily mean having the same perspective or conclusion. But the emotions and feelings that occur during a shared experience open the door to effective communication, another key component of mentoring. A shared experience does not necessarily mean that two people have it at the same time together. Two people can experience the joy of having children, the pain of divorce, or the loss of a loved one without incurring the experience at the same time. But the resulting emotions and feelings build a bridge, initially bringing two people together as a starting point to build a relationship.

Having a shared experience eases a person's wariness toward the other and assists in establishing credibility. An example would be three soldiers, two having frontline combat experiences while the third remained on base away from the heat of battle. The combat-experienced soldiers will form a quicker, deeper connection with each other much more easily than with the non-combat experienced soldier. They're all soldiers, but with a significant difference and perspective that forms each relationship. This example can be expanded into virtually every aspect of life.

Having a shared experience is not limited to age, gender, or ethnicity. A shared experience becomes the spark igniting the beginning of the relationship. Everything else is secondary. When mentees find they have several shared experiences with their mentors, they become the foundation for development of their relationship.

Once mentoring begins, there will be times when the mentor and the mentee create shared experiences, thereby solidifying and facilitating growth of the relationship. This camaraderie builds trust and opens the door of insight into the other person. The more trust, the easier it is for the mentee to be candid and address those personal issues impacting his life. Establishing mutual trust is part of the foundation for a vibrant, meaningful mentoring relationship.

EMOTIONS AND FEELINGS

Emotions and feelings are natural occurrences within a mentoring relationship. For this reason it is strongly advised that there be no cross-gender mentoring. Men should only mentor men, and women mentor only women. Back to the example of the three soldiers: in the military today it is common for women to have combat experience and to incur debilitating physical and emotional wounds. While a woman and a male soldier may have shared combat experience, the emotions and feelings accompanying this experience can cause an unhealthy and unstable relationship because men are wired differently than women. God did this at the very beginning with Adam and Eve and it continues today and into the future. In analyzing and meditating on the relationship between Naomi and Ruth, it becomes evident what God wanted accomplished could not have happened had either one been a male interacting with a female.

Another reason not to engage in cross-gender mentoring is the different roles each gender has within a given society and culture. Repeated exposure and participation in these society-mandated roles affects the mindset of a person and their acceptance of their role. In twenty-first century American society, acceptance of homosexuality raised the level of contention over accepted roles. The secular culture rejected the Biblical mandate pertaining to homosexuality, thereby allowing same-sex marriage as well as cross-sexual counseling and mentoring. Several denominations in America have accepted this secular deviation and have allowed these deviations to become part of their misguided spiritual counseling and mentoring.

An effective mentor must be mature, knowledgeable, experienced, emotionally balanced, have leadership qualities, confidence, discretion and empathy. In spiritual mentoring, put at the top of the list: acceptance of Christ's salvation, His authorization, spiritual maturity in Christ, a humble spirit with willingness to follow the guidance of the Holy Spirit, and God's personal authorization and commission. All of which brings us to the matter of age.

AGE

Sadly, in the 21st Century of American culture it has become the norm to displace a person once they reach a certain age. People who have experienced termination in the workforce at age 50 or older quickly learn how difficult it is to obtain new gainful employment. A stigma is attached that resembles a scarlet letter or flashing neon sign stating, "Too old; no longer qualified; out of touch; no longer relevant." Instead of being able to use the combined knowledge/experience to his chosen profession, the over-50 worker is put out to pasture or relegated to lesser meaningful positions or tasks. Many baby boomers of the 60's would say, "It's a bummer, man!" Indeed it is.

Thankfully, God doesn't treat His creation the way the world does. In fact, nowhere in the Bible does God state He has an age requirement, a retirement age, or even an early retirement plan. In fact, the opposite is true. Moses was approximately 80 years old when God said; "Hey, Moses, have I got an offer for you, let's talk." Moses was initially startled and he turned down God's proposal, but later accepted; and the rest, as they say, is history—and God didn't even have to spring for lunch. What a deal! Before Moses, there were Abraham and Sarah—what an example of God choosing those whom He favored to carry out His plan and purpose. Here's an example of two oldsters involved in changing the entire world!

Moses enjoyed a vibrant, strong, and enlightening relationship with God. To have this special relationship with the Lord God Almighty, it's necessary to surrender one's will to His. Moses declares this in Deuteronomy 6:4-9:

> *"Hear, O Israel: The Lord our God, the Lord is One! You shall love the Lord your God with all your heart, with all your soul, and with all your strength. And these words which I command you today shall be in your heart. You shall teach them diligently to your children, and shall talk to them when you sit in your house, when you walk by the way, when you lie down, and when you rise up. You shall bind them as a sign on your hand, and they shall be as frontlets between your eyes. You shall write them on the doorposts of your house and on your gates."*

In reading this passage, can you sense Moses' passion, enthusiasm, and pleading to the Jews? He was challenging them to become mentors. No doubt, the experiences, tests, and trials that Moses experienced during the first 80 years of his life factored into this passage.

Moses is saying that we should surrender our will to God's, 24/7/365. This commandment was not limited to just the ancient Jews, but is applicable to anyone who accepts Christ's salvation. The main qualification is to love God with all of who we are. This comes about with age and through life's experiences, tests and trials, success and setbacks, deception and temptation and learning, humility, and heart-felt thanksgiving. This passage can be summed up in the modern language of, "Each one, teach one." Not only is this passage a commandment, it comes with great responsibility.

MENTORS MUST BE DILIGENT

A word of particular note in the Deuteronomy passage is *diligently*. The dictionary defines this word as, "Marked by persistent, painstaking effort." Another translation from street jargon is, "It ain't going to be easy." It wasn't easy for Moses to be a leader and mentor to God's chosen people. Along the way, this man of God was bombarded with irritation, frustration, and at times even anger with the actions and inactions of the Jews and their refusal to surrender to the will of God. Yet Moses remained steadfast and persistent in following God's directive for him. Moses carried out God's plan and purpose without demanding that God make it easier or release him from his assignment.

NO DEGREES NECESSARY

Being chosen by God to be a mentor doesn't necessarily mean you need a college degree, or must have completed seminary training, or must be a member in good standing of a particular church or denomination. God measures the heart and graces those who earnestly seek Him, obey His commandments, have a humble spirit and a willingness to take that step of faith, as did Abraham. Our Heavenly Father prepares His mentors through tests, trials, pain, and suffering. He also blesses His mentors with the discernment, wisdom, and discerning spirits as they are necessary for mentoring His way.

Repeated doses of life experiences can result in a spirit of brokenness and an attitude of humility that God wants in those whom He chooses to be His servants. Humility is the opposite of pride, arrogance, and control—the evil factors that resulted in the devil being forever cast from heaven and denied eternal relationship with the Godhead. These same character traits of the First Great Fall are part of a person's sinful nature that begins at birth. They are traits the devil wants people to embrace and use throughout their entire life. Living a life based on pride, arrogance, and control results in missing out on a personal relationship with Christ—the greatest treasure man can receive.

Mentors are assigned to cut through their own pride, arrogance, and control, thereby allowing the Holy Spirit to use the mentor to model how personal relationship with Christ is vital to becoming a true follower of Christ. This was true of Moses, Paul, and the other Apostles. First came their individual brokenness, followed by surrendering to the Lord's will. Then they were empowered by the Holy Spirit to take action, carrying out God's plan and purpose for their lives. For Moses, Paul, and people today, first comes conviction, then transformation, then authorization from God to move forward in His power and blessing.

FIVE ESSENTIAL CHARACTER TRAITS

Moses, Paul, the Apostles, and anyone who truly is a follower of Christ Jesus today exhibits five traits necessary in surrendering one's will to Christ's:

1. A willing spirit
2. Courage
3. Persistence
4. Self-control
5. Humility

First, is a willing and cooperative spirit, letting Christ have His way in every aspect of their life.

Second, is exercising courage. It's not easy carrying out God's plan and purpose and often the temptation is to stop, turn around and to give-up.

Third, is by manifesting persistence. This requires tenacity, steadfastness, and determination to overcome adversity, discouragement, setbacks, and the spiritual warfare impacting one's emotions and feelings to give in.

Fourth, is controlling one's emotions and feelings that result in a positive attitude giving thanks, glory, and honor to God for being assigned the very task that can be daunting (read Isaiah 6).

Fifth, is the realization you are totally dependent on God's grace and mercy to carry out His assignment and become His follower. Self-reliance and independent action are tools of the devil. God rewards an attitude of total dependence on Him with wisdom, discernment, and power to see into the spirit world and overcome the deceptions of the enemy. As reference, read and study Jeremiah 29:11.

A Biblical example of living in pride and arrogance is found in Luke 18:9-14 when Christ spoke the parable of two men who prayed. I encourage you to read this passage then meditate on it and let the Holy Spirit fill your heart with discernment and wisdom. This passage addresses many people who have college degrees or completed seminary school and rely on intellectualism (not intelligence) to be a Godly servant. Their cerebral intellectualism approach and haughtiness is very similar to that of the Pharisee. There isn't a sincere humble bone in their body.

Let's take a minute to explain the difference between intelligence and intellectualism. Intelligence is the capacity to acquire and to apply knowledge. Intellectualism is the pursuit, development, and adherence to ideas in the abstract form. Intelligence is taking what is learned and applying it in practical situations. Intellectualism is keeping ideas in theory only, without any practical application or testing to determine validity. Intellectualism is rift with pride, arrogance, and control--all of which are attributes of the devil.

Advocates of intellectualism do not make good mentors despite the fact many will go ahead of Christ and engage in mentoring on their own or even make vain attempts to teach mentoring. When these prideful and arrogant people attempt to mentor, the mentee empowered by the Holy Spirit early on will discern who they really are and cease further involvement with them. When prideful and arrogant ones attempt to teach mentoring, their efforts ring out as hollow theory only, with no personal, battle-tested experience to add authenticity or credibility. "Experts" espouse intellectualism.

An example is found in the world of athletics when a person wears the uniform, learns the plays, but spends their time on the sidelines, never really playing the game. These are "wanna-bes" who often try to project themselves as real players. This is very common in other pursuits other than athletics. The parable in Luke 18:9-14 is Christ's way of exposing an "expert" who relies on intellectualism as opposed to being a humble follower. Read these passages carefully and remember the definition of who is an expert. Jonah, Balaam, and the Pharisees are examples of those who attempted to negotiate, manipulate, or interpret God through their intellectualism and not surrender their will to His. God rebuked them just as He rebukes modern-day counterparts. It's a matter of "when and how" His rebuke comes about, and not a question of "if."

Those who believe their intellectual, cerebral approach to the Bible is sufficient to serve the Godhead don't understand who God is looking for in choosing His ministers. God looks at the heart and wants to see compassion, empathy, and caring. This is why some of the better mentors come from the ranks of those who have endured alcoholism, drug abuse, sexual abuse, divorce, pornography, co-dependency, prison sentence, and other things that once took them out of relationship with God. Those who have surrendered their addictions to Christ have experienced the compassion and restoration of Christ, and use this for effective mentoring.

To be fair, not every person who has suffered addictions or abuse and other life experiences makes a good mentor or is chosen by God to engage in His ministry of mentoring. It's still God's choice and His alone, not man's. God always searches the heart, not the mind. It's not that these people can't become good mentors; it's that they are gifted for other ministry, or perhaps they won't surrender their will to God's thereby allowing Him to use them in His greater plan and purpose. Pride becomes an insurmountable barrier that is self-imposed by one's own choice.

Here are some questions to consider:

Where in the New Testament does it state that Christ looked favorably on the Pharisees or Sadducees?

Another question: what was Christ's attitude and teaching about the Pharisees and Sadducees?

Final question: how does Christ really see you in regards to being His servant?

Read Luke chapters 11 and 12; they are very sobering when answering these questions. In Luke 11:42-45, Christ rebukes the Pharisees for hindering and robbing the common people of the truth of God's Word that leads to having an eternal relationship with Him. James 3:1 is another sobering reference. In Luke 17, the good doctor teaches those things that really matter and emphasizes the sin of causing others to stumble. Luke fully understood that battle testing results in both the understanding and the courage of forgiving, rebuking in love, being faithful, preparing spiritually, and doing it Christ's way.

TIME FOR INTROSPECTION AND MEDITATION

Introspection at this point is good. Take some time and meditate on your current relationship with the Godhead.

Are you of a humble spirit similar to the tax collector in the parable Christ spoke about (Luke 18: 9-14) or are you more like the Pharisee?

How many times have you jumped ahead of Christ into areas the Holy Spirit did not direct you and what were the results?

Are you playing the religious game similar to that of the Pharisee?

Are you guided by your own intellectualism rather than the Holy Spirit?

This is a perfect time to "man-up" as the street jargon says, and go before the throne of Christ Jesus who sits at the right hand of the Father in full power, authority, and glory, and simply say, "Christ Jesus, my Savior, King and Shepherd, I want to follow You and be Your servant. Holy Spirit, lead me to repentance from my prideful, arrogant, and controlling ways. Cleanse and purify my heart." Do this and the door opens to Jeremiah 29:11.

Jeremiah 29:11

*"For I know the plans I have for you," declares the Lord,
"plans for good and not for evil,
plans to give you hope and a future."*

ॐ

CHAPTER 3: WHO IS THE MENTEE?

In our story depicting secular mentoring, the Roman youth, Flavius, is the mentee, but mentoring is not limited to involvement with youths, teenagers, or young adults. Mentees are not limited to those individuals going through the educational process.

By definition; *a mentee is anyone in need of understanding for coping with struggles and life changes.* Therefore this includes everyone. In spiritual mentoring, a mentee is *anyone who hungers for the Lord and seeks a closer relationship with Him.* These really aren't flippant answers because everyone, regardless of age, gender, profession, religious affiliation, geographic location, educational background, or experience level, has various mentoring needs throughout life's journey. A need or deficiency is a void incurred by what life, the world, and the devil do to a person. It is important that the mentor focus on the practical aspect of the mentee's need. The mentee wants relief, resolution, or guidance. They are not interested in, nor want the intellectual answer (academics) from the mentor. The spiritual mentor must always show the *practical* application of Biblical principles and tie these principles to his/her own life experiences. In doing this, the mentee gets a true understanding of Biblical principles. This combination gives shape, form, and life to God's Word in a manner that goes directly to the mentee's heart. This motivates the mentee's quest for more understanding of God.

The mentee seeks God's face and this leads the mentee to seek a deeper relationship with the Godhead and that is the essence of the Great Commission. It's interesting that Christ's commandment is to make disciples (learners, followers). It is not *per se* an evangelizing directive. The conviction comes only from the Holy Spirit. Once the lost one accepts Christ's eternal salvation, the shift is to become His follower and to carry out His plan and purpose. This is where mentoring is so valuable. The mentor has the responsibility to do it His way.

If you've never experienced hurt, pain, suffering, questioning, or disillusionment, then you may not ever have been mentored. Spiritual mentoring can and should address these issues. A Biblical perspective assists the mentee to gain spiritual maturity and to hear the voice of the Holy Spirit for counseling, teaching, comforting and guidance. Spiritual mentoring guides the mentee in separating from the secular world's cultural values, habits, and goals to being a follower of Christ with His values, teachings, and commandments. Spiritual mentoring addresses the need, shows the spiritual application, then, provides a solution that will honor God and not the worldly culture.

A mentee can be a mentor's child, sibling, friend, acquaintance, or even a perfect stranger, at first. It bears repeating that a mentee should *always* be a member of the same sex as the mentor. The issues impacting a mentee are such that an effective God-honoring resolution comes about from the same gender perspective. Having the same gender perspective assists in establishing understanding and the ability to get to the core of the issue. God wired men and women differently for His purposes, and man needs to stay within God's constraints—no exceptions. Cross-gender mentoring opens the door for the devil to deceive by means of emotions and feelings that become sensual, worldly, and not of God.

The Bible states that when a man and a woman become married, they become one in spirit, establishing a covenant relationship. The married couple share many life experiences, tests, trials, and tribulations together, yet may retain different perspectives along the way. When issues arise that put strain on a marriage, it is advisable for the couple to seek out a member of the same sex to confide their feelings and emotions. Both spouses become mentees.

The issues may prevent the couple from reaching a God-honoring solution when there is no wise counsel from a God-appointed mentor. Sadly, in the early part of the twenty-first century, the American divorce rate of Christian marriages equaled that of the secular world—one out of every two marriages. The devastation and ripping apart resulting from divorce has a great impact on the couple's children, family members, and close friends. No one is immune; everyone has a need. Everyone benefits from the guidance of a God-appointed mentor.

WHERE DOES THE MENTEE COME FROM?

Finding a mentee isn't the difficult part. God will guide the mentee to His chosen mentor. The mentor must be prepared to listen and then answer God's call when it comes. The vast majority of the time it's the mentee who seeks out the mentor and not the other way around. This reflects the conviction of the Holy Spirit and the individual's compelling desire to grow, or to repent from the ways of the world and its deceptive culture.

Mentees include those who are spiritually new in Christ and need guidance and direction in establishing their relationship with the Godhead. Mentees may be those who are lost, or Christians overcoming addictions, recovery from divorce, death grief, backsliding, or having difficulty in the workplace with unethical or deceptive practices. Mentees are those who are impacted by spiritual warfare that affects their walk with the Lord. Mentees may be inmates adjusting to life within prison walls, or adjusting to life on the outside after prolonged incarceration. The devil attacks everyday practical aspects of living, and the mentor must counter this attack with practical Biblical applications to be truly effective.

A mentee may be a pastor seeking direction in leading his congregation. A mentee may be a mentor struggling with burnout. A mentee is anyone seeking how to follow Christ, draw closer to Him in relationship, and separate themselves from the ways of the worldly culture and influence. A prime example of this is found in Acts 8 with the Ethiopian eunuch who verbalized his need to understand Scripture. His hunger and thirst for God was satisfied by the mentoring Philip. A mentee may be a lost soul who needs understanding and help for repentance. Assisting the lost soul in one of life's rough moments can be the spark that leads that person to accepting Christ's salvation.

Repeat this sentence: "*I* am a mentee; *I* have a need." Mentors are also sometimes mentees, not "experts." "Experts" never need mentoring—just ask them. Mentors realize their total dependency on Christ, through His Holy Spirit, to guide them in their God-chosen ministry. It is God alone who provides the necessary tools and strength to fulfill His commandment of the Great Commission.

There are classes available in both secular and Christian environments that teach an individual how to be a counselor (a part of mentoring). People who attend these classes learn techniques about life issues and become certified to counsel without having the actual life experience themselves. The counselor's effectiveness is often curtailed when they have no personal experience in these life issues. The lack of a shared experience severely limits the ability of the counselor to connect with the client because there is no common bond. Experience is a major plus and is part of God's training for His chosen mentors. Mentoring from a no-experience position is merely exercising intellectualism and the result often isn't effective or God-honoring.

THE BACKGROUND EXPERIENCE FACTOR

Background experiences establish an early connection with a mentee and influence the mentee's decision regarding his or her selection of a mentor. Mentees always look for those who have shared the same pain or a related pain as a potential mentor because that shared pain creates credibility, which leads to trust. Mentees never select a mentor whom they cannot trust.

When mentees cease a mentoring relationship, the primary reason cited is that the mentor didn't understand them or their perspective emotionally, spiritually, or physically. The mentor merely wanted to put forth his point of view and get the mentee to subscribe to it as well. This illustrates the importance of connecting, being on the same page as the mentee. Not being able to relate results in frustration for the mentee who then ends the mentoring relationship. Many times the impression left from this negative experience causes the mentee not to seek another mentor for quite some time.

Studies indicate that medical patients' main frustration with doctors and medical personnel is that they don't listen, understand, or empathize with the psychological impact of their ailment. This is commonly referred to as the doctor's "bedside manner" which factors prominently into a patient's obtaining another doctor or simply stopping treatment and communication with the doctor. Often the patient will confide with the nurse, however. In spiritual mentoring, a mentor's "bedside manner" is crucial to sustaining both the mentoring relationship and the mentee's growing relationship with Christ Jesus. Spiritual mentors certainly shouldn't be like the doctor with the detached bedside manner, nor should they perceive themselves that way. The spiritual mentor should strive to be more like the supportive nurse, available and listening.

In the Old Testament, Moses had sympathy and concern for his people, the Jews. His lack of control over his emotions and feelings led him to murder a fellow Egyptian. This act caused him to seek refuge in the desert where he was befriended by Jews led by Jethro. Moses then spent 40 years learning and experiencing the Jewish way of life and culture. This was necessary because the first 40 years of Moses' life were spent as an Egyptian with an entirely different set of mores, customs, traditions, and lifestyle.

Moses was mentored by Jethro, and when God determined Moses was ready, He assigned him to lead the entire Jewish nation (nearly three million!) out of bondage. Had Moses not experienced the Jewish culture and the feelings and emotions of bondage, he probably would not have been chosen by God to lead the Jews out of Egypt. The Jews simply would not have followed him. Even with their shared background experience, Moses still had difficult moments in leading the Jews to the Promised Land. Imagine what he would have done during those difficult times had he not been experienced with the Jewish mindset. The other main point to remember is that Moses did not elect to lead the Jews out of Egypt; God chose him and equipped him for this formidable assignment. This applies to mentoring and should never be forgotten!

THE WHEN AND WHERE OF MENTORING

Once God's Holy Spirit leads the mentee to the chosen mentor, what follows is determining when and where the mentoring will take place. Since mentoring is a relational process and not a single event, proper care should be utilized in selecting both the location and the time for each designated session. Mentoring should be sensitive to time but should never be dictated by the length of time. The time element is dictated by the mentee's desire to seek Christ Jesus and to grow in spiritual maturity. The attitude and involvement from the mentee in seeking relationship with Christ determines the duration of the mentoring relationship.

Allowing the mentee into the decision-making process for the when and where of the mentoring sessions shows the mentor's respect for the mentee. This respect leads to trust and helps sustain a good mentoring relationship.

Each mentoring session should be based on both the mentee's and the mentor's respective time schedule. Many mentees and mentors are employed, and their respective working schedules are the most common factors in determining the mentoring session. It can become a juggling act, and both the mentor and the mentee must be willing to make a sacrificial adjustment to allow mentoring to take place.

Sometimes a mentoring session can be scheduled to coincide with breakfast, lunch, or dinner. Other times, it may be held over coffee, either during the week or weekend. It is better not to have a scheduled session later in the evening. Developments in the mentoring process may be such that the issues involved do not lend themselves to a restful night's sleep. Whatever time is agreed upon, allowance should be made when issues cause the session to go beyond its normal time allotment. Certain issues will be carried over from one session to another. The greater the impact of the issue on the mentee, the more time is needed to work out the emotions and the impact the mentee is feeling. Some issues can be resolved quickly, but may also lead to more complex issues. The mentor and the mentee should agree to give the more complex issues more time and effort for resolution.

When the mentor and the mentee become relaxed and comfortable with each other, it's not uncommon for multiple sessions to take place during a week. Respective work schedules often require that each session be structured within an hour's format. Some issues may require longer time periods; others don't. The importance is to stay focused on the issue and not ramble or otherwise become sidetracked. Ineffective use of time often leads to frustration, which can either stall or end the mentoring relationship.

There may be an emergency development that requires an unscheduled session, but these are the exception rather than the rule. Should a mentor be called by the mentee on such an occasion, the mentor must first ask qualifying questions to determine the nature and extent of the emergency before agreeing to meet with the mentee. Some of these "emergency" situations may be resolved via telephone communication. If the request is a true emergency, the mentor is obligated to seek professional assistance as the primary intercessor and the mentor becomes secondary, yet still involved.

If the mentee gets into the habit of repeatedly calling the mentor with so-called "emergencies," it probably is best that the mentor suggest the mentee seek professional counseling. There may be mental health disorders involved which the mentor isn't qualified to address. An emergency as defined by the mentee may not be a life or death emergency, but a reflection of the emotional impact an issue or situation has on the mentee. It often reflects the mentee's inability to make decisions.

The secular world's protocol in counseling is the one-hour time schedule. This is based on money and not necessarily the needs of the mentee. Spiritual mentors should never seek payment for the God-given opportunity to be His servant in building the relationship He wants with his special creation. Paul never charged for being Christ's servant, and those who did charge suffered the consequences. Those who are licensed psychologists do charge for their services, and they should. This type of counseling is different from mentoring and the two should not be confused as being the same. Should a pastor charge for any advice, he immediately becomes a Pharisee and out of the will of the Godhead.

LOCATION, LOCATION, LOCATION

Finding a location for the mentoring session often is easier than determining the time of each session. Again citing the employment factor, a meeting place can be agreed upon that is close to each participant's place of employment. This may be a restaurant or coffee shop, a park, or other appropriate public facility. The rapid development of technology enables the use of computer emails, cell phones, telephones, and video conversations that can be effective in addressing the mentee's issues. It is NOT advisable to discuss private issues via any form of social media. Simply put, this is foolish, and provides the devil an opportunity to use unsaved individuals in destroying the mentee's relationship with Christ. If the mentee has alcohol issues, then, obviously, the location should not be a bar. Bars and social alcohol based clubs may be great places for evangelizing, but do not make for good mentoring locations.

If both the mentor and the mentee are not working, the twin issues of time and location are easily established. Should the mentor be semi-retired or retired, and the mentee still working, the scheduling often is easier, due to flexibility on the part of the retired mentor.

In line with this, a mentee with restrictions involving children imposed by state judicial laws must not meet in areas where children are present or nearby. This would be a parole violation that could result in the mentee's return to prison and charges brought against the mentor for aiding and abetting. The scheduling of mentoring in a prison is dictated by the correctional facility. This varies from state to state and facility to facility. Mentoring in a jail environment often has different rules than that of a prison.

Meeting in a mentor's home has both positive and negative points that ultimately the mentor decides whether or not to use the home as a meeting place. A mentor's spouse may be uncomfortable with having a session in the home. Children may pose a problem with meeting in one's home due to noise and distractions associated with active children. The mentor may initially not feel comfortable meeting with the mentee in the confines of the mentor's home. These same reasons also may factor in not meeting at the mentee's home. The key factor here is having respect for one's family as well as for each other. Should the mentee be a paroled child abuser, the mentor cannot bring the mentee into their home when children are present; again, this would be a parole violation on the part of the mentee and both the mentor and the mentee would face potential state charges.

An initial meeting between the mentor and the mentee may take place in one location but move to another location once both participants share their respective schedules. It's recommended that the initial meeting place become the location for regularly scheduled mentoring sessions.

Church buildings usually do not make for good mentoring locations. Some churches won't allow it, while others don't have a private space available to accommodate such sessions. Many times the mentor and the mentee do not attend the same church and that may eliminate each as a location, depending on the policy of the church's leadership. Church buildings also may not meet the time constraint for a meeting place because it takes too long to arrive there. Churches often have many activities going on that may become distractions during mentoring. This does not automatically rule out such locations. Again, it is left to the discretion of both the mentor and the mentee.

The important consideration to remember is to take time for scheduling, make sacrifices if necessary regarding time and location, and meet on a regular basis. Keeping the mentoring appointments as routinely predictable as possible will enhance the chances of both parties staying true to the commitment. Be similar to a mail carrier; meet regardless of rain, sleet, hail, snow, or wind. Don't let psychological or emotional distractions prevent you from meeting.

CREATE SHARED EXPERIENCES

Quite often, the mentor and the mentee learn they have shared experiences ranging from athletics, military, parenting, jobs, social functions, and of course the pain from spiritual warfare attacks by the devil. As already noted, these shared background experiences serve as a springboard to developing the relationship and make it easier for the mentee to trust the mentor. The resulting bond felt by both the mentor and the mentee becomes foundational to those issues that may be difficult, painful, or embarrassing for the mentee to address.

Shared experiences can also be *created* through involvement based upon similar interests. Attending a ball game, an art gallery, a concert, or involvement in a community outreach project is a good way to build a relationship and have it become a way to develop trust in the relationship. Creating a shared experience fosters friendship, fellowship, and bonding that make it easier for both the mentee and the mentor to present personal, sensitive issues to the other. This is what true relationship involves. The Apostle James in his epistle exhorts believers in Christ to be doers of the Word and shared involvement in a community outreach provides a good bond and modeling of Christian life for the mentee.

This being said, it's not mandatory for the mentor and the mentee to do things together. Sometimes this can become more of a distraction and can delay, impede or derail the mentoring process. Describing a shared experience and some of the details often is enough for the mentoring process to either get started or to continue.

Shared experiences become catalysts in breaking through barriers the mentee has suppressed over time. Once breakthrough is achieved, the mentee is willing to face the issue and determine the Godly resolution. In this respect, the mentoring then includes counseling. Good counseling is predicated on listening. There are times once the mentee airs the suppressed issue, he then accepts the godly resolution that may have been put on his heart earlier by the Holy Spirit. By listening, the mentor sees the involvement of the Holy Spirit and receives discernment and guidance on how to proceed in the mentoring relationship. Listening is central in many of the Proverbs of Solomon, in the Old Testament. And in the New Testament, we are also admonished, *"Be quick to hear, and slow to speak"* (James 1:19).

At this point, it must be stressed that mentoring is not confined to merely a Bible study. Spiritual mentoring should include Bible study, and referencing the Bible is necessary in seeking God's practical solution to an issue. But, be cautioned. The mentor must guard against using Biblical passages to give credence to the mentor's experience for the sole purpose of getting the mentee to subscribe to the mentor's perspective.

PUT PERSONAL ISSUES ASIDE

When meeting with a mentee, leave all your personal issues at home and focus only on the mentee's needs. Be mindful not to let any shared community outreach become distracting to the main purpose of mentoring—making disciples who earnestly seek relationship with Christ Jesus.

Many examples could be cited of how a mentor's personal issues resulted in his inability to control his feelings, thereby having a negative impact on the mentee. In some instances, the mentor could not focus properly on the mentee's needs and issues because of the distraction of his own issues, thus eliminating his ability to listen to the mentee. There have been times when a mentor's emotions from his own personal issues resulted in an outburst of irritation, frustration, or anger with the mentee resulting in the termination of their relationship. The best way for a mentor to control his emotions and feelings is to go before the Lord in prayer seeking the comfort, counsel, and protection of the Holy Spirit. Once the prayer is completed, the mentor then can proceed with the mentoring session.

The reverse is also true. A mentee's emotions/feelings and conviction of the Holy Spirit may result in outbursts, venting, and releasing of pent-up anger. In such instances it is imperative that the mentor remain calm, cool, and in control. When the mentee is allowed to vent, progress can be made in addressing and solving the problem. Once the venting is complete, the mentor has an excellent opportunity to pray with the mentee and take the issue to the foot of the throne of Almighty God.

In our secular story, Cato met at the home of Flavius. In Greek mentoring, the mentee went to the mentor's home and lived there throughout the designated mentoring period of time. In today's environment, mentoring doesn't take place in a home environment as in those ancient times.

It must be emphasized that mentoring is and should be personal. Twenty-first century technological devices ranging from computers to cell phone texting should not be replacements for personal, one-on-one involvement. Foster homes often are projected as sources for secular counseling and mentoring, but, sadly, in reality this is not the case. A high percentage of secular foster homes are in it only for the money while others want to dictate to the youth or to abuse them. Prisons are full of youths who experienced both such conditions.

CHAPTER 4: THE MENTORING PROCESS AND STRUCTURE

Because mentoring is based on a relationship with a mentee it becomes a process similar to any ongoing relationship much like a marriage, parenting, a close friendship, or involvement with one's parents. Now is a good time to define the word *process* to give meaning and form to what the mentoring process is about. *Process: A series of actions that achieve an end result over a designated period of time. Synonym: progression.* Mentoring is a *process* and not an event.

From our earlier story involving our three Roman characters, the end result or goal for Flavius was to be more like his father Marius, become an officer in the Roman military, and carry on valued family traditions. Flavius established the desired end result; and our friend and trusted mentor, Cato, was requested to assist in making this goal a reality. Quite the responsibility placed on Cato, who was willing to become involved in the lives of both Flavius and Marius. To achieve the desired result shared by Flavius and his father Marius, Cato knew it would take a series of actions over a designated period of time. At different intervals during this time-period, Cato would evaluate Flavius' progress to determine what changes might or might not be implemented. This is where Cato's experience and knowledge factor becomes crucial in mentoring Flavius.

The process between Cato and Flavius is the same in practical and spiritual mentoring today. A disclaimer is that in spiritual mentoring, it is Christ Jesus who has established the goal, which is a growing relationship with Him. Salvation has already taken place. Growing closer to God is now important, so that the mentee truly surrenders to Christ and submits to carrying out His divine will, plan, and purpose. In addressing and resolving practical issues, the mentee learns how the Godhead wants this done to bring Him all glory and honor without worldly, cultural manifestations.

The worldly process is partially determined by the mentee and the rest by the mentor who utilizes a series of techniques, experiences, knowledge, and wisdom to ensure achieving the goals desired by Flavius and Marius. But the spiritual process is determined by the counseling and the direction of the Holy Spirit. Both the mentor and the mentee must listen to and act on the counsel and the direction given by the Holy Spirit to ensure the mentoring process is in accordance with God's plan and purpose.

The designated period of time involved between Cato and Flavius is determined by Flavius's attitude, which affects how quickly and thoroughly he assimilates Cato's mentoring. Attitude in spiritual mentoring is everything. A selfish, prideful attitude by either the mentor or the mentee ruins the mentoring experience. Another factor in their process is how many obstacles arise that hinder or interfere with their process. Similar to that Irishman, Murphy, if anything can go wrong then it will go wrong. No doubt, Cato was aware of these probable obstacles and hurdles despite never knowing that Irishman. Cato had contingency plans to minimize any setbacks. Every mentor should have a "what if" plan just like our friend Cato. In spiritual mentoring, the backup plan should always come from the Holy Spirit. In spiritual mentoring, the devil will use evil tactics disguised as Murphy's Law for his deceitful intentions.

An effective mentor must have a plan and must structure a foundation to build the mentoring process with the mentee. To obtain an understanding of structure and planning within the mentoring process, here's an apt definition of structure: *"The manner in which parts are arranged, organized, or combined to form a whole."* In spiritual mentoring, if the mentee's issue is pornography and the Holy Spirit is convicting him of this sin, the structure for the mentoring process could include: confession (admitting), how/when it started, and learning this is spiritual warfare and sin which keeps the mentee from having a relationship with the Godhead.

The next step is to have a plan, which is defined as: *"A detailed outline indicating how a project or purpose is to be accomplished."* Organization and prioritization are necessary to create the structure.

The plan is the method of implementation. Structure comes first, then the plan. In the pornography example, after confession, the Holy Spirit impresses the need for repentance, and this leads to contacting the mentor.

Understanding and utilizing structure is necessary in spiritual mentoring. Many times the mentee has struggles that involve emotions and feelings that affect the decision-making process. The components of the mentee's struggle need to be arranged, organized, and prioritized. The mentor can do this in the initial meeting with the mentee or take time to develop it and present it to the mentee later. The mentor first asks the mentee a series of questions that indicate where the mentee's heart is. From here the mentor can proceed with the organization, structure, and eventual plan. This must always be Holy Spirit-led by the mentor and the mentee, praying for guidance and discernment.

There are occasions when a mentee may have several struggles that at first glance appear unrelated; but by giving them structure these elements can be combined in such a manner to resolve more than one struggle at a time. An example is a person who is unemployed and experiencing rejection after rejection of resumés sent to prospective employers. During this struggle, the person also gains weight and becomes more reclusive. In this particular example, the mentor should address the emotions and feelings of the mentee to determine how the mentee is able to deal with anxiety, worry, and self-esteem. This is where the mentor should refer to Biblical passages such as Matthew 6:25-34 in which Christ clearly addresses the issue of worry/anxiety. The Word of God becomes foundational to the problem resolution of the mentee, and advances the mentee in his growing relationship with Christ Jesus. The mentee learns how and why Christ Jesus commands His sheep (followers) to bring all their concerns to Him (seeking first God's kingdom). The mentor's personal experience with anxiety and worry become important and helpful to the mentee's understanding and accepting of the process to resolve this issue.

Gaining control of the emotions and feelings will enable the mentee to better cope with the priority issue of unemployment. In turn, the mentee is now able to address the weight problem and any other side effects that occurred stemming from the central issue. Addressing the weight problem first via diets or weight loss problems would not have worked because the core issue of unemployment was impacting the emotions and feelings which led to the weight problem. This is but one example, but the important thing to remember is that with every practical issue there is a corresponding spiritual one also.

Back to our earlier example of pornography. Say the mentee had low self-esteem, was shy, and had difficulty communicating with females or being around them. His biological urges were attacked by the devil when visually looking at photos or videos of naked women. He received demonic satisfaction that was reinforced by repeated action. In the secular and the spiritual examples all components must be addressed. The Bible provides many references to practical issues that can and should be dealt with in God's way that will honor Him.

Structuring the mentoring process includes time allocation. The obvious question is, how much time should a mentor spend with a mentee? Determining factors answering this question include the attitude of the mentee, the type of struggles and issues involved, and unforeseen developments. Attitude is everything for both mentor and mentee. Personality conflicts often determine if a relationship takes place, but also its duration. Some struggles and issues are resolved sooner than others. Should a person be involved with divorce, grief recovery, adjustment to life outside prison, and addictions, the mentoring process may be longer. Unforeseen developments impacting the length of time of a mentoring relationship could include illness, relocation to another town or state, or the mentee or the mentor becoming incarcerated.

Defining moments in the mentoring relationship will take place when the mentor and the mentee realize change is necessary, or that change has taken place. This doesn't mean that the mentoring process is complete. The initial phase of the mentoring process may last two weeks, three months, or one year or even longer.

During this time, many issues can be resolved to the mentee's benefit and Christ's satisfaction. The mentor's observation of the mentee may conclude that the mentee is on solid footing, meaning less time and fewer sessions are necessary. Of course, in spiritual mentoring, the prompting of the Holy Spirit will speak loudly in the hearts of both the mentor and the mentee to indicate a time for change. God's guideline for the designated time period is found in the Old Testament book, Ecclesiastes 3:1-8; *"To everything there is a season, a time for every purpose under heaven."*

Solomon tells us in this passage how important timing is to carrying out God's plan for our life. God provides cycles of life, each with its distinct purpose and designated time. When we rebel and disobey God or refuse His plan and purpose, the result is despair, depression, and torment. This is when a mentor has the opportunity to be God's vessel in righting the ship, allowing the mentee once again to enjoy the peace and joy God blesses His children when they obey and follow Him.

The essence of spiritual mentoring is assisting the mentee in having a closer relationship with Christ. When done God's way, the Holy Spirit does divine work in the mentee that manifests outwardly in such a manner that the mentor knows in his heart the mentoring can either lessen or cease altogether. The key is the Holy Spirit working in both the mentor and the mentee.

A prime example of the Holy Spirit working in both the mentor and the mentee is found in Acts chapter 8, with Philip and the eunuch. This passage states that it was the direction of God through the prompting of His Holy Spirit that caused Philip to stop his ministry and proceed down the desert road. It was the prompting of the Holy Spirit that led the eunuch to ask Philip for help understanding the scriptures. Philip listened and obeyed the voice of God. He asked the eunuch what he wanted, and then Philip ministered to him. Philip did not evangelize to the eunuch; this had already been done. The eunuch wanted and needed assistance in having a relationship with his Savior. He knew this in his heart. This desire was so strong the eunuch recited scripture aloud, in a sense pleading for help in understanding God's Word.

Philip utilized his God-given discernment, wisdom, and experience to meet the needs of the eunuch. Philip spoke only God's Word to his mentee. Philip stayed with the eunuch until such time the eunuch felt confident to continue back to his homeland. The Holy Spirit moved powerfully within the heart of the eunuch who declared his understanding of the Word.

Once back home, the eunuch shared the good news about Christ with his countrymen, resulting in thousands accepting Christ's salvation. Philip was divinely transported to another location where he continued evangelizing and mentoring. Read this passage and study it carefully and then compare it to the remainder of this guidebook. Also read Romans 10:17 and apply it to Acts 8.

One of the key elements of the mentoring process is for the mentor to establish the ground rules both he and the mentee must abide by without exception. These ground rules become the structure of the mentoring process/relationship between the two individuals. Everything has structure. Philip utilized his previous evangelizing and disciplining experience to create the structure needed with his new mentee, the eunuch.

Structure must be established from the beginning of the mentoring process to prevent the process from becoming merely a social event. The mentee has self-determined goals inspired by the Holy Spirit and the mentor should have the techniques appropriate to the mentee's goals so that they both stay focused on making progress leading to successful completion. If there are no structuring ground rules involved, the mentoring process will quickly deteriorate and ultimately dissolve. Chaos then becomes the "structure," and if allowed to continue, neither party can get the process back on track. Part of Philip's adherence to structure was how he focused only on the Word of God per the request of his mentee, the eunuch.

Without structure it's too easy to get side-tracked by rabbit trails that may be initiated by either the mentee or the mentor. These rabbit trails involve focusing on tangents rather than the core elements of the issue. The end result is that both parties experience negative feelings that cause the relationship to end. In spiritual mentoring, the mentor is to put God's Holy Spirit in charge and heed His guidance, direction, and counsel that is spoken to the mentor's heart. Our friend Cato would be relieved to know there is One who is all knowing and perfectly qualified to assist in the mentoring process.

The balancing act with structure is to not make the mentoring process rigid, confining, stifling, or anything that results in ruining the relationship. An inflexible type of mentoring does not allow the mentee to grow in Christ. The mentoring process should have flexibility and adaptability based on how the relationship with the mentee progresses. Flexibility and adaptability become valuable elements in growing the relationship. At a particular juncture in the mentoring process, either the mentor or the mentee will make a suggestion to do something that coincides with a positive breakthrough. Taking the time to get involved with whatever runs parallel to the new development will give an added dimension to the process and foster a deeper bond between the mentor and the mentee.

An example took place when a mentee made mention of his curiosity about an art exhibit of the famous painter Picasso. The mentee indicated he would like to attend the exhibit and learn about Picasso. The mentor suggested they attend together because he, too, was curious about Picasso. Following their attendance at the exhibit, the two engaged in a lively discussion followed by mutually agreeing to take a short painting class. The process of learning basic painting techniques opened new doors for both parties to share their thoughts and feelings about painting and modern art. They learned a different aspect about each other and this led to a deeper bonding between them. During these involvements the mentor should look for opportunities to show Christ Jesus to the mentee. One possible way would be to reflect how Picasso's artistic talent and skill can be parallel to Matthew 25, the parable of the talents and the three servants.

This is an example of a secular approach to mentoring. In the spiritual context, an example can be that both the mentor and the mentee read an inspiring book about Christ or an Apostle or other topic. After discussing the book, they agree to join an outreach program within their community. This involvement fosters the growth of the relationship. It is important to emphasize that reading spiritually-based material should not give way to merely doing a Bible study to the exclusion of mentoring. The mentor must always include the practical application, especially from the mentee's perspective and events occurring in the mentee's life.

Throughout their outreach effort, mentors should be very observant of the mentee's actions and ask pertinent questions to be sensitive to how the Holy Spirit is moving within the heart of the mentee. This should take place after each outreach effort and serve as a basis for the mentee to reflect and recognize how the Holy Spirit moved and instilled His blessing of discernment in the mentee.

These types of involvement become a breath of fresh air that injects life and a new element into the mentoring process just as it does with any relationship. The attitudes of both mentor and mentee foster this breath of fresh air. Had the mentor been rigid, confining, and inflexible, the air would have become stale and stifled his relationship with the mentee. (And Cato shouted, "Yes!) The mentor should not be averse to incorporating secular elements that are not sinful or part of deception that could lead to a temptation and then sin.

With all the different aspects to mentoring, it is highly advisable that the mentor and the mentee journal each session. This is not to say the mentor should take notes during each session; rather, write down the key points or takeaways very soon after the mentoring session has ended. There will be times when something is said or an issue arises that the mentor can suggest both he and the mentee immediately write down answers to the key elements; who, what, when, where, and why of the event or the issue. A short pencil is far better than a long memory, and journaling each session will assist the mentor in several ways:

1. Accurate recording of major points of the session. This helps the mentor stay focused on the key or primary issue with the mentee.

2. Properly note any quotable moments by the mentee and their emotions and feelings associated with that particular experience. This gives the mentor insight to who the mentee is, so the mentor won't say or do anything that would ignite the mentee's emotions in a negative way.

3. Provide a reminder for the mentor. This may range from adjusting scheduling, to researching elements of an issue the mentee is struggling with—for example, contacting a person or agency that is better qualified to meet the mentee's specific need.

4. Assist the mentor in preparing for the next session with the mentee. Referring to the completed session helps the mentor to pray to God for guidance and direction for the next session. Preparation is important to staying on course for the mentee's attaining resolution of issues and accomplishing their goals.

5. Create a documented method for the mentor to present to the mentee as a sign of progress in their mentoring relationship. There are times when the mentor should sit down with the mentee and review how much progress the mentee has made. Mentees often need encouragement to continue their process of developing a relationship with Christ and overcome the spiritual warfare involved.

6. Protect both the mentor and the mentee. The devil is out to rob, kill, or destroy all efforts of God's children to attain and retain relationship with Him. Part of the destruction process by the devil may include litigation. America especially is a litigation-oriented culture, and lawsuits occur for any reason. There is always a willing attorney to take on a case that is easy to win in a secular court of law. Documentation of each mentoring session provides evidence, the key factor in a judge's decision, to prove the innocence of the mentor should a lawsuit be filed by the mentee or someone associated with the mentee. To quote a time-worn cliché, "An ounce of prevention is worth a pound of cure."

7. Prevent any gaming or conning by the mentee. People aren't always who they present themselves to be, and journaling provides a means to ferret out those mentees whose purpose is to game or con a

mentor for whatever reason that controls their mind. Journaling is especially recommended in cases involving mentoring of inmates or newly released inmates. During their time of incarceration, inmates have access to learning judicial processes and procedures and in essence become the proverbial "jailhouse lawyer" and quite effective in filing lawsuits. Not every prison mentee will file a lawsuit against their mentor and this thought should not interfere with a mentor becoming involved with an inmate mentee. But due diligence and precaution are highly advisable. Litigation is not limited to mentoring inmates but to mentoring anyone. There's always a lawyer willing to bring forth a lawsuit, most of which are without merit, but which can have a huge impact, nonetheless.

CR

CHAPTER 5: CASE STUDIES

Thus far, the thrust of this narrative has been identifying and explaining mentoring and the elements of its process. Now is the time to put it together by giving illustrations, real case studies compiled by individuals actually involved with mentoring. These case studies provide insight as to how the mentoring elements have been used in mentoring situations, and how to analyze the effectiveness of the mentor.

The case studies have been selected on the basis of occurrence frequency and situations illustrating greater impact. There are situations and issues that are more frequent in mentoring regardless of gender and therefore are included as a reference guide. Many of the case studies utilized in this narrative have issues with a domino effect for the mentor and the mentee.

Each case study has been condensed to only the essential elements needed for illustration purposes of this narrative. Names of persons involved have been changed for privacy reasons. The reader of these case studies may believe they know either the mentor or the mentee of the particular case study. This is a possibility; but the probability is you don't know either person. This illustrates how common these issues are to life's struggles and experiences.

Many existing manuals, guides, and how-to books about mentoring limit themselves to the academic approach of merely identifying the subject matter and listing the what-to-do's. This guidebook utilizes actual mentoring case studies to show the practical implementation aspect. Hopefully, these case study illustrations (brief as they are) give life, form, and understanding to mentoring.

HOW TO USE THESE CASE STUDIES

As you read each case study, put yourself in the situation of the mentor. What would you do differently than what the mentor actually did? Write down what you would do and also your perception of the main focal points of the case study. In addition, take the role of the mentee and identify the spiritual needs as well as the emotions and perceptions associated with the issue. There are several discussion questions included, the purpose being to get the reader to meditate on the spiritual aspects of these various issues.

A separate section is devoted to the actual resolution that took place in each case study. Don't cheat by looking at the case study resolution first! This will lessen the value that can be obtained from participating in this section. In reading the resolution first, you only hinder your opportunity to develop as an effective spiritual mentor serving Christ Jesus and furthering God's kingdom.

Should you do the case studies as a group, have a discussion after reading each case study to share the various perspectives each member has. After discussion and writing down the perceived main points as they pertain to mentoring and being a follower of Christ Jesus, answer the questions. Then read how the case study was actually resolved and compare this resolution to what your group has come up with. While there will be differences between what you or your group perceive as the resolution to what really happened, bear in mind the main thing to consider is whether the resolution was truly God honoring, obedient to God's precepts, and furthered His kingdom.

This format gives insight as to who you are in the development aspect of becoming a mentor and following Christ's direction, not leaning on your own understandings, thereby causing problems in allowing God to carry out His plan and purpose in the mentee's relationship with Him. Enjoy this section of the guidebook.

 confoncon

CASE STUDY #1: TREVOR'S TROPHY

Celeste was twenty-one when she married Trevor after both had graduated from college. The two began dating during their sophomore year and their relationship grew quickly. They became engaged with both sets of parents approving their decision. Celeste often spoke freely with her mother about how comforting it was that she and Trevor shared the same values and perspective on life.

During their senior year in college, Trevor secured a good job through his fraternity contacts. Celeste obtained a job in the public relations department of a mid-sized company. Their respective jobs were with growing companies. Advancement opportunities were an important factor in their decisions to accept employment with each firm.

Five years into his employment, Trevor received two promotions, the final one becoming district manager that required extensive travel. Celeste, a former high school and college homecoming queen, utilized her attractiveness to advance with her firm. Her promotion came sooner than Trevor's and did not require extensive travel, but did mandate her appearance at many public functions and community involvements. Celeste became the main spokesperson for her company.

The couple did not openly discuss the impact Celeste's beauty had on each other's career advancements; nonetheless it was felt. Superiors and co-workers with both Celeste and Trevor often made comments about Celeste's beauty and poise. These comments made an impression in the minds of both Celeste and Trevor. There was an unspoken agreement to use Celeste's beauty as much as possible to further each other's career. The scenario was much like that of a B-movie plot, yet was indeed a real life situation.

After ten years with each company, Celeste began to change. Devotion to their respective careers resulted in not having children, something the couple had discussed and agreed on during their college time. This agreement was finalized when they opted to live together during college and Celeste began taking the pill to prevent an unwanted pregnancy. Now having children became a growing desire within Celeste. She felt unfulfilled. Reaching a plateau in her company and becoming more aware of the emphasis placed on her beauty added to Celeste's growing inner discomfort. Trevor avoided any discussion with Celeste on her emerging feelings and demanded that she attend the many social functions required by his company.

One day Celeste called in sick and was not available for an assignment by her company. She remained home recuperating from flu-like symptoms for a week, during which time Trevor became agitated because she was not available for a company-sponsored event. The occasion mandated the appearance of all the top company executives, which Trevor had now become. Celeste's supervisor was also irritated that she could not represent the company at an important event. This illness and the reaction by Trevor and her employer revealed to Celeste who she really was in the eyes of those she loved—merely a trophy much like the mounted heads that adorned the walls of a hunting lodge. Realizing this made Celeste emotionally sick, but gave clarity to the emptiness that was overcoming her emotionally.

Celeste realized she was at a crossroads. Either she could continue being the trophy of both her husband and her employer or she could make a change. She reflected how much of her life was spent as a trophy and that her mother was also a trophy wife. Now she saw with new eyes that several of her friends and colleagues at work were also trophies. Celeste was dumb-founded at how she had become a willing participant in this game. The shock effect of this realization was so profound she could not even cry. Instead she cried out to Christ Jesus for help. Growing up, she had attended church and had gone through the motions of being called a Christian but she never had made any effort to have a personal relationship with Christ. Now this relationship was what she realized she needed most.

Christ answered her plea, and for the first time in her life, Celeste felt relief, having asked Christ into her heart and accepting His eternal salvation. Trevor did not respond well to Celeste's announcement of accepting Christ as Lord and Savior, and over time he became agitated by how often she spoke about her new salvation. The couple still attended the same church denomination they had frequented during their college days. But now, Trevor felt Celeste was becoming a fanatic about Christ.

Their church accepted Celeste's desire to be more involved with church activities, and involved her in ways similar to that of her employer. At first, Celeste overlooked this similarity, but soon realized her church was no better than her employer. A second wave of shock and dismay flooded Celeste's mind and emotions. Celeste immediately went to the pastor to convey her observations, but his answer did not mollify her perceptions about the church. The pastor's response was similar to that of both Trevor and her employer.

During this meeting with the church pastor, Celeste took a bold move and stated she would no longer be a participant in the church activities. The pastor then informed Celeste she should look for another church to attend. Celeste left the meeting with an odd feeling. She wasn't saddened by the pastor's reaction but felt stronger that her perception of the church was correct. To her surprise she felt relief and not sadness, guilt, or anger.

While involved in one of the church activities, Celeste had met a woman with whom she felt a connection. Celeste felt compelled to reach out to this woman and speak to her about her situation. Rose agreed to meet with Celeste over coffee during which time Celeste unleashed all the details and her accompanying emotions and feelings. Rose listened silently and attentively to Celeste's story. After Celeste had finished, she asked Celeste if they could pray about the situation. Celeste was surprised by this but agreed, and Rose's prayer had a deep impact on Celeste so that she knew God had directed her to the right person to share her concerns. This meeting jumpstarted a friendship and mentoring that continues to the time of this writing.

Rose never dictated or castigated Celeste during their time together. She always listened to Celeste's concerns and asked Celeste to convey her feelings and reactions about the various situations they shared. Rose showed how different passages in the Bible illustrated similarities to Celeste's situation and how God provided a solution. There were times when Rose used an event or situation from her personal life experience to convey how Christ through His Holy Spirit moved her to a godly resolution and how He blessed her with discernment and wisdom. Rose pointed out how Celeste had turned to Christ first and allowed Him to lead her, and how this was resulting in Celeste drawing closer to Him in a stronger personal relationship.

There were times of difficulty in the mentoring relationship between the two women. Various issues were such that Celeste's emotions and feelings dictated her decisions. Rose accepted Celeste's decisions, but encouraged her to go to Christ in prayer and supplication asking Him for discernment, guidance, and wisdom. Sometimes Celeste would see the wisdom of Rose's admonishment and act on it immediately; other times

Celeste balked. The two women did not let these times of differences ruin their relationship.

A defining point in their mentoring relationship came when Celeste confided to Rose that she had quit her job and had informed Trevor not to expect her to be merely a trophy wife. Celeste joyfully shared with Rose how she had gone to God in earnest prayer and fasting seeking His counsel, guidance, and direction with her decisions on quitting her job and confronting Trevor. Celeste was ecstatic with how the Holy Spirit gave her power, strength, and direction concerning these issues. What truly impressed Rose was Celeste's statement that nothing would come between her and her personal relationship with Christ.

Celeste found that her employer quickly found a replacement, another trophy, and acted as if Celeste was a non-entity. There was no jealousy or anger towards her former employer over this attitude, but praise to God for leading her away from that environment. Celeste's decision to stop involvement with church activities led to her leaving the church. Rather than seeking a replacement church, Celeste opted to delve deeply into God's word. After a period of time, the Holy Spirit led her to become a lay-counselor to women coming out of abusive relationships. Celeste found this involvement rewarding and an avenue for her to use the discernment and wisdom God had blessed her with, to assist women in need. Her marriage with Trevor cooled, yet she remained committed to being his wife, but not his trophy. The couple did not have the children they wanted and it was only after Trevor's company moved him into a position of less authority and company involvement that his attitude towards Celeste changed. When the company merged with a competitor, Trevor was terminated and went into early retirement.

One day Trevor approached Celeste with tears, saying he had truly accepted Christ into his life and wanted forgiveness for the way he had treated Celeste during their marriage. The two embraced and cried together and began the process of mending their relationship. Celeste went to the Lord in joyful prayer, giving thanks to Him for protecting her, giving her divine strength, and using her during this difficult time with Trevor. Two years later, Trevor died from cancer. Rose re-entered Celeste's life as a mentor assisting her through that difficult time of grief recovery.

QUESTIONS:

1. How did Celeste's brokenness factor into her becoming a mentee?
2. Why did Celeste reach out to Rose?
3. Should Rose have counseled Celeste into seeking a replacement church?
4. Why did Rose re-enter Celeste's life a second time as a mentor?
5. What were Rose's qualifications to be a mentor to Celeste?

ৡৡৡৡ

CASE STUDY #2: EVE'S CONFRONTATION WITH HER FAITH

Eve is a woman who recently turned 50. This milestone was marked by a birthday party orchestrated by her husband who invited family and close friends to herald this momentous occasion. During this celebration, Eve's husband and several of her close friends toasted her by relaying how she impacted their lives with her encouragement, profession of faith, and getting them involved with several of the outreach programs in which she was a participant or team leader. One of the attendees was a younger woman named Stacy, in her late twenties, who lived next door to Eve. Shortly after Stacy and her husband purchased the home next to Eve and her husband, Eve befriended Stacy. Over the course of eighteen months, she witnessed to Stacy who had not accepted Christ's eternal salvation. Stacy listened and observed Eve and was on the verge of asking Christ into her life when a troubling event caused her to reconsider taking that huge step. Stacy had grown up in a family who only attended church on Easter and Christmas and were lukewarm to believing in Christ. They were very negative towards churches and denominations, viewing them as hypocrites.

The day after Eve's 50th birthday celebration, Stacy suggested that she and Eve have coffee at a favorite bistro where they often met and had great discussions. Stacy arranged a babysitter for their meeting. Eve detected there was something weighing heavily on Stacy, and therefore broached the question.

Eve: "Stacy, I sense there's something troubling you—am I correct?"

Stacy: "Yes, you are. Yesterday at your wonderful party, I listened to what the people said about you and I agree wholeheartedly with their comments. I could easily have added my own, but my words would have been redundant, so I kept silent but do want to say how much our relationship has meant to me. I value your friendship and how much you have helped me since we first got acquainted. Next to Stan, you're my best friend."

Eve listened to Stacy's comments and was glad to learn she was having a positive impact on Stacy and even anticipated that Stacy would use this opportunity to accept Christ's salvation. Eve's emotional anticipation of Stacy's step of faith caused her heart to beat anxiously in expectation. Eve was not prepared for Stacy's revelation of what was troubling her.

Stacy leaned towards Eve, looked around and quietly said, "I've been thinking a lot about what you've been telling me about Jesus and His love for me and desire to have relationship with me. I've been thinking about it so much that something from my past has come to mind that causes me to doubt if Jesus really can love me and forgive me for what I've done."

Eve responded to Stacy, "You're right about Jesus wanting to share all eternity with you and He will forgive all our sins no matter how bad we think they are."

With this assurance, Stacy then revealed to Eve the source of her emotional turmoil. "Eve, I'm admitting to you something no one else knows." Stacy paused and chokingly continued, "Shortly before we moved here, I had an abortion. Stan (Stacy's husband) was on his final deployment with the Navy and I was lonely and had an affair with a man with whom I worked. I knew from the beginning it was wrong and ended the affair but I had become pregnant. I had the abortion because Stan would know the child wasn't his because of his deployment. I was scared that if he found out, it would ruin our marriage. We've been together twelve years and I love him so much, I don't want to lose him." Stacy then looked up at Eve with watery eyes and slumped shoulders, waiting for Eve's response, not knowing how she would react.

The wait for Eve's reply seemed eternal and the air was filled with tension. Eve was completely taken aback by Stacy's confession and realized she had held her breath the entire time Stacy spoke about her affair. As Eve looked into Stacy's teary eyes, Eve's mind was racing with different thoughts and her emotions were like a pin ball being bounced from one end of the board to the other. Taking a deep breath and mentally fighting for control and composure, Eve sat upright then gave her reaction to Stacy.

QUESTIONS:

To the reader: Take some time to review and digest what has taken place between these two women before putting yourself in Eve's position. Write down what you think Eve would have said to Stacy. Here are key components to this case study to consider in forming your personal reply:

- Eve is a Christian, while Stacy isn't.
- The two women have established a friendship and relationship for one and a half years.
- Stacy believes she can trust Eve enough to seek her counsel on a very important part of her life.
- Stacy's comment of not telling another person about her affair and abortion indicates her shame and distrust to tell anyone about this issue. This reveals Stacy's reluctance to confide deep personal issues with other people.
- Stacy had not yet confessed the affair and abortion to her husband Stan.
- God's timing and the conviction of His Holy Spirit in Stacy was such that she was reflecting on the spiritual aspect of her affair and abortion and how it would deter from eternal relationship with Him.
- Should Eve respond as an evangelist first, or as a friend? It's stated that Eve witnessed to Stacy on several occasions during their 18-month friendship and Stacy's comments reveal Eve's words had impact on her.
- Stacy was clearly very emotional and even had second thoughts about telling Eve this part of her past.
- The age difference between the two women indicates part of their relationship is similar to that between a mother and a daughter.
- Stacy and Stan already have children.
- Stacy loves Stan and has the desire to remain married to him.
- Should Stacy go to Stan about the affair and the abortion? Should she reveal only the affair or should she remain silent and not tell Stan, because other than Eve and the man she had the affair with, no one else knows it took place?
- What other factors could be part of this situation?

ॐॐॐॐ

CASE STUDY #3: MAY THE FORCE BE WITH YOU

Maggie had been diagnosed with epilepsy within months after celebrating her 60th birthday. The diagnosis had both a positive and a negative impact on this child of God who had accepted Christ as Lord and Savior while in her early 30's. Over that time span, Maggie enjoyed a fruitful business career, being a wife and mother, and recently a grandmother. She loved the Lord and chose to serve Him mainly through her church's activities. Maggie's positive reaction to the diagnosis was faith and trust in the Godhead that this development was under His control. The negative impact was the perception that she could no longer do some of the activities she enjoyed doing with her husband her children and for herself. There was an element of fear associated with this, mainly that she would be rejected by those outside her immediate family.

This unrighteous fear soon was abated by the support she received from her friends and her church family. After living with epilepsy for two years, Maggie was asked to speak about her experiences and God's faithful provision to her at a church-sponsored women's conference. Maggie readily agreed, despite the fact the invitation did not come from her church, and she asked God's guidance in preparing her talk. The event drew over 100 women from various churches.

The event went smoothly and the Holy Spirit guided Maggie's words and provided her with passion, clarity, and insight into dealing with epilepsy as a godly servant. After completing her talk, Maggie was approached by a woman close to her age, who introduced herself as May. Their conversation did not last long due to the circumstances of the event but Maggie agreed to meet with May a couple of days later to answer May's questions.

Meeting at a popular coffee shop the two women quickly discovered they had similarities including a passion for M&M's candy. They laughed that the letter M coincided with their respective first names. Once a relaxed atmosphere was established, May confided to Maggie how much Maggie's talk inspired her and went to her heart. May confided that for the majority of her life she had low self-esteem issues and was drawn to Maggie concerning this based on Maggie's talk. This was a surprise to Maggie since self-esteem was not one of the elements of her talk.

Nonetheless, Maggie closely listened to May, sensing the angst of her situation. As Maggie listened, she realized elements of self-esteem indeed were brought out in her presentation, despite not overtly including them into the talk.

To Maggie's surprise, May asked if Maggie would be willing to help her with this issue. Maggie looked into May's eyes with understanding, clearly seeing a quiet pleading, near desperation, in May's request. Taking a deep breath, Maggie said she would be willing to meet with May and help her any way she could.

QUESTIONS:

1. Should Maggie engage in counseling May despite the fact she had no previous experience in counseling?
2. Should Maggie have asked for time to think about doing counseling and then discuss this with the church pastor who sponsored the event?
3. Why did May seek out Maggie rather than one of the church's staff members?
4. List the various ways God intervened in this situation, if you believe divine intervention really took place?
5. Assume you are Maggie; how would you counsel May?

పపపపప

CASE STUDY #4: BILL & RUTH'S QUANDARY

Bill and Harry had been friends for over thirty years, beginning in their teen years, and shared many experiences, both pleasurable and painful. Early in their friendship, both were non-believers in Christ, but labeled themselves agnostic rather than atheists. They had grown up in so-called Christian homes, but neither attended any church regularly, believing that if one lived a good, moral life, was a good-Samaritan living by the "golden rule," that was good enough. Bill married at the age of 20, and soon afterward began a family having two daughters and a son. Harry opted for college followed by a stint in the Air Force, fulfilling his dream of flying.

During his military service, Harry had a Damascus Road experience, at which time he gave up his sinful worldly life style and accepted Christ's salvation. Harry communicated this life change to his best friend Bill, and he spoke and wrote to Bill about life with Christ. At first, Bill thought Harry was joking, and poked fun at his conversion. Over time, Bill realized Harry wasn't joking, and Bill began to listen more attentively to what Harry said about relationship with Christ. After two years of listening to Harry, Bill had his own Damascus Road experience and accepted Christ into his life. The two friends now enjoyed a different type of friendship that included fellowship.

When Harry retired from the Air Force, he and his wife, now empty-nesters, moved to a community of 55,000 residents within forty miles of Bill and his wife, also empty-nesters. Their friendship grew, and more frequent personal visits, telephone calls, and e-mailings took place. The duo found themselves discussing God's Word and how He was working in their respective lives. Harry was able to serve as a mentor to Bill, disciplining him on a variety of these spiritual issues. There were times of disagreement between the two friends, but they remained steadfast in their focus on serving God and their spiritual bonding became stronger. Harry was gratified how much Bill thirsted for a growing relationship with Christ.

One day, Bill telephoned Harry requesting some time together, alone, as there was an issue Bill was struggling to resolve. Harry immediately agreed to meet with his friend, wondering what the issue could be. He prayed for God's guidance and discernment to be His servant when he met with Bill.

At their meeting Bill's discomfort was easily apparent, but Harry waited for Bill to speak about his troubling issue. Harry did not want to pressure Bill, especially not knowing what the issue was about. Bill did not waste any time with small talk. After they sat down with their coffees, Bill quickly informed Harry that Bill's youngest daughter was a professed lesbian and was intending to marry her partner. The daughter wanted Bill to give her away as in a traditional heterosexual marriage and also wanted Harry, whom she considered to be an uncle, to attend her wedding.

At this point, Bill sighed and looked at his best friend with troubled eyes and asked Harry what he thought about the situation, what Bill should do, and if Harry would attend the daughter's wedding despite the obvious sin of lesbianism.

Harry: "My friend, this indeed is a shock, I had no idea Amy was lesbian; but, please tell me, what are your emotions about Amy and your feelings concerning involvement with her wedding?"

Bill: "Ruth and I are beside ourselves. Amy informed us during her junior year at the university she felt she was a lesbian inside and was "coming- out- of- the-closet" about it. We told her it was against God's law and she should pray about this and seek deliverance from this sin. Amy got mad, said we weren't understanding, left, and didn't speak to us again for two years. When emotions calmed down, Amy reconnected with us and there was an uneasy truce about the matter. We never discussed it, but hoped Amy would change. When Amy did visit us, she never brought her lesbian partner to our home and we never discussed the issue. Ruth and I were stunned and embarrassed and didn't tell anyone about Amy's lesbianism. I'm sorry for not confiding in you about this, but I just didn't have the strength to say anything."

Harry: "Bill, you're my friend and we've been through a lot together, and I understand your reluctance to say anything about this to me or anyone else. I want you to know how much I appreciate your candor and will support you in any way I possibly can."

Bill: "Harry, I really appreciate your willingness to stand beside Ruth and I in this and honestly I wanted to say something about Amy to you earlier but was unsure if you would be understanding about it. With all the protesting and damnation type of preaching going on about homosexuality, Ruth and I were afraid you might side with the fanatics.

Many of our other Christian friends are condemning about homosexuality to the point of being vile, so that we don't know who will listen and help, or who will condemn and reject."

Harry: "I must admit, my friend, there was a time when I would have reacted to you, Ruth, and Amy in a condemning spirit. God opened my eyes to that attitude when I first began involvement with the prison ministry and association with the celebrate recovery program. I'm thankful for God's grace and discernment and repentance on this deception. So, how are you and Ruth feeling about being a part of Amy's lesbian wedding?"

Bill: "We're confused and torn. On the one hand, we know what God says about homosexuality; but Amy's also our daughter, our flesh and blood, and we do love her. The wedding's five weeks away, and we don't know how to handle this situation. How do we obey God and at the same time let Amy know how much we still love her? We're afraid that if we reject her, she will think of us as being like those Christians who say one thing about God's love yet do another. In twenty-five years of marriage, this is our toughest decision we have to make."

Harry: "This is tough, very tough, but I believe this situation can be resolved in a Godly manner."

QUESTIONS:

Dear reader, have you ever been in a similar situation or do you know someone who might currently be encountering this quandary? Please consider the following questions associated with this case study:

1. Were Bill and Ruth correct in their initial response to Amy's announcement of being a lesbian?
2. Should Bill and Ruth have sought professional counseling about this issue?
3. Were Bill and Ruth correct in accepting a reconnection with Amy based on a truce or should they have insisted on a reconnection only if Amy repented from lesbianism?
4. Should Bill and Ruth simply pray to God about this issue and not confide with Harry or anyone else?
5. Would it be advisable for Bill and Ruth to attend Amy's wedding and attempt to resolve the issue at a later time?

6. Should Harry even attempt to counsel or to mentor Bill on this issue or suggest they seek professional counseling?
7. Should Harry simply state he would not attend the wedding?
8. Since Harry isn't an ordained minister or pastor, is he qualified to get involved in this issue?
9. Are Bill and Ruth correct in their assessment of Christians being condemning about homosexuality or are they reacting to their emotions and feelings?
10. Would your emotions and feelings impact your response to Bill?

These are a few of the many questions that can be posed about the people involved in this situation. Take some time in answering these questions and ponder others that may come to mind.

৵৵৵৵

CASE STUDY #5: MARK & MARSHA GET RIPPED

Mark and Marsha met at a party and immediately there was a physical attraction that led to having sex with each other. Mark didn't contact Marsha after their liaison, and Marsha didn't appear concerned with his lack of interest in seeing her again. The two saw one another at a local movie rental outlet, and again the physical attraction led to another night of sex. This time the two decided to meet each other on a semi-regular basis while remaining free to date other people. This took place for a short period of time until Mark suggested they become "exclusive." Marsha agreed, and within three months they moved in together.

Marsha was a divorced mother of two children. Mark took to them early in their relationship, and the children were happy whenever Mark was around. This pleased Marsha, and it was a contributing factor in her decision to move in with Mark. Mark had never been married. Coming from divorced parents, he was reluctant to have a long-term relationship with a woman. By moving in with Marsha and remaining unmarried, Mark felt free to leave should their arrangement become uncomfortable to him.

Both had full-time jobs, and they shared similar interests and the same circle of friends who easily accepted their co-habitation. It appeared they were the perfect couple and in love with each other. After seven months of living together, Marsha announced that she was pregnant. This was a shock to Mark who had not planned on having any children. Emotionally, he was still adjusting to a monogamous relationship and was unsure if he wanted a long-term relationship with Marsha. He also feared being a father, having been influenced by his own parents' divorce. Being pregnant was also a shock to Marsha who was on the pill and did not want to have another child.

The couple discussed the situation at length and agreed that Marsha would continue with the pregnancy and they would remain living together. Marsha's other two children were young enough that they didn't understand or know about marriage, so that didn't appear to be a big problem. Marsha's parents both had been married twice before and they liked Mark and were agreeable with their decision. Mark's parents had remarried other spouses soon after their divorce and his mother was happy that Mark was going to be a father. Mark's dad did not like the decision and strongly suggested Mark should convince Marsha to have an abortion. This caused an argument between the couple that created a barrier in their relationship.

Marsha delivered a healthy boy, and she and Mark continued living together another year at which time they decided to get married. Mark discovered he loved being a dad, even changing diapers, and he resolved to work as hard as he could to be a good husband and father. Marsha appeared happy and her boss arranged that she could work out of her home.

A recessionary economy occurred seven years into their marriage, resulting in Mark's being laid-off and Marsha having to resume full-time employment to pay their bills. Mark sent out dozens of resumés and took part-time work, but no full-time employment came. Mark became discouraged, yet took it upon himself to take care of the children and do as much of the domestic duties as possible so that Marsha wasn't overloaded. Mark became accomplished at cooking and child rearing. The recession lingered in their community, and Mark took full-time employment in a field that didn't pay as much as his original career position. Their growing family and assorted bills created financial difficulties that led to repeated marital arguments.

During this time, Mark felt the conviction of the Holy Spirit and asked Jesus into his life. Marsha indicated she believed in God but showed no signs of joy over Mark's salvation. The two began attending a local church but their marital difficulties continued. Marsha's attitude took a paradigm shift, and she began spending more time at work or with a couple of her friends. Mark also discovered Marsha was having an affair with a male co-worker. Devastated, Mark confronted Marsha with her behavior, and was shocked when she said she was filing for divorce and wanted Mark to move out of their home.

Stunned, Mark didn't know what to do or say. He simply left the house to sort things out. He contacted a good friend, Ray, the assistant pastor of the church he attended, to seek his advice. The friend agreed to meet with Mark and discuss the situation. After learning about the impending divorce filing and Marsha's demand that Mark leave their home, Ray suggested that Mark tell Marsha he was staying and that she could move out. Ray stated this action could convince Marsha to reconsider her divorce decision and work on reconciliation.

Mark did this, and within three days the sheriff's department sent deputies to evict Mark from the home. Marsha also filed a restraining on Mark that prevented him from contacting her or the children. She cited verbal abuse as cause, and the judge agreed by imposing the court order. Mark found a small apartment and contacted an attorney friend, a Christian who also attended Mark's church. The divorce proceedings began, and Mark became increasingly distressed. His attorney did not communicate with him and even appeared to be stalling in efforts for Mark to have contact with the children. After two months the restraining order was lifted, and Mark regained contact with his son, but could not have contact with Marsha's other children. Not being allowed contact with his step-children deeply grieved Mark. During discussion with his attorney, Mark felt the attorney was intimidated by Marsha's attorney and wasn't truly representing him effectively.

During the time leading up to the divorce court date, Mark questioned the advice given by Ray. He began sharing more of his emotions and feelings with another friend, Jim, who was a Christian and who also had been divorced. In addition, a second friend Mark knew from a shared racquetball interest, a non-Christian named Dan, also entered the picture as an advisor and one who had also experienced divorce.

After listening to the different advice given by his three friends, Mark stopped seeking advice from Ray and spent more time listening to Jim and Dan. Marsha's attorney was making the divorce proceedings tougher, and Mark's attorney did not seem competent in dealing with these developments. Exasperated, Mark confided to both Jim and Dan he felt like killing both Marsha and her attorney.

When Jim heard Mark's statement about killing both Marsha and her attorney, he interrupted the conversation and suggested they pray about it. At first, Mark was reluctant to do so, wanting to continue talking about the divorce, but he relented and allowed Jim to lead the prayer. Jim placed one hand on Mark's head and the other on Mark's shoulder. In a controlled but emphatic voice, Jim commanded all demons of harassment who were attempting to deceive and to destroy Mark to leave in the name and the cleansing blood of Christ Jesus who had sovereignty over them. Jim then took the hand he had placed on Mark's shoulder and raised it toward heaven, stating praise and glory to Christ, and giving thanks for His supreme power over all forces of evil. Jim then asked the

Holy Spirit to open Mark's eyes to the deception of the enemy and to provide discernment, guidance, and counsel to Mark.

After concluding his prayer, Jim looked at Mark who appeared less tense. Mark sighed and softly said he was very frustrated with the developments of the divorce and thanked Jim for the prayer. The remainder of their time together went smoothly and Jim suggested they meet again later that week. Mark agreed and they parted.

Dan's reaction to Mark's words of frustration prompted him to get involved in another way. He contacted Mark, and the two met the day after Mark's session with Jim. Dan opened the conversation by telling Mark he needed to get a different attorney. He gave Mark the name of the attorney he used in his own divorce.

Immediately after his meeting with Dan, Mark called the attorney recommended by Dan. Once the second attorney accepted Mark's case, the divorce proceedings changed dramatically. The proceedings had limped along for seven months, but when Mark's new attorney came onboard, the delays ceased, a court date was established, and the cloud of confusion was removed from Mark who turned his attention to his son and to his work. Marsha was prohibited from limiting the contact Mark had with his son, and she stopped making demands for child support while the divorce proceedings were ongoing.

Both Jim and Dan attended the court hearing in support of Mark. Marsha's parents were there in support of her, and appeared uneasy, tentative, and did not make any contact with Mark. The only other people in attendance were the attorneys, the judge, and the court reporter. The courtroom was big, creating an echo effect, and Mark felt cold the entire time the hearing lasted.

The proceedings lasted only fifteen minutes because the details involving the divorce had been hashed out, argued, and finally agreed upon prior to the hearing date. The judge asked both Mark and Marsha if they understood and agreed with the settlement. After they voiced their understanding, the judge ruled the divorce granted, and left the room.

Over the next eight years, issues pertaining to child custody caused problems between Mark and Marsha. Several of these issues resulted in more court hearings. During this time, Marsha's new husband (the co-worker she had the affair with) interfered by influencing Marsha against Mark and his visitations with his son. There were also times when Marsha's new husband attempted to impede Mark's employment and also filed a false charge with the church Mark attended. That resulted in the church refusing Mark's continuation with three church ministries. Marsha stopped attending church altogether.

Mark relied on his fellow Christian friend Jim for advice in each of these harassing issues. Mark also began more in-depth personal study of the Bible. He ceased attending the church where Ray was assistant pastor, opting instead for the teaching of a radio minister he began listening to during the early days of the divorce proceedings. The combined personal study, listening to the radio minister, and conversations with Jim led to Mark's surrendering to Christ Jesus.

Divorce is one of the top three issues and conflicts that arise during mentoring; therefore, a mentor must be prepared in dealing with this element should it become part of the mentoring relationship with the mentee.

QUESTIONS:

1. What do you think happened between Mark and Ray that ended their relationship?
2. Do you believe Mark's first attorney represented Mark in a godly manner?
3. Why did Mark make the chilling statement about killing Marsha and her attorney, especially while receiving spiritual advice from both Ray and Jim?
4. Did Mark receive sound spiritual advice from either Ray or Jim?
5. Should Mark have sought advice from a non-Christian such as Dan?
6. Why didn't Marsha celebrate with joy over Mark's salvation?
7. Marsha stated she believed in God, but if she did, why did she engage in pre-marital sex with Mark and later move in with him and ultimately have an affair while still married?
8. Do you believe Marsha really accepted Christ's salvation?
9. Why did Mark and Marsha continue to have marital problems after he accepted Christ into his heart?
10. Should Mark and Marsha have gone to their church pastor for advice with their marital issues?
11. Was the church correct in ending Mark's participation in church ministries?

12. Was Mark correct in deciding not to seek another church but do his own personal Bible study?
13. Where was God in this situation?

❧❧❧❧

CASE STUDY #6: PHIL & SUSAN DOUBLE THEIR BET

Susan grew up in a loving Christian home. Following her high school graduation, she began attending a local community college with her best friend Jan. The two formed a girls' Bible study for young Christian women who were attending the same community college.

After completing two years at the community college, the two friends transferred to a nearby university within 100 miles of home. During her second semester at the university, Susan declared a major in music teaching with a minor in secondary education. Upon receiving her degree, Susan applied to the university's graduate program for a master's degree in a relatively new field utilizing music therapy for autistic people. She would begin her master's program in the fall.

That summer, Susan met a young man named Phil who was visiting a friend her home town. Phil lived in the town where Susan would be doing her master's study. Phil had graduated earlier that spring from another university, but secured employment as a high school teacher and coach. He was working as a youth counselor and coach in Susan's hometown, and the two of them began casual dating that summer. Susan's friend Jan was dating Phil's best friend Wayne, so most of that summer the two couples spent quite a bit of time together. It was no surprise when Jan and Wayne announced their engagement. They asked Susan and Phil to be their respective maid of honor and best man at the upcoming wedding planned for the next spring.

Jan and Wayne's wedding proceeded as planned, and after their honeymoon they took up residence in Jan's hometown, thereby allowing them to continue socializing with Susan and Phil. Their social dates were not that frequent because Susan's study requirements became more demanding. Susan did continue dating Phil, who greatly assisted her in her master's studies. Phil was very supportive and would spend much of his free time doing research for Susan. Within a year, she obtained her master's degree. The university was so impressed with her music work with autistic students they offered her a post-graduate assistant position with a monthly stipend. While associated with the university, a private company learned of Susan's innovative work and offered her a lucrative position to develop a course study they marketed to schools and organizations that dealt with autism. The company made Susan their main spokesperson in these efforts.

Having secured well-paying jobs, Susan and Phil decided to marry. They asked Jan and Wayne to be their respective maid of honor and best man. Six months later, the wedding took place.

Two years into their marriage, Susan and Phil learned they could not have children because of an abnormality with Phil. Jan and Wayne had their second child during this time, and being "favorite aunt and uncle" seemed okay with Susan and Phil. Susan's position of working with autistic individuals grew, and she received state recognition for her efforts and innovative programs. Phil became the head football coach at the high school where he taught. In his second year, the team finished second in state competition.

Dismayed that they could not have children of their own, Susan and Phil discussed the possibility of adopting a child born in a foreign country. The process was tedious, expensive, and often frustrating; ultimately, the couple dropped out to consider other options. After a period of time, they agreed to put adoption on hold until they could become emotionally refueled.

Shortly after deciding to table adoption plans, Susan began noticing changes in Phil. At first, they were barely perceptible, but then became more obvious. Phil's sense of humor became dulled, he wasn't as active in their church outreach programs, and wasn't as enthusiastic to interact with Jan and Wayne. The only areas where Phil remained normal were in his coaching and following both college and professional football and basketball. Susan went out of her way to console and accommodate him whenever possible. Jan and Wayne were cognizant of Phil's behavior change and also how Susan was enabling Phil. When Jan and Wayne attempted to talk with Susan and Phil about this situation they were politely rebuffed.

One day Susan attempted to withdraw cash from their joint checking account at an ATM machine and discovered there wasn't enough money for her withdrawal. This was odd because Susan had made a deposit into that account five days earlier and was sure there was enough money in the account. Susan went to the bank and found out the account was nearly drained. That evening after dinner, Susan questioned Phil about the bank account.

Phil hung his head and softly told Susan he had withdrawn the money without telling her. The funds were used for his own purposes of betting on college and professional football games. He lost on all of his bets. Shocked, Susan could not speak. Phil said that he had been betting small amounts on different games for quite some time. He promised to replenish the account with money from a private savings account. The money was deposited into the checking account, and Phil assured Susan he would not let it happen again. Susan was satisfied with Phil's answer and promise.

Three months later, Susan learned of another depletion of the joint checking account. Again, Phil confessed that he had bet on professional basketball games and got carried away. Once again, he replenished the checking account with money from his savings, but Susan was more concerned about Phil's behavior. This time, Phil wasn't quite as contrite as the first time and he did not promise to stop his gambling. Susan did not question Phil on his changed behavior.

Periodically, she would check the joint account and found numerous withdrawals by Phil. Quietly, she began to replenish the account with money from her personal savings account. She loved Phil dearly and felt he was just under strain from his coaching and teaching duties. She perceived their inability to adopt was also having an impact on the man she loved. Susan also felt obligated to Phil for all the times he helped her while she was studying for her master's degree. Susan also felt threatened that if she were to confront Phil about his gambling, he might elect to leave or otherwise get mad at her for jumping to conclusions about a problem that didn't exist. Besides, Phil remained attentive to Susan and was very considerate of her.

Phil's gambling escalated to the point that one day he informed her he had lost a big bet and needed two thousand dollars to cover the loss. Shocked, Susan told Phil she needed time to process what was happening. Phil insisted he needed the funds, stating it was urgent, otherwise he could get into serious trouble. His facial expression and tone of voice alarmed Susan and she agreed to give Phil the money.

The next day Susan telephoned Jan and asked to see her as soon as possible. The two met at a restaurant, and right away Susan told Jan the entire story about Phil's gambling. Much to Susan's surprise, Jan informed Susan that Phil had approached Wayne for a loan because of a gambling loss. Wayne agreed to loan the money to Phil, and later, Phil approached Wayne again for another loan. This time, Wayne informed Phil he would not loan him any money. That was when Phil asked Susan for two thousand dollars.

Susan and Jan realized Phil's gambling problem was much bigger than anyone realized. After discussing more details about Phil's behavior, they agreed it would be best to discuss this with Wayne, and explore what avenues could be taken to help Phil. After their discussion, Susan went home and confronted Phil about his gambling. She emphatically stated she was closing their joint checking account and that Phil should seek professional help because his gambling had become a big problem. Sternly, Susan indicated she would no longer provide Phil money for any gambling debts.

That weekend, Jan and Wayne arrived unannounced at Susan and Phil's home and confronted Phil about his gambling problem. Phil admitted to getting in over his head, but explained it was the circumstances and developments of the college and pro football seasons that led to his difficulty. There were several upsets that resulted in Phil's losses. He was adamant that his gambling wasn't the problem they accused him of, and that he could and would stop making bets.

Phil wasn't able to control his gambling. Eventually, Susan was contacted by the couple's credit union about defaults on a sizable personal loan Phil had taken out. Susan was near tears on learning this devastating news. She requested some time to digest this news and later met with the bankers and agreed to pay Phil's defaulted loan. During her meetings with the bankers, Susan stated she would no longer repay any loans incurred by Phil. She closed all joint accounts held with the credit union. The credit union concurred with Susan's decision. That evening Susan angrily confronted Phil about the events with the credit union and her decision to no longer pay any of his debts.

Finally, Susan informed Phil that he must seek professional counseling for his gambling addiction or she would file for divorce. Phil sat silent after hearing Susan's demands, then agreed to everything she said. Phil contacted Wayne who helped arrange professional counseling. Phil began attending a support group. Three years had elapsed since Phil first acknowledged his gambling to Susan.

QUESTIONS:

1. What do you think was the cause of Phil's gambling?
2. Why did Susan allow herself to be a part of Phil's gambling addiction?

3. Should Wayne have confronted Phil about his gambling when he first became aware of the problem?
4. Was the unannounced confrontation with Phil the proper way of approaching his gambling problem?
5. Were there other influencing factors, other than the default loans, that caused Susan to procrastinate in confronting Phil's gambling addiction?
6. How did Phil's addiction impact his and Susan's relationship with God?

* споспоспоспоспо*

CASE STUDY #7: YVETTE'S INFERNO

Yvette had dreamed about becoming a mother since the age of 12 and believed she would have multiple children. Quietly, she kept this desire to herself, not sharing it with her sister or her parents. Only after she had accepted Christ's eternal salvation 10 years later, and married in the same year, did she share this with the Lord God Almighty, pleading with Him to bless her with multiple children. One month past her first wedding anniversary, the good news came that she was pregnant and would deliver a girl. One year after Alisha was born, Yvette became pregnant again, and this time it would be a boy.

During her second pregnancy, Yvette met Sarah, a young woman who also was pregnant, and the two became friends. The two would get together often and found they had another bond in addition to pregnancy. Sarah revealed she, too, was saved by God's grace. Both women delivered healthy babies and continued with their friendship, going to parks and children's events together. Yvette was thankful for Sarah's friendship, and greatly appreciated her spiritual maturity and the different ways Sarah was able to explain passages of Scripture that Yvette struggled to understand.

When Alisha celebrated her fourth birthday, she became ill. Things did not improve, and the family physician strongly suggested Alisha be taken to a specialist. A series of tests were conducted and the results shook Yvette to her core. The specialist informed Yvette and her husband Dan that the prognosis was a fatal form of cancer. The distraught couple clung heavily to each other and asked the doctor if treatment was a possibility. When the doctor answered yes, but not to put too much hope in the treatment, the couple emphatically stated they wanted to begin as soon as possible.

Sarah was heart-broken on hearing the news about Alisha and assured Yvette she would be there for her. Sarah would look after Alisha's little brother Peter during those times of hospital treatment. She would also bring by lunch or dinner for the family and do errands for them when the treatments drained them of their energy. Sarah would spiritually mentor Yvette during this time; and later, Yvette would admit Sarah's efforts were comforting and consoling. In addition to Sarah's personal ministering, Yvette and Dan joined a support group through their church. The group regularly made stops at the hurting couple's home. Each member of the group would go from room to room praying earnestly and the group leader, a woman in her early 40's, would pray over Yvette and Dan. Each time the group left, the couple felt a peace, a calmness, and fortified to deal with the situation.

The couple, Sarah, and the support group were convinced that God's mighty hand of healing would rest on Alisha, it was just a matter of time, and they were anxious for that healing to be complete. One month before Alisha's fifth birthday, she went to heaven sometime during her night's sleep. Yvette found her daughter's body early in the morning after entering Alisha's bedroom convinced today would be the day of healing. Yvette let out a shout "No, No, No" and began crying at the side of Alisha's bed. Dan rushed into the bedroom and immediately knew what had happened. Shaking, he knelt beside Yvette with one arm around her small shoulder and the other grasping Alisha's now cold hand. After some time, Yvette struggled to her feet and called Sarah who immediately rushed to her friend's side. Dan called 911, and shortly thereafter, an ambulance came to the home. The paramedics began examining Alisha's body while the devastated parents looked on in disbelief, numb, and silent. One of the paramedics quietly told the couple that Alisha was dead.

Alisha's body was transported by ambulance to the hospital, and then to the funeral home. During this time, Sarah and the support group began assisting Yvette and Dan with making funeral arrangements. After the burial, Yvette relied more on Sarah who readily made her time available to console and minister her friend.

Yvette's grief was deep, and her emotions were a mix of faith, doubt, and confusion. At one point, she finally confided to Sarah how angry she was that God didn't fulfill His promise of healing Alisha. Startled, Sarah asked Yvette what promise was made to Yvette concerning Alisha. Yvette said that during one of the support group's home visits, several Bible passages were given to Yvette and Dan that indicated Alisha would be healed. Sarah began asking more questions, and from Yvette's answers, she realized that extra help was needed to deal with Yvette's anger.

QUESTIONS:

1. Was Yvette correct in stating that God promised a complete healing to Alisha?
2. Did the support group give correct Bible passages to Yvette and Dan?
3. Was the praying and prayer time a waste of time?
4. Did Sarah adequately minister to Yvette?
5. What questions and answers led Sarah to seek another minister to deal with Yvette's anger?
6. What factors led to Yvette's anger with God?

ৰ্ক্চৰ্ক্চৰ্ক্চৰ্ক্চ

CASE STUDY #8:   HENRY'S CALL TO DUTY

Terry and Henry worked for the same company in different departments. Terry was director of sales and marketing, while Henry was director of accounting. Both were in their early forties, married with children, and shared similar interests in fishing and bicycle road riding. They were Christians, but attended different churches. On a regular basis, the two would get together and go fishing or take a bike ride, at which time they would share their thoughts and relay different developments about family and church. They had occasional lunches together at work, but their respective schedules and duties did not allow for regular conversations during the work week.

Just before beginning one of their bike rides, Henry announced he was getting involved with a new program initiated by his church pastor. The program was mentoring, and was to be aligned with a national organization that assisted churches in establishing mentoring programs. The director of the mentoring program assured the church pastor that his program would increase church attendance, create more involvement in church activities, and bring in new congregants. Henry went on to say that his church pastor was excited about what the program could do for the church and was eager to get this program implemented. Henry was to be a member of the mentoring team and would go through a training process conducted by his pastor who had received similar training from the national organization.

Terry listened as Henry explained his involvement with the church sponsored mentoring ministry. When the two stopped for a short break on their extended ride, Terry asked Henry how he decided to become involved with the proposed new ministry. Henry indicated the senior pastor and the newly appointed church ministry director had approached him and several other men of the church about joining this new ministry. Terry nodded his head and said he wished Henry well in his new endeavor, and the two friends continued on their bike ride.

Several weeks later on another bike ride, Henry enthusiastically told Terry that a total of ten men had stepped forward to become mentors, and their four week training program had just completed. Henry was already assigned his first mentee, a man named Jake who also attended the same church as Henry. They planned to meet the upcoming week.

Henry said he felt involvement with Jake would go smoothly and that the two would become friends.

Over the next six months, Henry and Jake routinely met once a week. Henry followed the guidelines set forth by the national mentoring organization which was essentially a Bible study with questions for each man to answer. The questions were meant to be thought-provoking, eliciting comments leading to a better understanding of the Bible. Jake proved to be receptive to this format, and Henry was pleased to instruct Jake about the Bible.

Periodically, Henry would relay his mentoring developments with Jake to Terry, feeling that Terry would understand and approve of Henry's new mentoring ministry. Henry knew of Terry's own involvement with mentoring and was pleased they now shared another interest. Terry always listened attentively when Henry spoke of his mentoring, but he did not make any suggestions to Terry concerning the mentoring with Henry.

Six months into his mentoring with Jake, a development occurred that shook Henry to the bone. Henry's wife Joan had developed a close friendship with Jake's wife, Pam. Both women were involved in various church activities including choir and Sunday school teaching to the children of church members. In addition, they periodically got together for lunch.

At one of their lunch outings, Pam asked if she could share a concern with Joan who readily agreed to hear what Pam had to say. Pam revealed that she was uneasy with a marital situation that had come about during her marriage with Jake. Pam believed this situation wasn't right and wanted advice from Joan. The situation was pornography that she and Jake indulged in on a regular basis.

The horrified expression on Joan's face caused Pam to quickly assert the pornography did not include anything with children, bondage, or exotic sex methods. Pam also said that Jake and she were not into sex with other partners. She said that when Jake first revealed his involvement with pornography, he showed her how certain forms of it could enhance their sex life. At first, Pam was reluctant to participate, but over time had come to enjoy some of the things that Jake liked. However, she participated in others to please him despite not feeling comfortable with them.

Joan was not only stunned about this confession, but also that Pam was a professed Christian. Fighting for breath and to retain her composure, Joan at first couldn't speak, and merely looked at Pam, whose eyes were locked on Joan's. After what seemed a lifetime, Joan told Pam how surprised she was to learn this, and asked why Pam felt compelled to disclose this information.

Pam said that part of her reasoning was that she felt close to Joan, and valued her discernment, and also that she no longer felt comfortable participating with Jake in his pornography. Pam indicated how much Jake enjoyed his Bible study time with Henry and wondered whether Jake had mentioned anything to Henry about the involvement with pornography. When Joan stated that Henry had made no mention of Jake's pornography issue, Pam requested that Joan share this information with Henry in the hope that he could counsel Jake into stopping what was now escalating and threatening to ruin their marriage.

Joan received an additional shock when she asked Pam why she and Jake did not seek Christian counseling over this issue. Pam revealed that Jake really wasn't a Christian and only went to church with her as part of their agreement with his pornography. Pam said that while Jake enjoyed the Bible study, he felt no compulsion to step forward and become a Christian. Jake's main interest level was not to become a Christian. He wanted to learn more about Christianity to satisfy his intellectual curiosity and personal philosophies. Joan readily agreed to speak with Henry about all that Pam had revealed to her.

In the privacy of their bedroom, Joan told Henry everything that Pam had revealed to her earlier that day. Henry sat speechless and motionless for what seemed like an eternity. Finally, Henry raised his head, sighed, and told Joan he was beside himself in learning this aspect about Jake. Henry indicated that during all the mentoring sessions with Jake, plus their fishing excursions together, Jake gave no indication he was involved with pornography or that he wanted help in stopping his involvement with that sin. Equally shocking to Henry was that Jake was not a Christian, despite his interest and participation in the mentoring Bible study. Joan asked Henry what he was going to do. Henry replied he would discuss this first with the church mentoring director, get his advice, and proceed from there.

The mentoring director was aghast at what Henry told him. When Henry finished his depiction, there was a long silence in the room. The mentoring director told Henry they should meet with Jake to confront him about his pornography involvement, his not being a Christian, and deny him from attending further sessions.

Two days later, Henry met with Jake for their usual weekly mentoring session. When Jake arrived for the meeting, Henry immediately introduced him to the church's mentoring director. Jake did not appear concerned about the addition of the mentoring director to their regular meeting. Henry, on the other hand, was nervous, almost to the point of agitation. He had never been in such a position before in his life and he didn't know what to do. He was having great difficulty controlling his emotions, and was thankful the mentoring director was taking charge of the meeting.

The mentoring director wasted little time in addressing the issue of Pam's revelation about Jake not being a Christian, and his involvement with pornography. Jake sat motionless and stoic. He surveyed the room of the restaurant and very calmly leaned towards the mentoring director and quietly spoke that his personal life was of no concern to the mentoring director and that he had no business interfering in his life. Jake then turned his head towards Henry and calmly stated he did not see any need for further contact with Henry. Jake then stood up, turned, and walked out of the restaurant without looking back at the two men who were following his movements.

Once Jake was out of sight, the mentoring director looked at Henry and said they should notify the senior pastor of these developments. Pam and Jake stopped attending the church, much to Pam's dismay. They also ended all involvement with Joan and Henry, despite Joan's efforts to contact and maintain a friendship with her.

QUESTIONS:

1. Was Pam under the conviction of the Holy Spirit that caused her to reveal the pornography issue with Joan?

2. Should Joan have persuaded Pam to seek professional counseling rather than get Henry involved?

3. Did Henry take the right course of action by seeking the advice of the church's mentoring director?

4. Was the mentoring program genuine?

5. Was the church mentoring director correct in being present with Henry when confronting Jake about his not being a Christian and the sin of pornography?

6. Did the mentoring program incorporated by the church correctly address this issue?

7. Why didn't Jake reveal himself as a pornographer and not being a Christian to Henry early in their mentoring sessions?

8. Should Joan and Henry have discussed this issue with Pam and Jake first, before seeking advice from the church mentoring director or senior pastor?

9. Should Henry even have gotten involved with Jake over this issue?

10. Were Henry and the church's mentoring director correct to confront Jake over this issue in a public restaurant without giving Jake advance notice of their intentions?

ও৵ও৵ও৵ও৵

CASE STUDY #9: TWO MAGPIES HARMONIZE

Denise and Janet had been friends nearly twenty years, enjoying several shared interests, especially swimming and singing. Singing was the vehicle that sparked their friendship, and the two women sang in the same church choir and a small group that consisted of four women, all from the same church. In addition to singing at their church, the group sang at different community events. They were also popular in several surrounding towns. Their singing engagements did not interfere with the raising of their respective children and other family involvements. The friendship between the two women led to their families participating in different activities together. Denise and Janet were as close as two sisters despite the fact that Janet was six years older than Denise.

When the two magpies, as they referred to themselves, reached their 40's and their children entered that often tumultuous period known as the dreaded teenage years, they often compared notes and offered advice to each other. Denise had two boys, while Janet was the mother of two girls and a boy. The two magpies agreed that their shared activity of swimming was the main outlet that enabled them to remain sane in sometimes insane situations. One situation took their friendship into an entirely different arena that impacted them for life.

Janet returned home from work one day and found that her oldest daughter, Chloe, age 17, had left her purse on the kitchen counter. The family cat had overturned the purse and several of its contents were strewn on the counter. When Janet went to replace Chloe's things she noticed an object that surprised her and caused great concern. On the counter was a packaged condom. Janet stared at the package for what seemed a lifetime. Thoughts of disbelief flooded her mind. Neither she nor her husband Eric ever imagined that any of their children would engage in premarital sex. Now the unthinkable appeared to be a reality. Janet's disbelief turned to anger. She heard Chloe in another room, grabbed the condom package, and quickly went to confront her daughter.

Seeing the expression on her mother's face and the packaged condom in her hand, Chloe immediately became defensive. Janet added to her defensiveness by demanding an explanation for why the package

91

was in Chloe's possession. At first, Chloe attempted to defuse the confrontation by saying it really wasn't hers but a friend's who gave it to her because Chloe was curious about them having never seen one before. Janet's reaction was to call Chloe a liar, and she demanded the truth.

Realizing she could not lie her way out of the confrontation, Chloe disclosed the truth. She and her steady boyfriend, a young man a year older than she, had been thinking about having sex together. Chloe insisted she was still a virgin. Janet stood silently staring intently into Chloe's face. Janet's intensity and silence caused Chloe finally to reveal that she and her boyfriend had engaged in premarital sex twice. Grasping the bedroom chest of drawers tightly, Janet fought for control and as calmly as possible demanded the name of the boyfriend.

A second wave of shock rocked Janet when Chloe stated the boyfriend was the son of one of their church's highly respected elders. Both Janet and Eric had great respect for this family and felt their oldest son was a role model for other young people in the church. Janet felt devastated and betrayed.

Summoning all her strength, Janet informed Chloe that she would have to relay this revelation to Eric, and then they would decide what proper course of action would be taken. Chloe slumped down on her bed, no longer able to look her mother in the eye.

Eric sensed the tension in their home when he returned from work and was anxious to find out the reason for this heavy cloud. Once told of the condom package, Eric merely stared into space in disbelief and shock. He quickly felt hurt, betrayed by this oldest daughter and her boyfriend whom he had used as a role model and assistant in several church youth activities. He and Janet sat in silence on their patio for a long period.

Finally, the two dismayed parents began discussing what they should do, and came into agreement that Chloe was grounded (taking away her driving privileges). She could no longer have any relationship with her boyfriend and Eric would inform the boyfriend's father of the situation. Eric also was to inform the church youth pastor of this situation and inform him that Chloe could not participate in youth activities for a while. Janet added she felt Chloe should receive counseling at a nearby facility that had a reputation for assisting young women in premarital relationships. This facility was Christian-based, and Janet felt a neutral counselor would be best for Chloe. Eric agreed. When their plan was implemented, the two parents were in for additional shock.

Eric arranged a meeting with the boyfriend's father. The two met at the church after an elder's meeting. Eric was confident that he and John (the boyfriend's father) would come to a godly solution concerning this issue. On the contrary, John became defensive and angry towards Eric, saying this was an effort to discredit both him and his family before the church. John defiantly accused Chloe of initiating the sexual encounter. He ended their meeting by stating that Eric should have been a better godly parent to his children. Stunned, Eric left the church and did not notice the stares from the youth pastor and the senior pastor as he walked out of the facility. Prior to the meeting with John, Eric had informed the youth pastor of the situation. The youth pastor insisted on knowing the young man's name and Eric obliged. Reluctantly, Eric had disclosed the boyfriend's name to the youth pastor, wanting instead to speak with John about this first.

That evening when they were alone, each relayed the day's events. Janet had arranged for an initial counseling session for Chloe the next day after school. She looked wide-eyed at Eric as he relayed the meeting with both the youth pastor and John. Before any discussion could take place, the phone rang, adding to the tension already in place in their situation.

The telephone call was for Janet. The caller was John's wife Marge. Marge immediately was accusatory towards Janet and angry because the youth pastor had called them earlier, informing them their son could no longer be a part of any youth activities at the church. The senior pastor was calling a meeting of the board to confront John and discuss his continuation as a church elder. Marge concluded her diatribe, informing Janet they were going to consult an attorney to determine if any legal action could be taken against Janet, Eric, and Chloe. Eric's response to this call led him to take Janet's hand and the two prayed fervently to God for His divine help.

Representatives of the counseling facility made Janet and Chloe as comfortable as possible, and within a short time they were told the counselor would see Chloe. Janet was not allowed to participate in this meeting. Chloe's emotions were at a high level as she proceeded down the corridor to the counselor's office. She momentarily stood at the door wanting to turn and leave, but she knocked on the door and entered the room.

Surprise filled the small counseling room when Chloe saw the counselor was her friend Denise. Equally flabbergasted was Denise, who nonetheless was able to motion for Chloe to sit down. The next few minutes were very awkward. Finally, Denise took a deep breath and informed Chloe she had no idea who her client would be and attempted to assure Chloe that the meeting was not a set-up arranged between Janet and her.

Sensing Chloe did not believe her, Denise asked if she could provide evidence that would assure Chloe and change her mind about the meeting. Chloe cautiously gave her permission, but felt angry just the same. Denise then calmly disclosed part of her testimony that made Chloe actually shudder.

As a 17-year old young summer camp counselor, Denise had become infatuated with a fellow male counselor. The two spent every available minute together, and on the final night engaged in premarital sex. The young man assured Denise he would contact her later and they would continue their relationship. He assured Denise he eventually wanted to marry her but needed time to get things arranged. He said he very much wanted to meet her parents.

It never happened. When Denise did not hear from her lover, she attempted to contact him, and found out the telephone number he gave her was a pizza place and nobody there had ever heard of him. Stunned, Denise, nonetheless, felt that her lover would contact her and explain the misinformation. Again, it never happened.

Denise went through her senior year of high school not dating, still hoping to hear from her lover. It never happened. Her emotions led her to the local Air Force recruiter where Denise felt getting away from everything would help her overcome her feelings of rejection. Denise qualified for a good position as an air traffic controller and was told she needed a physical examination prior to reporting for basic training. Denise never went to basic training because the physical exam revealed she was HIV positive. Rocked, Denise could not believe this could be the case. Nonetheless, she was not accepted into the Air Force and elected to earn a degree in accounting instead.

While in college, Denise said she met her husband, but they nearly parted ways when he proposed to her. She tearfully told him about her HIV, expecting him to reject her. To her surprise, Chad said this news did not stop him from wanting to share his life with her. The two married and within three years were able to adopt the first of their two boys.

Softly, Denise said that intimacy with Chad was allowed but that condoms were necessary to protect Chad and to prevent any pregnancy that could have devastating results on their offspring. Denise concluded her testimony by saying that despite their deep friendship, Janet was totally unaware of Denise's HIV situation or that she was a volunteer counselor of the facility. Denise then asked Chloe if this was enough to overcome her skepticism.

Rocked by Denise's testimony, Chloe sat a few minutes, wide-eyed, staring into Denise's face and adjusting to what her mother's perceived "older sister" had just told her. Finally, Chloe extended her hand to Denise and asked for her counseling.

There are numerous questions associated with this case study. Purposefully, no questions are posed below, to allow you and your group to identify the spiritual issues, religious influences, and the nature of the case. This is an opportunity to compose your own questions. Reflect on them, then discuss them, especially as to how mentoring can or did take place.

QUESTIONS:

What questions would you pose regarding this case study?

 తతతత

CASE STUDY #10: NATE NAVIGATES CHURNING CHURCH WATERS

Nate and his wife Teresa moved to a midsize city and explored eight different churches before settling on a church they felt comfortable attending and becoming involved in with the different church outreaches. Soon after their seventh anniversary of association with this church an event took place that rocked their boat.

Nate was mentoring a man in his mid-thirties who had difficulty living a Christ-centered life. While still in his teens this man, Buck, had an experience with a church that ended in his relationship with Christians and church attendance. In Buck's words, the church was nothing but a bunch of hypocrites and he questioned many of the church members' salvation including that of the head pastor and his wife.

Twenty years after leaving that church and living what he believed to be the Christian life, Buck was transferred to the same city and company where Nate worked. Buck was assigned to the same department as Nate's, and the two soon established a friendship. When Buck learned that Nate was a Christian, he informed his new friend he wasn't interested in any church or association with any church groups. At first, Nate did not question or probe Buck's feelings concerning church and Christians, and decided to build the friendship.

Two years after their initial introduction with each other, Nate was able to speak to Buck concerning spiritual issues. Buck was surprised to learn that he and Nate had similar values and thoughts concerning religion. They both believed that the focus should be on having a vibrant relationship with Christ Jesus rather than putting a church or a denomination at the top of the list.

Buck often would initiate conversations with Nate concerning different passages and books of the Bible. Nate would listen, then engage in thought-provoking dialogue with Buck. Buck especially appreciated how Nate could take Scripture and explain the practical application to everyday living. Often, the two men picked out different situations at work where they could use and manifest practical applications of the Bible.

On one occasion, Nate was especially pleased to witness how Buck approached an unsaved soul concerning a difficult issue taking place in his life. The man close to Buck's age was struggling with war-time experiences he had had in the Army while deployed in Iraq. The man expressed disgust over how the different Muslim factions were fighting each other as well as the American forces at the same time. The man clearly expressed his anger with religion, including Christianity, since many of his fellow soldiers professed to be Christian, yet he said their actions were as bad as those of the Muslims they encountered.

Buck explained to this man about having a relationship with Christ Jesus. He acknowledged how often religion would attempt to disguise its man-made intent as being part of Christianity or that many religions and religious cults maintained they were the only true vehicle to believing in God.

Before and after each session Buck had with this skeptic, he would consult Nate and seek his guidance and clarification. Buck was enjoying his conversations with this man and told Nate how much he felt spiritually alive. Buck also enjoyed the prayer time he and Nate shared.

In the spring of the year, Nate found himself in a different and difficult situation with both Buck and the man Buck was mentoring in an effort that the man would accept Christ's salvation. A group of self-proclaimed Christians based in Kansas arrived in the city and immediately made headlines with video exposure, protesting a funeral of a soldier who had recently been killed by ambush in a part of Iraq where Buck had been stationed. This group numbered twenty and held up protest signs at the church where the deceased soldier's funeral was taking place. The group was very vocal, chanting protests about homosexuals in the Army and how the deceased soldier was going to hell. The protestors taunted the people who were going into the church for the funeral service.

Earlier in the week, Buck had heard of this protest, so he planned on attending the church funeral to see exactly what the protestors would do. Witnessing the protestors and seeing the shock and hurt on the faces of the deceased soldier's family and friends, Buck got angry and confronted the protestors. Soon a shouting match ensued between Buck and the leader of the protestors, and Buck grabbed one of the protestor's sign and broke it in two. Buck then began to shake and weep, and turned to leave. Buck's actions were recorded by one of the television crews assigned to cover the protest and the reporters made an effort to interview Buck, but he refused. Nonetheless, the video of his breaking the protestors' sign and his weeping made the evening news broadcast.

The next day, Buck went to the family of the deceased soldier and informed them he had been stationed in the same area as their son. The family invited Buck into their home, and soon the family vented their anger, shock, and frustration with these un-Christ-like protestors. Buck shared his sympathy along with their anger, and, after a short time, he left.

Buck telephoned Nate about the situation to discuss the events and Buck's high level emotions and feelings concerning the protestors. With tears in his eyes and a halting voice, Buck explained his visit to the deceased soldier's family, and how inadequate he felt attempting to answer their questions of why the protest, especially when their son was not a homosexual, and in fact was about to become engaged to his high school sweetheart. Buck continued with how his feelings of anger triggered a very strong urge to strike the protestor whose sign he broke. With a deep sigh, Buck stated he didn't know how he would address his actions with the man he was attempting to accept Christ's salvation. It was clear that Buck was at a very low point emotionally, spiritually, and physically.

Nate listened to Buck a long while before he spoke to his friend. The two friends mainly agreed the protest was senseless and should never have taken place. Using his Bible as a reference, Nate went to several different passages of Scripture to explain the real importance of Christian living was to be a true follower of Christ Jesus and to carry out the plan and purpose God has for each of His special creation. Nate also described two personal experiences that were similar to what Buck was going through.

Buck listened attentively. When Nate had finished, Buck softly thanked his friend for his advice and said he would continue to talk to his unsaved friend about accepting Christ's salvation. Nate stated he would continue to assist Buck in his evangelizing efforts.

Two days after the protestors left the city, both Nate and Buck were summoned to a meeting with their pastor. Much to their dismay, the pastor indicated his agreement with the protestors against homosexuality and reminded the men of their denominational stance on this issue. The pastor stated he would not intervene with the family of the deceased soldier, nor would he file a complaint with the denominational regional office for a reprimand to the Kansas based protestors.

When the pastor had finished, Nate stood and announced he did not agree with the pastor's decision and that effective immediately he was no longer associated with that church. Buck also stood up and said he would never set foot in any church of that denomination ever again. Both men walked out of the church.

QUESTIONS:

1. Do you agree or disagree with the protestors?
2. What Biblical references apply to the protestors?
3. Did Nate do an adequate job of mentoring Buck?
4. Should Buck continue evangelizing his unsaved friend despite his emotional state of being?
5. What Biblical references did Nate use to console Buck and to admonish him?
6. Do you agree/disagree with the pastor's statements and stance?
7. Should the denomination have intervened with the protestors?
8. Were Nate and Buck justified in their walking away from their church?
9. Should denominationalism have even entered into this situation?
10. Was Nate a good mentor to Buck?

ॐॐॐॐॐ

CASE STUDY #11: THE CASE OF THE DISILLUSIONED DETECTIVE

June 7th was a milestone day for Doug, as it marked his twentieth year as a police detective in what now had become home for himself and his family. Prior to moving to the community of 65,000, Doug had ended his military career in criminal justice, but wanted to stay in his chosen field of endeavor as a civilian. After searching several months for the right sized community with the amenities they desired, he, his wife, and their two children moved. It all came together when Doug was accepted on the police force. At the time of his application, the community totaled 51,000 and a manufacturing facility announced plans to build a branch plant near the town.

The community's growth resulted in the need for additional police officers. The chief of police was impressed with Doug's credentials and his interview. So, he offered Doug the position of detective. All Doug had to do was go through the state's police academy. The money was good and the quality of life met his family's needs, so the decision was made. Within three years he was promoted to chief of detectives and lead investigator. The department's professionalism became known throughout the state and Doug and his detectives at times were solicited to conduct investigations for smaller surrounding communities that could not afford their own staff of detectives.

As Doug drove to work on the morning of his career milestone, he reflected on his choice to accept the position. He never regretted the decision, nor did his wife. They quickly fell in love with the community, making it their chosen home. Doug suspected that once he got to his office, there would be a celebration in his honor. He chuckled at this thought and actually looked forward to some of the usual celebration activities. At age 52, he was comfortable in his position with the police department, but was giving retirement some consideration after a combined 34 years in criminal justice. Doug had earned the respect of his fellow detectives, plus the patrol officers, and was regarded as being fair, honest, with a straightforward and no-nonsense approach. A devoted follower of Christ, Doug's intent every day was to let everyone see Christ through him and to use his God-given talents to glorify Him.

Part of Doug's duties was to train other detectives. One trainee stood out, and Doug made him his assistant. Chuck was 15 years younger than Doug, but with a sharp investigative mindset. It was a pleasure for Doug to work with Chuck, especially now that Chuck had accepted Christ's salvation. When not involved in work duties, the two spent time together discussing the Bible and Chuck's growing relationship with Christ. Doug's emphasis was illustrating how God's Word should be utilized in dealing with life issues in a way that he might remain obedient and faithful to God.

One day at work, Doug noticed the office environment was subdued. Immediately, he was summoned to the chief of police's office. In the chief's office were Chuck, the district attorney, and his chief assistant.

There were no smiles, just somberness. Doug was motioned to take a seat and the chief went straight to the point. Earlier that morning, four bodies had been discovered dead in their home in what was an upper middle-class neighborhood. In addition to the family members, the family dog also had been killed. Murdered were the two parents, one son, and the daughter. Another son survived because he had stayed overnight at a friend's house.

The chief informed Doug the murders were brutal. In addition to each being shot twice, they had been stabbed multiple times. The dog, which had been shot once in the head, had not been stabbed. The gunshot to the dog's head resembled that of a mercy killing. The media had already been at the scene of the crime and began reporting the event. The chief informed Doug that he and another detective were assigned to the case and would report directly to both the chief and the district attorney.

Chuck was taken off the case because the victims were friends of Chuck and they attended the same church and had occasionally socialized together. Street patrol officers had control of the scene. Three detectives were also present, and the coroner's office would remove the bodies after Doug and the new detective had viewed the scene. Doug and the assigned detective then left to do their work.

Despite years of experience with homicides, there are those cases that make one's gut cringe. Doug and his new partner felt prepared for this particular case, but once on the scene, each man's emotions were impacted. Forensics was their job, photographing each body and the various rooms the victims were found in. In addition, each room of the house was also photographed and inspected for any evidence the perpetrator had left behind. There is always evidence; it's a matter of carefully observing, searching, and collecting what is there.

The crime scene crew was thorough, and after Doug and his partner had inspected each room where the victims were slain, the coroner's people were allowed to remove the bodies, including the dog's. Doug immediately instructed the other detectives to canvas the back yard, garage, vehicles, closets, and other rooms of the house, and the trash. Doug and his partner then embarked on interviewing the neighbors. After viewing the crime scene, both Doug and his partner wondered if this case would align with the statistics that a high percentage of homicides are committed by someone who knows the victim.

When the two detectives returned to their office and began the process of sorting through the evidence and the crime scene photos, plus the interviews, it appeared it was a house invasion gone violent. Doug sat at his desk pondering some of the photos searching for more clues and anything that would give insight to who the killer was.

Knowing Chuck's personal involvement with the victims, Doug reached out to him to have lunch and discuss this involvement. Chuck was grateful for this opportunity and readily accepted the invitation. Doug could see the angst in Chuck's face, his body language, and his tone of voice. Chuck stated he and his wife had met the victims at a school function in which their respective children were involved. This, plus shared church activities, resulted in the families getting to know each other more intimately and occasionally socializing together at picnics, BBQ's, and church outings. Chuck said it was difficult to understand why God would let this brutal murder happen.

Chuck stopped his narrative at that point. Doug indicated that because of this personal involvement, he could not authorize Chuck's participation whatsoever in the case and said Chuck would not have access to any of the evidence or findings from the investigation. Chuck protested at first, but finally nodded his head in agreement and understanding. Doug then informed Chuck he would be re-assigned to other cases should they arise. At that point, Doug received a call on his cell phone from the coroner's office indicating the initial report was completed, and the meeting with Chuck ended.

Doug telephoned his new partner to meet him at the coroner's office. Once there, they were ushered into the room where the examinations of each victim took place and the coroner gave them a report of what type of gun was used, the angle of shots each victim received, and the number of stab wounds. The wounds would be analyzed to determine which were fatal in nature and other details like the angle of thrust and what type of knife was used.

It wasn't easy viewing the bodies and looking at the detailed photos of each victim but the report shed light on who the murderer could be. The photos provided proof of what type of knife was used, which was already in the hands of the police department. It was easily found in the home during the initial search. There were no fingerprints on the knife, but it was clear from the microscopic bloodstains it was part of the murders. Other pieces of the puzzle began to come together, which led the two detectives to have another interview with several people associated with the crime. Doug re-interviewed the surviving son, and his new partner spoke with the son's friend and his parents and neighbors. One of the assigned detectives found a shotgun in a wooded area that bordered the family's property. The gun was turned over to the forensics department.

Back at their office the two compared notes and the consensus was to have the surviving son come to the police station for interrogation. The maternal grandparents of the youth had arrived and demanded an attorney be present during the interrogation. Doug was seasoned with interrogation techniques and was not intimidated by having an attorney present. The assistant district attorney was also present. Doug and the youth were alone in the interrogation room while the youth's attorney and the assistant district attorney sat in another with audio and video of the interrogation room.

Doug was gentle, soft-spoken, yet skillfully demanding in his questions. Only once did the youth's attorney raise an objection. The big break-through came when Doug approached the subject of the family dog. Doug learned the dog had been a gift as a puppy to the youth. Doug attacked the emotional involvement the youth had with the dog, repeatedly asking how he felt about the manner in which the dog died. After 45 minutes of questioning, the youth confessed and admitted to the killings. At age 15, the youth could be tried as an adult in the state court system, which the assistant district attorney informed the youth's attorney would be the case. Immediately the teenager was taken into custody.

After the youth's arrest, Doug allowed Chuck to review the evidence and the testimony. They met for coffee and Doug could see by Chuck's body language he was in turmoil. After a short time, Chuck informed

Doug he was having trouble with his relationship with Christ, the reason being the murder case. He disclosed to his friend and mentor he couldn't stop focusing on why God could allow such a tragedy to happen. Chuck relayed that he knew what the Bible said, thanks to Doug's mentoring, but nonetheless he felt disappointed and angry towards God. Chuck insisted that he needed time to sort through this on his own and didn't want to meet for mentoring, but was hoping he and Doug could remain friends.

The two men looked at each other in silence, then Doug stated he was okay with Chuck's wanting to back off from the mentoring, and said he understood Chuck's feelings of being angry with God. Doug said he would keep Chuck in his prayers concerning this issue and that most certainly they would remain friends and colleagues. At that point, Doug informed Chuck that after this trial he was going to submit his resignation from the police department.

Shocked, Chuck stared wide-eyed at Doug in disbelief. Doug asked Chuck to keep this announcement private until Doug had sufficient time to inform the chief of police. Doug added that the governor had approached him to take over the state's bureau of investigation that was mired in scandal. Doug concluded by saying this decision was in the works for some time and the murder trial was a non- issue in his decision and that he was going to recommend Chuck to the chief of police to become the next chief of detectives. With that, the two men stood up, hugged each other, and went their separate ways.

QUESTIONS:

1. How do you relate to Doug's statement of wanting everyone he came into contact with to see Christ through him?
2. What specific ways can not only Doug but you also let the world see Christ through you and use God-given talents to glorify Him?
3. Was Doug correct in not insisting that Chuck continue with their mentoring since he was struggling over being angry with God?
4. Did Chuck's being angry impede his relationship with Christ or affect his salvation?
5. Should Doug have ceased all involvement with Chuck after learning of his desire to stop the mentoring?
6. Was Chuck's issue the result of spiritual immaturity or simply a form of temper tantrum?

7. Should Doug have recommended Chuck seek advice from someone else concerning his issue with Christ?
8. Was Chuck under spiritual attack?
9. Should Chuck have continued the mentoring and used this to resolve his issue over being angry with God?

ৡৡৡৡ

CASE STUDY #12: TRISHA'S FINAL BATTLE

Trisha was on top of the world. Her husband had recently received a promotion that ensured they would not have to relocate their family to another city as his employer initially indicated would take place. She and husband Jason had established roots in their small metropolitan city that was a regional hub. They enjoyed the lifestyle and believed the total environment of the community was conducive to raising their son and daughter.

In addition, Trisha had just been promoted within her company, and now would be the project manager for the new clients her company was actively pursuing. All this was taking place within two months of celebrating her 32nd birthday. She and Jason celebrated their career advancements by taking a weekend holiday, just the two of them. Trisha's co-worker Sheila offered to keep the kids, allowing Trisha and Jason their romantic getaway, which proved to reinforce their commitment to each other. When Trisha returned to work, she was floating on a cloud, happy, and content. Eagerly, she dived into her new duties at work, receiving commendations from her co-workers as well as her supervisors. Trisha wasn't merely happy with her life; she was ecstatic.

Ten months after her promotion, Trisha began to experience fatigue, and one day while showering, she felt a lump in her left breast. She had sufficient knowledge about abnormalities to recognize she needed to get an examination. Later that day at work, she was able to obtain an appointment with her internist doctor. In her mind, Trisha believed there was nothing to the lump; but, nonetheless, she wanted the examination to verify her opinion and to ease her emotions.

Two weeks later, she had the examination and to her horror her doctor broke the worst news possible—she had breast cancer. Stunned, Trisha felt numb and unable to speak. Her doctor arranged for a series of chemotherapy treatments that needed to begin immediately. Trisha could not go back to work that day, and she phoned to tell her boss. She drove to a park she liked, and sat on a park bench next to the lake, staring at the calm waters in front of her. She had a lot to think about and to process, and this setting was the perfect place for her.

As she took in the serene vista before her, the doctor's words echoed repeatedly in her mind—breast cancer, breast cancer, breast cancer. Trisha had read enough about this dreaded disease. She knew it could be terminal, but also that many women had survived. Trisha sighed and felt a peculiar irony, remembering how she had participated in a local breast cancer awareness and fundraising walk-a-thon. She remembered some of the stories by women survivors and how encouraging they were and the special bond each had with other. It all seemed surreal to Trisha, but the reality was she had the disease and must battle it with all her reserve and strength.

That evening after the kids were asleep, Trisha broke the dreaded news to Jason. Earlier, Trisha had prepared her words to ease the impact, but when she sat facing her husband, all she could do was blurt out, "Honey, I've got breast cancer." The result was that Jason sat motionless, staring wide-eyed at his attractive wife who was the love of his life and the mother of his children. Trisha waited for Jason to respond to her announcement as the reality of the situation impacted her. Tears began to form in Jason's eyes, and he took hold of her hand. Choked up with emotion, haltingly, he said he would do anything to help her during this time. The couple hugged each other and sat silently until it was time to go to bed.

Sheila was the only person Trisha initially confided in about this new development, telling her when the chemotherapy sessions would begin. To her surprise, Sheila informed Trisha that she, too, had battled breast cancer, as did her mother and an aunt. Sheila emphatically told Trisha that she would be there for her anytime Trisha wanted to talk about her disease. Trisha felt an overwhelming sense of relief from these words, and knew she needed another woman to confide in and lean on.

For several months, Trisha made repeated trips to the special cancer clinic for the chemotherapy treatments. As the treatments progressed, Trisha often felt a reluctance to continue. They were unpleasant experiences. Through it all, Sheila was intuitive to what Trisha was experiencing physically, emotionally, and mentally. Trisha was very appreciative and thankful for Sheila's friendship and encouraging presence. The two women became closer as a result of the disease, much closer than Trisha had experienced with any of her other friends. She and Sheila had a special bond that was similar to the women she had encountered or observed at the fundraising walk-a-thon. Sometimes Trisha would reflect on this bond and realize not only how special it was, but also how those who have never had that shared experience are relegated to mere observer status and can't completely understand. Although Trisha cherished and valued their special bond, at the same time she wished it could be under different circumstances.

The grueling experience of the chemotherapy treatments ended and Trisha had an appointment with her doctor for the results. Jason took time off from work and went with her to the doctor's visit. Together they held hands and silently waited for the doctor and the verdict. The news was good—the cancer was in remission—but precautions still needed to be taken to make sure. Trisha and Jason were elated with the news. On the way home from the appointment, Trisha cell phoned Sheila with the good news. Later, the two special friends had a celebratory lunch. Trisha knew this bond with Sheila would last a long time and she was thankful for this relationship. Trisha was also glad life could now get back to normal.

Five years later, Trisha began to experience some of the same symptoms she had encountered when first diagnosed with the cancer. A cold chill ran through Trisha's body at the thought the cancer could be back. Again, she arranged an appointment with her doctor. It seemed déjà vu and was not a pleasant thought. On the way to the doctor's appointment, Trisha realized how tightly she had gripped the steering wheel of her car. Throughout the appointment Trisha was tense, on edge, and anxious. The doctor informed her that tests and biopsies would be taken and he would have the results later. Trisha opted not to tell Jason or Sheila of this new development until after the test results were known.

Time became a heavy weight as Trisha waited for the test results. The doctor did not mince words with her when he told her the cancer had metastasized to her bones. There was no cure; her condition was deemed terminal by the doctor. Shaken, Trisha fought back tears and struggled to retain control of her emotions. Somehow, she uttered the words that she wanted a second opinion and the doctor arranged for her to meet with another oncologist.

Trisha informed both Jason and Sheila of the new development. They, too, were shaken and stunned, but at the same time supportive to Trisha. Jason accompanied his wife to her doctor appointment, and the wait this time was excruciatingly long. The second oncologist confirmed his colleague's diagnosis restating it was terminal; but said there was no definite time frame before the cancer took her life.

Jason and Trisha went to the same park Trisha had been to earlier when first diagnosed with breast cancer. The two sat silently for some time as the sun glistened off the water. It seemed ironic and out of place to hear the cheerful chirping of the birds as the couple contemplated the worst news imaginable. Trisha relayed to Jason that the first doctor had given her the name of a support group of women who also were encountering the same situation. Now, she would contact them. She would also continue to seek support from Sheila and, of course, her most important ally, Jason. Tearfully, Jason said he would do whatever was necessary to assist her and acknowledged that other women who were experiencing the same fate probably would be better than he in certain scenarios.

The couple held onto each other while sitting on the park bench and agreed they would not inform their children at this time. At ages 8 and 10, the consensus was they were too young to understand and there was no need to worry them. They also agreed that despite having accepted Christ Jesus into their lives years earlier, they did not feel comfortable seeking advice or solace from a church. This was reinforced by the fact they had not attended a church in quite a while. For the next hour they merely sat on the park bench, holding each other tightly, staring out on the shimmering water.

Trisha did call Sheila, and the two met over coffee to discuss the new situation. As Trisha relayed to her friend the details of the doctor's meeting and the plan she and Jason decided on taking, Sheila sat silent, intently watching her friend, observing her body language and listening to her words. When Trisha was finished, Sheila took her hand and simply said that she would be there for Trisha. Sheila also stated she felt it was a very good idea for Trisha to attend the support group of other women who were experiencing the same issue and that they would be helpful.

Tentatively, Trisha entered the room with other women who also had metastasized breast cancer and quickly was put at ease by the smiling faces and warm welcome. When she walked out of the meeting, Trisha felt relaxed, relieved to know these women would be of great comfort to her. After describing the meeting with Jason, he, too, was relieved and no longer anxious and said he felt these women were just what Trisha and he needed. The next day at work, Trisha excitedly detailed the meeting to Sheila who also said the support group would be great for Trisha.

For the next two years, Trisha met once a week with her support group. She became a mentor to another woman named Meg who had just learned she too had metastasized breast cancer. Trisha became her confidant just as Sheila remained Trisha's. The sharing, learning, coping, and hoping grew among the women. Jason benefited as well by Trisha's attitude, and the two felt they were growing closer together in a manner totally unexpected. It was a period of time where love abounded and God's grace and mercy was manifested in ways none of the participants had experienced before.

Six months after celebrating her second anniversary with the group, Trisha was called home by her loving Heavenly Father and Almighty God.

QUESTIONS:

1. Were Trisha and Jason correct in not immediately telling their children about the terminal cancer?
2. If you were Jason, what ways would you support your dying wife or would you feel over whelmed and at a loss of what to do?
3. Do you think Sheila spiritually mentored Trisha and do you think she also mentored her in other ways as well?
4. How do you think the women's support group assisted Trisha?
5. How did Trisha mentor Meg?
6. Should Jason and Trisha sought comfort and help from a church?
7. If your spouse, sibling, child, or parent informed you of having a terminal disease, what would your actions be?

CⓇ

CHAPTER 6: SPIRITUAL WARFARE

This chapter is inserted now to better understand what every person who answers God's call to their specific ministry encounters—spiritual warfare. This happens to mentors and mentees at various junctures during their relationship. Each of the narrated case studies contains numerous bouts of spiritual warfare. In mentoring this will always be. The following is a guideline of principles surrounding spiritual warfare, although these are not intended as definitive or exhaustive explanations of this subject.

These guidelines are taken directly from the Bible and are without denominational mantra. There are numerous books available pertaining to spiritual warfare, but similar to other subjects, some miss the point entirely because of denominationalism, while others approach the topic from an academic perspective. The academics don't have the personal experience, and as such are theorists who misinterpret spiritual warfare. Assuredly, some who read this chapter will agree with the stated premise. Others will reject it in favor of their denominational stance. All denominations have stances that influence how the topic of spiritual warfare is handled. Academics may or may not accept the principles in this chapter.

The purpose of including spiritual warfare in this mentoring guidebook is to mentors or mentees who follow Christ's commandment of taking the gospel to all. Fulfilling the great commission is a vital part of mentoring, and they will encounter spiritual warfare at some point in their endeavors. Similar to any chosen ministry, God will direct one's path by using talents, skills, and spiritual gifts appropriate for effective mentoring. Because the enemy of God, the devil, opposes all God's purposes, expect spiritual warfare to occur during any stage of carrying out God's ministry.

Spiritual warfare is the result of the current war between the devil and the Sovereign Godhead. This war began before the creation of the earth and of man. Nobody knows exactly when the war began, but the Bible states that the angel Lucifer wanted to be as God. He refused to accept the fact there is only one true God. He revolted, resulting in being cast out of heaven and losing eternal relationship with the Sovereign Godhead. The devil is forever banished and condemned by Sovereign God.

Lucifer's pride, arrogance, and treacherous desire for control were the factors for what is referred to as the Great Fall and the beginning of The Great War. The war will continue until Christ returns. This war is the basis of all wars that have taken place throughout history and of all wars that will continue until Christ's coming. All wars on earth resemble this spiritual, heavenly war. This spiritual war, with earth as its battlefield, includes soldiers on each side, and numerous casualties.

Spiritual warfare for the purposes of this guidebook will be centered on definition, Biblical examples, preparation, and how to combat the tools of the devil.

DEFINITION

Spiritual warfare consists of the tactics utilized by the devil to prevent all human beings from having eternal life and relationship with the sovereign God.

Let's break down this definition for better understanding. First is the word *tactics*. This term is commonly referred to in military operations and indeed the definition of tactics fits within the scope of spiritual warfare. The dictionary defines *tactics* as the technique of securing the objectives designated by strategy, especially the art of deploying and directing troops in coordinated maneuvers against an enemy. In spiritual warfare the commander designs the technique and the deployment of the troops. The tactics used by the troops of the evil commander, the devil, are designed to rob, kill, and destroy any and all relationship with God and his chosen people. By attacking all human beings, the devil is attacking God because the devil wants to supplant God.

The righteous commander, Sovereign God, also has a stated objective and tactics to achieve His will, plan, and purpose. Sovereign

God's tactics include using his soldiers as ministers to overcome the evil tactics employed by the devil. Rather than to rob, kill, and destroy, God wants to redeem, renew, and give eternal life to man, His special creation. This was God's will at the time of the Great Fall, was the intent when He created Adam and Eve, and why He gave His only begotten Son as a sacrifice. The sacrifice of His Son, Jesus, and His victory over death and the devil, resulted in Christ now being our field commander in this earthly battlefield.

The devil's strategy, technique, and coordinated maneuvers in spiritual warfare consist of the flesh, the world, and efforts of his demonic forces. The flesh, our inherent human nature and our five senses, coupled with emotions and feelings, impact and influence our thoughts and decision-making. The world is the culture in which one lives and includes the rituals, traditions and mores that are deemed necessary for acceptance and continued membership. References to the devil include Satan himself, and the demons that have chosen to follow his evil ways.

BIBLICAL EXAMPLES OF SPIRITUAL WARFARE

Spiritual warfare began before man was ever created. In Genesis 2:9b, the Word of God states: *"...and the tree of the knowledge of good and evil."* This phrase implies that evil existed when the devil was cast from heaven, severing his eternal relationship with God some time before God created man and woman. No human knows how long before God created man and woman that the devil was cast from heaven. Also of particular note is that no mention of the devil is made in Genesis until *after* God created man and woman. When God placed Adam in the Garden of Eden, He gave him a commandment (Gen. 2:15-16) to take care of the garden and not to eat of the fruit of the tree of the knowledge of good and evil. Sometime after issuing this commandment (Gen.3), the *devil initiated spiritual warfare* against mankind, beginning with tempting Eve to doubt God's command. She tried the forbidden fruit and gave it to Adam who was with her, and the rest is history. Of particular emphasis is the fact that neither Adam nor Eve had any concept of what evil was until they ate the forbidden fruit. In these early chapters of God's Word, it is learned that the devil hates God and man (Genesis 1:26-27), and is relentlessly determined to rob man of God's blessing (Genesis 1:28-31), beginning very soon after man's creation.

How is it, then, that the devil is allowed to go against God and man, His special creation, to involve mankind in spiritual warfare with such deadly consequences? After all, God proved His sovereignty by casting Lucifer out of heaven. And for a period of time God had exclusive relationship with Adam and Eve in the Garden. The answer lies in Genesis 2:15-17, when God showed Adam the tree of the knowledge of good and evil and instructed him not to eat of its fruit or he would surely die. This passage lets us know that Adam was blessed with the freedom of choice. Lucifer also had this freedom of choice; otherwise, he would not have had freedom to rebel.

Adam could obey God and do what God desired, or he could rebel against God, as the devil had done. God gave Adam the freedom of choice; otherwise, Adam and all of mankind would be like robots whose obedience would be hollow and meaningless. The devil fully understood this based on his own experiences with God. The devil jumped at the opportunity to tempt God's creation into disobeying God and to suffer the same fate of losing relationship with Almighty God. The tactics employed by the devil against Eve and Adam are the same tactics he uses against all human beings of the past, present, and the future. Mankind today does not have the same experience as Adam and Eve did—the chance to avoid knowledge of evil. Man now has knowledge of evil. It is through Adam's fall, and our inheritance of that sin nature through him.

Another Biblical example of spiritual warfare is found in the Book of Job 1:6-12, when God gave the devil permission to harass Job, test his faith, and prove the sovereignty of God. From the dialogue between God and the devil to the depiction of Job's trial and suffering, the Word of God instructs mankind that spiritual warfare indeed is real. It is also very nasty and deadly. The commanders are God and the devil, and the troops are either those who choose to believe and follow God, or those who choose to follow the devil. Again, the key is to understand the concept of choice and its ramifications. It's important to note how many other people were impacted as a result of this test to one man and one woman. This fact is a good reference for considering why things happen to people who seemingly are not involved in a particular evil situation.

In Matthew 4:1-11, the Word of God teaches us another important fact about the devil and spiritual warfare. In this passage the devil tempted Jesus much as he did Eve and Adam. This reflects the diabolical purpose of the devil in that he did not change his tactics, and he did not respect or fear Christ the incarnate Son of God. These verses indicate that the devil tempted Christ in ways that were personal to Him and the plan and purpose God had for Christ on earth. This passage shows us that the devil will tailor his deception and temptation to the unique personalities of men and women, and to the intended plan and purpose God has for each individual. There may be some similarities in God's chosen plan for His children that overlap between individuals, but there are distinct differences that reflect the personal plan God has for our lives. The devil always attacks on the personal level and aims at those areas of weakness of that individual.

The final Biblical example of spiritual warfare used for definition purposes is found throughout the Book of Revelation. In chapter 12:10 the Word of God states that the devil has access to God but also that *Christ Jesus is seated at the right hand of God the Father in all power and glory.* Christ's authority and purpose includes returning to earth a second time for the final victorious battle against the archenemy of God and man, His special creation. Witnessing Christ reunited with Abba God infuriates the devil and fuels his anger to keep mankind from experiencing relationship with the Trinity and having eternal life.

Both the Old and the New Testament repeatedly have examples of spiritual warfare, showing its main components of deception, temptation, and finally, sinful action. The important thing to grasp is that spiritual warfare is a reality. It affects all human beings beginning at birth, regardless if they later accept Christ's salvation or continue living in bondage to their sinful nature. This spiritual warfare continues until physical death. When one chooses to accept God's chosen personal ministry, spiritual warfare is soon to follow and will continue until physical death, even if that person ceases doing God's chosen ministry.

Also of note is that spiritual warfare is not limited to those who accept Christ's eternal salvation. Spiritual warfare is inherent from birth with every human being. With deception, using the ways of the world and the flesh, the devil attempts to convince the unsaved there is no need for repentance. Believing this lie and living this lie makes the unsaved person less of a target for the enemy, for the devil then has achieved his purpose. The last prophet to herald the coming of Christ, John the Baptist, understood this very well and fervently urged the lost to repent.

When a person does accept Christ's salvation, other deceptive tactics are implemented to keep that individual spiritually immature and to refuse acceptance of God's call to personal ministry. With both the unsaved and the spiritually immature, the devil doesn't have to waste his time, energy, or fire power, because they pose no threat to his objective of keeping humans from relationship with the Godhead. The unsaved scoff at the idea of God and eternal life. And the spiritually immature are content with their own salvation and see no need to pursue a growing relationship with Christ. Spiritually immature believers see no need to pursue God's chosen ministry for purpose and meaning in their earthly life's journey.

Those individuals who answer God's call to His chosen personal ministry find themselves in the cross-hairs of the devil's scope. They are subjected to spiritual warfare tactics intended to neutralize their efforts and ultimately to get them to abandon the ministry God elected them to carry out. Understanding this, it is wise to prepare for the battle.

PREPARATION FOR SPIRITUAL WARFARE

Once believers come to grips with the fact that spiritual warfare exists and is directed specifically towards them, they encounter a crossroad. They either attempt to battle the varying tactics employed by the devil in their own power and effort, or they realize their total dependency on God and ask His Holy Spirit for guidance, counsel, and supernatural power for victory. These are the only two choices available in this deadly spiritual war. Relying on one's self is to choose the way of pride, arrogance, and control. Asking the Godhead for assistance, guidance, and direction comes only by totally surrendering one's will to that of God's. It's also admitting one's total dependency on God and the realization that we can do all things only through Christ Jesus who strengthens, empowers, and directs. This is pleasing to God.

This choice is depicted in Proverbs 3:5-8. *"Trust in the Lord with all your heart, and lean not unto your own understanding. In all your ways acknowledge Him, and He will direct your path."* Victory is guaranteed when a person heeds the wise advice given by Solomon and trusts in the Lord. However, when a person chooses to follow the ways of the world and its deception, failure is guaranteed. Trusting in God, being totally dependent on Him, is the first step in combating spiritual warfare. The second step is to make a concerted effort to study His Word. This doesn't mean merely listening to a preacher give a message on Sunday, nor does it mean occasionally reading the Bible. Neither does more attendance in a Bible study necessarily mean studying God's Word.

Studying the Word of God means reading and praying for discernment of His Word, researching explanations and meanings through different commentaries, and meditating on what is spiritually revealed. Studying God's Word includes repeatedly praying and asking for clarification, discernment, and wisdom. This form of meditation is *not* the same as eastern religious and philosophical approaches where you sit in a certain position and focus on meaningless chants that serve only to dull one's opportunity of connecting with The Holy Spirit. Meditating, or deep reflection, is very important because it is a special time of taking all of one's questions and concerns to the Holy Spirit to receive His counsel, spiritual revelation, guidance, and direction.

Spiritual warfare is directed at every aspect of a person's life. As such, one needs awareness to take the necessary steps to eliminate its diabolical intent. This does not mean that a demon or the devil is directly involved in every bad or negative occurrence in one's life. The Apostle Paul wrote that we battle the flesh and the world in addition to the devil and his demons. The flesh is our sinful nature that we are born with and continues to be a thorn embedded in one's emotions, feelings, and thoughts even after accepting Christ's salvation.

A person is subjected to moments of adversity when the emotions and feelings may cause such a stirring within the body that the mind wrongly interprets these stirrings and results in negative or sinful action. Triggers of feelings and emotions fire the bullets of emotional pain, hurt, discouragement, despair, and anger. Ever get mad when someone cuts you off in traffic and you react by cursing them or making an obscene gesture? Have you ever gotten angry and verbally lashed out at someone for disagreeing with you, then later felt bad about doing so? Have you ever gone along with the crowd with some form of action despite uneasy feelings, or knowing that the action was wrong? Have you joined an organization or club to be with friends, even though what it stands for does not honor God? Have you ever rejected a person based on a difference of political affiliation, race, or because they belong to a different denomination?

These questions are examples of the subtle nature of deception, the number one tool of the devil. It was deception directed toward Eve that led to her disobedience of God's command. It was deception that caused Saul to persecute followers of Christ based on religion and culture. It is deception that leads one denomination to believe they are more spiritual than other denominations. Deception is why unsaved heathens call

Christians hypocrites. It is deception that causes Christians to act in the manner of a hypocrite. It is deception that causes an individual to align with religion rather than pursue a personal relationship with Christ.

Deception is first directed at one's senses (touch, sight, taste, smell, and hearing) then one's mind (thoughts and decision-making). The two intermingle to the point it's sometimes difficult to separate the flesh from the culture (the world). This is why the devil can appear like "an angel of light." He seldom appears unveiled as who he really is; if he did, it would be much easier to reject him and his efforts to destroy one's relationship with God. Take some time to reflect on how the devil has deceived you into ungodly behavior. As Jeremiah lamented, *"The heart is deceitful and desperately wicked. Who can know it?"* (Jeremiah 17:9) We need to let the Holy Spirit search our hearts and show us any evil that hides there in disguise. As David the psalmist said, *"Search me, O God, and know my heart; try me, and know my thoughts; And see if there be any wicked way in me, and lead me in the way everlasting."* (Psalm 139:23-24) This is a humble willingness to be corrected and instructed by God. If we can't be honest with ourselves, we are being deceived.

After reading the definition of spiritual warfare, the various Biblical examples of how it has taken place throughout time, and its deceptive nature, the first step in preparation to combat spiritual warfare is *acknowledgment*. Acknowledging and accepting the fact that spiritual warfare indeed *exists* is the first step to successfully overcome deception. Often this isn't easy for an individual. Yet recognizing spiritual warfare is directed towards *us* is even more imperative.

False illusions that spiritual warfare isn't very important, is an impediment that many people must still overcome. The unsaved heathen may have a high degree of education, yet insist that spiritual warfare is merely a figment of the imagination of a person subjected to antiquated religious belief systems. Christians may not be properly taught about spiritual warfare, and therefore are dubious of its impact on their relationship with God and His plan and purpose for their lives. There are Christians who believe that spiritual warfare affects only non-Christians. The saddest group is Christians who don't believe that spiritual warfare even exists.

These false impressions of spiritual warfare can, and often do, go with a person to their grave. The Bible instructs us that all of mankind will be judged and held accountable for their actions. The ramifications of ignoring or denying the deception of spiritual warfare will be one of the big confrontations each human will have when they come face-to-face with the Mighty and Sovereign God.

Anyone attempting to become a mentor or any other God-chosen minister must first accept, then prepare for, and seek God's supernatural strength to stand firm in spiritual warfare. A person who does not do these things will not be effective as a ministry servant of Almighty God. The price for this neglect is very grave. God has a ministry for everyone who chooses to follow Christ Jesus; God chooses, directs, defines, and empowers His chosen ones.

COMBATING SPIRITUAL WARFARE

At this point it's best to list the tools for combating spiritual warfare:

1. Relying on the power of the Holy Spirit. Christ told His Apostles on the day of Ascension that He would send a new Counselor who would indwell them and guide them to all truth. (Luke 24:49 and John 14:16-17) It is the Holy Spirit's job to open the eyes of our hearts that we may see the truth and reject the deception of the devil. Put your trust and faith in the Holy Spirit and not in yourself, a denomination, or a specific church.

2. Asking the Holy Spirit's guidance and discernment through prayer and petition and listening for His counsel, guidance and direction. Go to God first and let Him direct you where He wants you to go. God never leads anyone into sin.

3. Obeying God's commandments and rejecting the ways of the world (the culture). Social groups, political parties, denominations, and religions are not the answer. Many times the devil uses these institutions as tools of deception. Man's focus should always be on God first.

4. Surrendering our will to that of the Lord God Almighty. Sometimes this is easier said than done, especially when the flesh attempts to persuade us that what we're doing isn't that bad. The pleasure associated with our sensory perception often confuses us into believing that what we're doing isn't wrong. Our intellectual reasoning jumps in and tells us to logically believe or do something that presumably makes sense. That person then adheres to scientific data that he allows to override God's Word. God's own words in Isaiah 55:8-9 tell us He is above all of man's sense of reasoning: *"For My thoughts are not your*

119

thoughts, neither are your ways My ways, says the Lord. For as the heavens are higher than the earth, so are My ways higher than your ways, and My thoughts than your thoughts."

5. Pleading the name and the blood of Christ Jesus. There will be times when spiritual warfare gets intense and the devil does things to confuse, agitate, or instill fear into one's being. When this happens, calmly and verbally in an audible voice reject the devil and his demons and his efforts and command him to stop in the name of Christ Jesus who conquered sin and death by His Holy blood that washes you clean. James 4:7 gives the assurance, *"Therefore submit to God. Resist the devil and he will flee from you."* This passage goes beyond rejecting sinful behavior or temptation. James is speaking to followers of Christ Jesus who are doers of the Word and who are actively and repeatedly engaged in true ministry. James knew, by divine revelation and his personal experience, the intensity of the devil to impede anyone from carrying out God's purpose. In verse 6 of Chapter 4 of his epistle, James states that God is opposed to the proud, but gives grace to the humble. Pleading the name of Christ Jesus is a manifestation of humility and utilizes the authority Christ bestowed on His followers.

When verse 6 is combined with verse 7, James instructs that pride is the core of sinful behavior and God is opposed to pride today just as He was when Lucifer first exercised it and was cast down from heaven. Pride is the highest form of idolatry. When the devil uses pride as the deception to lead us to act on temptation, human effort alone is not enough to combat this form of evil. When pride raises its ugly head, it takes divine power that only the Sovereign God has and is eager to give to nullify the efforts of the evil one. Not only is this passage truth (also found in Rev. 12:10-12), it's also a promise and a guarantee from the Sovereign God of the universe. Why be foolish and not take advantage of one of God's gifts to you? It's a simple matter of choice.

God's Holy Spirit gives advanced revelation at the height of the moment when pride is about to be manifested. This often comes in the form of discernment and conviction that is felt in one's heart as well as mind and body. It is at that precise moment the person being tormented by pride should immediately stop whatever action is about to be taken, and verbally plead the name and the power of Christ Jesus. Once this is done, the mind, the body, and the heart experience relief, peace, and joy. At that moment, the devil and his hounds of hell retreat in anguish, gnashing their teeth over their unsuccessful tactics. This doesn't mean these purveyors of evil won't be back; they will. But in all subsequent attacks, the servant of God is more ready and fortified to again rely on Christ Jesus to repel the attack.

Despite the urging of the Apostle James, this simple yet supernaturally powerful tool to resist the devil and his demons isn't taught to many Christians today. Even in many seminaries and Bible colleges, verbally rebuking the devil and his hounds from hell is thought of as primitivism, superstition, or denominational tradition and observance. Overlooking the power and the ease of what James implores us to use when encountering evil is an example of deception. Not employing this technique of rebuking the prince of darkness and demons robs us of enjoying the joy and peace that come from the power of Sovereign God. Ultimately allowing the devil to instill unrighteous fear into one's being, and harboring it, grieves the Holy Spirit. This bondage causes a person to stop carrying out the plan and the purpose of God, and effectively eliminates the storing up of treasures in heaven. Bondage negates effective ministry.

The first phrase of James 4:7 tells Christians to *"submit to God."* By submitting to God and verbally rebuking the devil and his evil intentions, we put *all* our faith and trust in God Himself. We acknowledge His sovereign power and our total dependency on Him and allow Him to fight the spiritual battle for us. Remember that the devil spent countless time as an angel of God, thereby having access and relationship with the Holy Trinity. He also has had centuries of time to observe man. Realizing this fact, it's easier to understand how devastating his deceptive tactics are against man doing God's ministry. Overlooking or not understanding the personalization of this tactic, results in allowing the devil access and influence over one's life. Read 1 Peter 5:8-11, meditate on it, and research what commentaries have to say about this passage. Then decide what course of action you want and need to take.

Two other words in James 4:7 are noteworthy. They are *"resist"* and *"will."* The dictionary defines *resist* as *"to actively oppose with force and to remain firm in refraining from or giving in to or enjoying the substance."* This definition certainly has spiritual applications and correlates to 1 Peter 5:8-11 and other passages throughout the Bible pertaining to following God and obeying His commands. The definition depicts that resisting must be continuous, and often requires force and perseverance, because the enemy is relentless in its attacks. There is also a cautionary aspect to this definition. The battlefield tactics are subtle, not easily seen or understood, and often appear fun or pleasurable. When the Apostle James chose this word, it was not a flippant choice. James knew that to resist requires great effort and often isn't easy.

The other word is *"will."* Our friend the dictionary again supplies apt definitions of this word. One of the top listed meanings for this word states, *"something decided on by a person of supremacy."* The spiritual application parallels the opening verses of the book of Job. The devil can do nothing without the permission of God and *is* under His authority. Another part of this definition says, *"diligent purposefulness (determination); self-discipline (self-control)."* Again, the spiritual ramification is for a person to repent (change) from those activities and actions that are harmful to relationship with God. The self-discipline aspect includes repeatedly telling the devil and his demons to flee and stop their harassment. The devil knows those "triggers" (weak points) that influence a person's decision making. He will attack them at different times to get the desired results of sinful action and disobedience to God. Imparting self-discipline is part of the assigned duty and power of the Holy Spirit. Man cannot consistently generate self-discipline. This is evidenced by people who cannot overcome addictions ranging from alcoholism to weight control. How many times have you heard or been involved with an individual who has attempted to overcome these personal habits, only to incur setbacks despite following a man-made method guaranteed to work.

Another way of looking at this definition of spiritual warfare and God's empowerment is this: "When God gives a blessing, no man or principality can take it away from that person; but he can give it away." Too often a person gives away the blessing, only later to become angry with God for his plight. This is what the devil hopes we will do during those times of harassment and spiritual warfare. It's all a matter of choice. This is evident in the Old Testament stories of Isaac and also Jacob and their offspring. Samson certainly illustrates having a great blessing and assignment and giving it away through his worldly lustful pursuits. The reverse of this is Daniel and his three fellow followers of God who resisted the worldly culture of Babylon and remained obedient to God. All four were blessed beyond their expectations. The final example is that of the Apostle Paul. No other recorded follower of Christ Jesus in the Bible encountered the magnitude of hardship, persecution, and spiritual warfare as did Paul who remained steadfast in his faith, trust, and obedience to Christ Jesus.

In more recent history, Martin Luther is an example of someone whom God blessed with discernment, wisdom, and supernatural power to battle the demonic forces that controlled the Roman Catholic Church at that time. Luther relied on the Godhead and successfully battled the physical and the spiritual warfare tactics thrust at him. Luther did not give away God's blessings to him, and the result changed world history. For a while, the devil gnashed his teeth over this until such time he was able to reintroduce deception into the minds of Christians who later chose denominations and sects over a unified church body following Christ.

Even as these words are written, there are followers of Christ in the early 21st century who are resisting the devil, not by means of their own strength, but in the power of the Holy Spirit. They are retaining their earthly blessings while building up many treasures in heaven, as well. Unfortunately, there are many, many more Christians who are giving up their blessings by not taking the steps necessary to receiving them from God's willing and generous Hand.

CHAPTER 7: CASE STUDIES ANALYSIS

The previous chapter pertaining to spiritual warfare was necessary to provide a better understanding of the deceptiveness and the subtleness employed by the devil to rob, kill, and destroy the plan and the purpose of God being carried out by man, His special creation, you and me. The preceding chapter on spiritual warfare is meant to assist you in participating in the following case study analysis.

Now each case study will be analyzed to reveal how the mentor handled the situation, and also will provide discussion of the questions asked at the end of each case study. Hopefully, you didn't jump ahead to the analysis prior to pondering the questions and your own answers. If you did so, it may greatly detract from the intended learning experience. It also may have caused you to overlook the underlying spiritual warfare involved in each case.

While the case studies have certain dramatic aspects to them, nonetheless they are real. At some point, a mentor will encounter different tie-ins of his own ministry to these case studies. The focus isn't on Hollywood-style drama. They are real examples of how the devil works today.

As each case study analysis is revealed, take your time and don't rush through it to get to the next one. Take time individually with your answers and approach to the particular issue and situation, and compare them to what actually took place. After doing your individual comparison, share your answers and approach with another individual or group in discussion.

Shared learning is invaluable in making your mentoring time effective and God honoring. Please be considerate of each other's answers and focus on the essentials of carrying out God's assigned ministry, His way, to further His kingdom. How each mentor handled the given situation cited in these few case studies was based on their spiritual maturity and experience at the time. Your answers and approach will reflect your spiritual maturity and experiences. Each case study analysis also indicates if mentoring took place, or didn't, and how the situation provided an opportunity for mentoring.

It's okay to compare approaches, but not in a condemning manner. Any comparisons should be founded on God's Word and not on opinion, or denominational influence. Take your answers and analysis to God in prayer and meditation asking the Holy Spirit to teach, counsel, and direct your path in mentoring.

If you engage in a group discussion of these case studies, add your own examples of involvement in life issues and make them available for discussion. Enjoy this special time and may it be a blessing to everyone.

સ્ર સ્ર સ્ર સ્ર

ANALYSIS: CASE STUDY #1, **TREVOR'S TROPHY**

The analysis of this case study begins with answering the five questions posed at the end of the brief narrative about Celeste. The key to analysis of this study is the word *pride*. Compare the spiritual definition of pride with both Trevor and Celeste in mind. This will provide insight to their decision-making. It was stated in the case study that both Celeste and Trevor had attended a denominational church while in college; yet neither had truly accepted or asked Christ into their respective lives. A commonality to all churches, denominational or otherwise, is that some or many of the attendees are not really saved. This was the case with Celeste and Trevor.

Celeste's brokenness was essential for her to ask Christ into her life as Lord and Savior. This brokenness was precipitated by the Holy Spirit, opening Celeste's eyes as to who she was in her relationships with Trevor and her employer. The Holy Spirit also revealed her pride to her. She was not aware of how she was valued until that fateful moment of conviction by the Holy Spirit. There is always a form of brokenness that precedes asking Christ to be Lord and Savior. Without brokenness there can be no transformation.

After experiencing this spiritual brokenness, Celeste asked Christ into her life as Savior and again the prompting of the Holy Spirit led her to Rose as a mentor. This is very important to know and to follow in the ministry of mentoring. Rose did not seek out Celeste because Rose did not know Celeste's heart at that given time; only God did and He directed Celeste to Rose. Celeste was ready, eager, and in need. The Holy Spirit conveyed this to Rose who, in turn, accepted God's assignment of mentoring Celeste. Had Rose initiated the action to get Celeste to agree to become a mentee, ultimately Celeste would have psychologically felt coerced into this action and stopped the relationship. Question 2 is answered here in the statement that it was the Holy Spirit who prompted Celeste to reach out to Rose.

Rose realized her primary role as a mentor was to get Celeste on the right track of seeking a deeper relationship with Christ Jesus. Counseling Celeste to seek a replacement church wasn't even a factor in her responsibility. God had blessed Rose with spiritual maturity to know in her heart what Celeste needed to do. This spiritual maturity included Rose's own personal experience of being in Celeste's situation earlier in her own life. This is very, very common among God's appointed mentoring ministry.

Rose re-entered Celeste's life at the prompting of the Holy Spirit. A mentor may have impact and leave a positive impression in the heart and the mind of a mentee, but may not be assigned to that same mentee a second time. In this particular case, God again led Celeste to Rose, primarily because Rose had experienced the pain, the trauma, and undergone the process of grief recovery. In essence, Rose could effectively minister to Celeste from the heart—not merely from theory or intellectualism gained from taking a class in grief recovery. Ministering authentically to someone who is actually experiencing the many different facets of the pain and grief cannot rely on theory.

The secular world and the Christian community emphasis is often centered on qualification. In the secular world, a degree or a license are the two more commonly accepted means to determine qualification. In the Christian community, it is usually receiving a seminary education followed by licensing from a denomination or other organization. In true ministry, it is God who is the qualifier, issues the license, bestows the degree, and anoints for His chosen ministry. Christ Jesus did not ask or require His disciples to be Pharisees or Jewish Rabbis when He called them to follow Him. Christ knew their hearts, and that led to their becoming His Apostles. The Apostle Paul was a Pharisee and well educated; yet when asked by Christ to follow Him, Paul had to forsake this previous stature and position and learn how to follow Christ and conduct His ministry.

It's important to note that during their first mentoring relationship, there were times of disagreement between Celeste and Rose. This was due to Celeste having to rethink her position on issues ranging from living in a secular world to being a follower of Christ. Rose had to teach, counsel, and show Celeste how to identify these stumbling blocks (deception) that were impeding Celeste's growing relationship with Christ. Once identified, Celeste then was able to ask the Holy Spirit to help her in repenting (changing, turning around).

What ended the mentoring relationship between Celeste and Rose was a very telling statement Celeste made to Rose; that Celeste realized she was merely a pawn, a trophy to both her employer and her husband, and she no longer was willing to accept that limited and demeaning role.

This first part of Celeste's statement was big; but even bigger was that Celeste saw how the Holy Spirit was working in her and that she did not want to have anything interfere with her personal relationship with Christ. Rose correctly assessed Celeste's spiritual maturity and knew from that point on, Celeste would grow through her involvement with the Holy Spirit. Another aspect of Celeste's focus on Christ Jesus was her statement she wanted to study God's Word, meditate on it, and let God bless her with discernment and wisdom, all of which are part of that special bonding with God through a growing relationship with Christ. Rose was always available as God's servant should Celeste ask for assistance.

Later, Celeste was chosen by God, in His perfect timing, to be a mentor to women involved with abusive relationships. Her personal experience in this arena became part of her qualifications for God to open that door to be His minister to women in spiritual, emotional, and physical need. This illustrates how God works and to be prepared to answer God's call when it comes.

It cannot be emphasized enough about the *experience* factor in mentoring. In this case study there are two women who were chosen by God to be His ministry vessels. The emotions, spiritual warfare encounters from their respective experiences, the brokenness, and finally the humility are key components to effective mentoring and other true ministries. All these components jelled to make both Rose and Celeste receptive to doing God's work. It was easy for them to surrender their will to God's. Those who practice intellectualism (theorists only) are too prideful, arrogant, controlling, selfish, and unwilling to surrender all of themselves to God's will and beckoning. They are like the rich young man who could not forsake his worldly possessions to follow Christ. In another context, intellectualists know all the answers, but they forgot the question—"Will you follow Christ?"

❧❧❧❧❧

ANALYSIS: CASE STUDY #2, EVE'S CONFRONTATION WITH HER FAITH

A total of thirteen considerations were given at the end of this case study to ponder for determining how Eve would respond to Stacy. This particular scenario is common in mentoring. There comes a defining moment that either takes the mentoring higher or it causes a complete breakdown. Mentors must be prepared for these defining moments. Here is what took place:

For two years, Eve had been a member of a group comprised of Christian women from her church who combined with several other churches to picket a local abortion clinic. Eve's pastor, as well as her women's small group leader, had passionately used Scripture as justification for picketing the abortion clinic and the doctors and nurses who worked there. Early in their picketing, one of the local television stations, two radio stations (one Christian format), and the local newspaper reported on the group's efforts. Eve was even interviewed twice at this stage of the picketing. Despite the notoriety and the exposure, the abortion clinic remained open. There were a few times when the group encountered backlash from members of the community for their picketing. Eve and the other group members considered this backlash a reaction of the devil and felt compelled to continue their efforts. Their pastor encouraged them to continue their picketing. Eve personally believed that the doctors, nurses, and the women who had the abortions would burn in hell for disobeying God's view on killing, ruining the body as His temple, and playing God. Eve was very adamant about her conviction, and on a few occasions her belief had resulted in heated arguments with her family members and others in the Christian community outside her home church.

Stacy's confession and revelation hit Eve right between the eyes and she felt hurt, disappointment, and anger towards Stacy. Eve's anger swelled up inside her that she had to fight to retain control in formulating her reaction to Stacy. As Eve looked into Stacy's face, she felt that she was seeing an entirely different person than whom she thought she knew. The combination of committing adultery and abortion were issues Eve could not accept. Her emotional reactions prevented her from hearing God's voice of guidance and direction.

Eve looked Stacy in the eye and began to preach to her the same Scripture passages she had been taught by her pastor and her small group leader pertaining to how abortion is a sin and that God hates abortion. With each passage, Eve's voice became stronger, more emphatic, and she felt a rising level of confidence that this was what Stacy needed to hear so that she could repent of her sin. Eve was so focused on her words she failed to see Stacy's facial expression change. Her teary eyes dried and began narrowing as she looked at Eve. Stacy's lips compressed, her jaw hardened and tightened.

Stacy realized the woman who was preaching to her was not the friend she thought she knew the past one and a half years. Before Eve could finish, Stacy interrupted her, citing lateness for an important appointment, but assuring Eve she would call her later to finish their discussion. Eve felt confused and troubled by Stacy's reaction, but believed Stacy was receiving the conviction of the Holy Spirit and nodded her head and said she looked forward to continuing their talk.

Stacy never contacted Eve again. She stopped going to the women's Bible study group Eve had gotten her involved with and refused to have any interaction with Eve. Any time Stacy encountered Eve, she would politely say she couldn't talk because of a busy schedule. Other times, she would simply ignore Eve and not return her phone calls. Stacy's actions were troubling and disappointing to Eve who could not understand why Stacy was giving her the cold shoulder, refusing to have contact despite the overtures Eve put forth. Eve informed her small group about her concerns for Stacy and they all agreed Eve had handled the situation properly. Two women from the small group attempted to contact Stacy who ignored their phone calls as well. After three attempts, these women stopped their efforts. Eve continued picketing the abortion clinic; and based on Stacy's confession, she felt more convinced this was the right thing to do.

Nine months after their final meeting, Stacy was driving to an appointment and encountered heavy traffic. At a stop light, she began channel surfing the car radio and stopped on a Christian station that was broadcasting a daily message by a nationally respected Bible teacher. His message was on forgiveness, and Stacy felt drawn to his every word. When the light turned green, Stacy quickly found a parking spot and stopped to listen to the inspiring words coming to her. After the teacher was finished, Stacy felt relief and suddenly tears began to flow down her cheeks and her lower lip quivered. A very strong feeling came over her and she cried out, "OK, God, I believe you are speaking to me. I can't live with this guilt anymore about my past and if you're real, I ask that you let me know and help me. I need you, Jesus, to change my life."

Immediately, Stacy felt warmth she had never felt before; there was also a feeling of peace, relaxation, relief, and a sense that a heavy weight had been taken off her shoulders. Stacy realized she was laughing, and her tears were of joy and happiness. She realized she had never felt so good in all her life. Using her cell phone, Stacy called and cancelled her appointment, and drove to a nearby park where she sat absorbing this new-found sensation. After a while, Stacy realized she had been at the park several hours and that it was time to return home.

When Stacy walked into her home, Stan was already home from work and was preparing dinner for the family. As he looked at Stacy, his earlier concern gave way to surprise. Stacy's expression and body language told him something positive happened and he was eager to find out what took place. After dinner and with the children in bed, Stacy initiated the conversation, relaying to him everything that had taken place earlier that afternoon. Stan beamed with joy and delight, knowing that Stacy had accepted Christ into her life with His salvation. This was an answer to prayer. On his deployment at the time, Stacy had the affair and became pregnant, but Stan had accepted Christ's salvation while at sea. Stan had written Stacy about accepting Christ into his life, and after his deployment he had talked to her more about his experience. Stacy had listened but remained non-committal to the idea of believing in Christ. The more she interacted with Stan when he returned from his deployment, she experienced a definite change in his character by the way he treated her, their children, and people they socialized with. Stan's change in thinking and reacting to different topics caused Stacy to look at Christian faith differently. Stacy did not see the hypocritical actions in Stan she had been taught by her parents.

Stan became more involved in reading the Bible, listening to different radio teachings about Christ and the Christian life. He never had pushed Christ onto Stacy; but repeatedly prayed for her on a daily basis. Stacy did not object when Stan suggested getting their children involved in Christian groups geared to their age levels, but she did not get involved. This arrangement continued for three years and nine months until that fateful afternoon when Stacy had her personal encounter with Christ.

Four months after her conversion, Stacy summoned the courage to confess to Stan about her earlier affair and abortion. It was the most difficult time of Stacy's marriage to Stan. She hoped he would understand, but her earlier experience with Eve caused her to question if revealing her past would ruin her future with Stan and end their marriage. Her revelation to Stan was gut-wrenching. There were moments when her throat constricted, her lips dried, her heart raced, and she initially stumbled to voice her revelation. With each sentence, she would haltingly look at Stan to gauge the impact it was having on him. The more she talked the more confident she became and she was buoyed by Stan's body language. Stacy left nothing out, including her earlier meeting with Eve and the resulting feelings and emotions she had.

After Stacy had finished, she felt immense relief but remained cautious about Stan's reaction. She didn't have to wait long. When Stan looked at her, Stacy saw his love and compassion, and he moved from the end of the sofa towards her and gently took her into his arms, tightly hugging her and whispering in her ear that he loved her. The couple shed tears of relief, joy and happiness, and knew in their hearts their marriage would endure. Stacy's biggest boost came when Stan said that God had forgiven him of many sinful experiences in his unsaved life and that he forgave Stacy for her adultery.

Stacy became involved in a Christian-based recovery support group where she learned other women also had experienced the agony of abortion and the rejection by various Christians. Some had experienced a relationship with God, while others were struggling with different aspects of surrendering themselves totally to Christ.

One year after attending this recovery group, Stacy became a group leader and also a "sponsor" or mentor to other women impacted by abortion—ministering not only on abortion issues, but divorce, anger, always listening to learn the hidden emotions of the women who became her mentees. Stacy always offered love, encouragement, compassion and shared prayer with each of her mentees. There were also those times when Stacy had to admonish and hold her mentee accountable, but this was presented in a kindly, non-condemning manner.

Stacy regularly would find out who was considering having an abortion and discuss with the woman why she was thinking of having this procedure. Other times, Stacy would obtain the names of women who had gone through with the procedure at the same clinic Eve and her friends continued to picket. Stacy would meet with these women, inform them that she too had the procedure and shared coffee with them, allowing each woman the opportunity to pour out their emotions concerning the procedure.

Stacy felt this was a God-given ministry whereby she could share her experience and assist different women who were going through the same private hell. Stacy would keep a journal of each session with her mentee and took the reoccurring main points, compiled them into a booklet that she gave each woman at their initial meeting. This non-threatening information proved to put the woman at ease and opened the door for further contact.

On some occasions, her involvement with the mentee resulted in the woman asking Christ into her life. Other times, the woman remained cool to discussing or listening about Christ. Unfazed, Stacy would continue mentoring the woman in a practical manner, letting the woman see Christ through her character, and demeanor. *"I realized that my experience, the pain, the struggles, and the suffering could be used to help other women going through what I did. I try to impress upon the women I deal with that if God can forgive me of my actions, He can forgive them as well, if they just give Him a chance."*

This case study is complete for our purposes. Now it's time to analyze what happened and how it pertains to mentoring and to spiritual warfare. The first focus is on Eve.

Eve blew it big time. God gave her an opportunity to minister, and instead of following Christ by reaching out to Stacy by listening to her pain, her struggle, and letting the Holy Spirit direct her, Eve opted for modern-day legalism. Eve quoted memorized Scripture, but she took it out of context and generalized without considering Stacy as an individual in need of God's grace. Eve's approach was based on the superficial teaching received from her pastor and small group leader.

Eve failed to perceive the sensitivity of the situation. In the New Testament, Christ is often characterized by the word compassion. As defined in the dictionary, compassion is: having a sincere concern for the suffering of another by giving aid, support, and showing mercy. True followers of Christ who surrender their will to His become blessed with this attribute and as such more Christ-like. Eve showed no support (encouragement), and definitely showed no mercy towards Stacy.

Eve was spiritually immature and therefore ill-equipped for effective ministering to Stacy, or anyone else. Eve was very "churched" and followed the directives of her pastor, a false teacher, and the small group leader who was the pastor's shadow. Eve relied on her emotional reaction to the encouragement and teaching of her pastor and small group leader. She did not study or meditate on God's Word on her own. Failing to do this prevented her from hearing the quiet voice of guidance, counsel, and direction of the Holy Spirit. Eve in essence had become an idolater. She put man ahead of God.

Eve was partially correct in her belief that Stacy was under the conviction of the Holy Spirit. What Eve didn't do was pray and petition the Holy Spirit for guidance and direction to be God's vessel to Stacy at a critical juncture of Stacy's life. As a result, Eve was the exact opposite of Proverbs 3:4-6. She leaned on her own understanding (her flesh and the culture).

Eve had no clue that spiritual warfare was taking place, probably because she wasn't properly taught about this reality. What Eve didn't realize was that she, too, was under the conviction of the Holy Spirit.

Compare Eve to the lazy servant Christ referred to in His parable of the talents. You will need a commentary as reference that details this lazy and wicked servant to see the bigger picture involved here.

Eve grieved the Holy Spirit by creating a barrier with Stacy through her legalistic (Pharisee) reaction to Stacy's plea for help.

Eve fell victim to the deception of the devil by following her strong feelings that were reflective of the sinful nature humans are born into. The flesh is a tool of deception the devil uses repeatedly with great success and he doesn't have to exert any effort in the process.

Now it's time to focus on Stacy:

Stacy was under the conviction of the Holy Spirit, but didn't realize it at the time. She approached Eve, not from desperation, but as a source of hope that Eve would supply the answers to what she was feeling and experiencing. Stacy felt she could trust Eve. Trust is a big factor in the mentoring relationship and it's very fragile.

Stacy stopped Eve's diatribe and all communication with her, seeing her as just another one of "those Christian hypocrites" she had encountered at other times in her life. Eve was long on accusing but very short on listening.

135

Stacy's reaction to Eve created a barrier for the Holy Spirit to initially intervene and get Stacy to act on His earlier conviction to accept Christ's salvation. Nine months went by before Stacy's heart softened to hear the prompting of the Holy Spirit.

What was intended for evil, God turned to good, just as is found in the Book of Genesis, the story of Joseph. When Eve failed to obey God and allow Him to use her as part of Stacy's accepting Christ's eternal salvation, He used another approach to reach Stacy via the message of the radio teacher. When God's divine plan is in action, He will overcome all obstacles to achieve His plan.

The experience with Eve factored into Stacy's and Stan's wariness of the Christian community. This wariness became a benefit during their visits with different churches. God's gift of spiritual discernment allowed them to see the deception associated with those churches and they refused to let this deception gain a foothold in them.

Stacy's heart, love for God, and desire to serve Him resulted in His blessing her with a powerful ministry, being a godly mentor, and being more Christ-like. Unlike Eve, Stacy's ministry came from God and not from man.

Stacy's willingness to follow Christ allowed Him to draw her closer to Him. Her willing surrender to Christ resulted in a deeper relationship with Him. In return, Christ blessed her with wisdom, perception, discerning spirits, and His spiritual power to thwart the efforts of the devil. Stacy became a valuable soldier in Christ's army, gaining victory in the battlefield on earth.

Compare Stacy's method of dealing with the issue of abortion to that of Eve. Which was more effective? Now meditate on the parable of the talents for a clearer picture and understanding of God's perspective on these two women.

A significant factor in comparing Eve and Stacy is *experience*. Eve had academic teaching through her church and knew Scripture but had no compassion, an essential component to effective ministry. Eve's adherence to the intellectual, academic approach to God's Word resulted in her knowing *about* Christ but not knowing *Him* and receiving Him into her heart. Whatever previous experiences and struggles Eve may have endured did not serve as a springboard to compassion. Stacy's pain, struggles, and experience resulted in her looking at other women with the needed compassion and understanding to help them.

Everyone will have pain, suffering, and adversity throughout life on earth--that's a given. Some will allow Christ to turn this into compassion to serve Him and carry out His plan and purpose while others will not. It goes to one's freedom of choice. This is why some people remain weak Christians while others become true followers of Christ and receive rewards, as two of the servants did in the parable of the talents.

Eve's conviction led her to believe she was participating in a ministry. Her pastor and small group leader reinforced this idea and she felt good about her efforts. Unfortunately for Eve, God saw it differently and His attempt to open the eyes of her heart to see the deception of the devil went unheeded. Eve engaged in man's definition of ministry, but not God's.

It's evident Eve's pastor and small group leader had no experience in true ministry and relied on intellectualism to perpetuate their opinions about God's Word. In essence, by following these two leaders, Eve committed idolatry but failed to realize this was happening. As an idolater, Eve could not hear the prompting or the pleading of the Holy Spirit. As of this printing, Eve has not changed and her adamant stance on abortion has led her to increase her angry efforts against abortion and all those involved in it.

చాచాచాచా

ANALYSIS: CASE STUDY #3, MAY THE FORCE BE WITH YOU

As a noun, *self-esteem* is how individuals view themselves. An individual develops this inner perspective by utilizing talents and skills that usually bring forth positive results. Success leads to additional involvements, which result in others giving approval and reinforcing one's achievements. Positive feedback and acceptance become springboards for a person to continue various involvements.

Low self-esteem occurs when there is no positive reinforcement or approval. The person's negative emotions, based on unrighteous fear, take control. Now the individual feels fearful of failure, rejection, and the unknown. Involvements become less, the person becomes more introverted, and seeks only those involvements where he or she can blend in and not stand out in any perceived way.

This was the situation with May. Her self-esteem was shattered by a series of events and remarks from her family, friends, and teammates. As a teenage girl, she was ridiculed by her parents and this was reinforced by several acquaintances at school. Nobody took the time to reassure May that what she did was acceptable or worthy of approval.

May's low self-esteem distorted her view of life and she lived with almost constant unrighteous fear of failure and rejection. Any unknown outcome of any circumstance so paralyzed her emotionally that she either had great difficulty doing various tasks or refrained from getting involved altogether. This lasted 47 years, until she heard Maggie's presentation. While May's low self-esteem issues began at age 13, it can occur much earlier in life. Parents, siblings, other family members, and friends or acquaintances can add fuel to the devastating fire of fear, failure, and rejection. The person receiving this ridicule is shocked to hear it from loved ones, and this loss of trust heavily influences them the rest of their life.

Maggie was correct in agreeing to counsel May. Maggie's personal experience with epilepsy resulted in God blessing her with His discernment, wisdom, and discerning spirits that served to equip her for counseling May. God often takes one's life experiences, adds His blessings, and stamps that person "certified" to be His vessel and servant.

Maggie didn't need to ponder her involvement with May. The Holy Spirit had been working in her prior to this agreement. Maggie's agreement to give her talk to the women was an indication of her willingness to follow the guidance and direction of the Holy Spirit. Read Acts 3 when Peter and John intervened with the lame man. There were hundreds of beggars in the temple on a daily basis, yet Peter and John were drawn to this particular individual. Why? Because they were led by the Holy Spirit. In line with this Biblical passage, Maggie didn't need approval from the sponsoring church pastor; all she needed to do was say yes to the Lord and go forth as His servant, which she did.

Again this goes to the prompting of the Holy Spirit. Maggie was initially surprised when May said Maggie's words dealing with self-esteem went to her heart; yet May was totally unaware the issue of self-esteem was part of her presentation. Maggie was no more aware of what God had planned than the lame man was in Acts 3—that Peter would heal him that day and change his life forever.

Of note is that the two women used a brand of candy that tied to their first name initials as a beginning to a relationship. It was a small, seemingly insignificant statement, but was the springboard to a deeper relationship. This took away the fear factor and the devil lost his advantage in preventing May and Maggie from connecting and carrying out God's plan.

May and Maggie continued their involvement for several years. Initially, they met once a week; but as May's relationship with Christ grew stronger, these meetings lessened to once a month or when May felt the need to consult Maggie. During this less frequent meeting period, Maggie never pressured May into meeting and did not force her views on May. Maggie was a true mentor by listening, seeking God's direction, and being His servant to May. Maggie was content with how God was drawing May to Him, and she had the wisdom not to interfere in their growing relationship.

ৡৡৡৡ

ANALYSIS: CASE STUDY #4, BILL AND RUTH'S QUANDARY

In mentoring to make disciples, there will be times of discord that may be harassment from the devil or a special time of testing from God. In either scenario, the bottom line is choice, or how a person makes their final decision. Should a person choose to follow Christ and emulate Him, then that resolution will be based on understanding, discernment, and blessed wisdom received from the Holy Spirit, through studying and meditating on His Word.

This can be capsulated in the word *choice*. You choose either principle or preference. Our friend the dictionary defines preference as: *"using a standard of truth that is more desirable in making a choice."* The dictionary uses the word *"a"* because in the secular mindset truth is relative. Science has a standard of truth; philosophy and law have another standard; and religion has yet another standard. The majority of time these relative standards do not mesh--creating confusion, discord, and arguments.

The definition of *preference* in essence deems desire (wants based on emotions) as the foundation for making all choices. This definition reflects what living in the flesh is all about. It's that me-first attitude of self-centeredness; that I'm right and there's no reason to consider any alternative. This definition also incorporates the worldly culture that shapes and influences a person's preferences. If enough people (usually a minority) make enough noise (gaining media attention) about their preference, others soon jump on their bandwagon, resulting in more people accepting this premise as truth and one that is preferable to them in decision making. This dynamic becomes two legs of the stool of spiritual warfare the devil eagerly and consistently uses. The third leg of the stool is not questioning one's acceptance of preference.

Preference is contrasted to principle. As defined in the dictionary, *principle* is: *"moral or ethical standards or judgments founded on a basic law rather than desires."* This definition is as close as the secular dictionary comes to admitting that God's laws are sovereign over all aspects of earthly living. The dictionary implies what God openly states— that His law is basic and irrefutable, will not change, and withstands the onslaught of objection and scrutiny. Hello, dictionary, this is what is taught in the Bible. God's laws become a rock-solid foundation the Bible repeatedly references to withstand the deception and temptation of the devil and for having relationship with Him.

In the worldly culture, laws and philosophy do not remain constant. Their premise and foundation is based on change (evolving) that is inherent to the desires and whims of whoever shouts the loudest that their cause is the best and will make life easier. The acceptance of this loud-speak permeates politics and religion, making their foundational standards similar to drifting sand—unstable and incapable of withstanding hurricane winds of destruction, confusion, deception, and temptation.

How Bill, Ruth, and Harry dealt with the hurricane storm of homosexuality differs dramatically from how the world elects to address this issue.

Harry's suggestion was that Bill and Ruth must remain steadfast on God's principle concerning homosexuality, despite the emotional involvement of Amy being their daughter. Any deviation from God's principle would send a message to Amy that God's truth and law was the same as man's, and would render it ineffective in addressing her preference to homosexuality. Harry indicated to Bill that spiritual warfare was at work, and both Bill and Ruth should realize that Amy's eternal salvation was at the heart of this issue. Bill and Ruth should view themselves not just as parents, but as God's vessels and messengers to Amy.

Another part of Harry's godly solution was that Bill and Ruth needed to manifest true love to Amy and continue to refrain from any condemnation or legalism associated with their final decision. True love can involve tough love. It was also offered that Amy needed to see the fruit of the Spirit from Bill and Ruth and God's precepts in action, meaning they should walk the talk. Harry also suggested that Bill and Ruth's answer to Amy could be God's weapon to cut through the deception that had taken over Amy's thinking and mindset.

Harry recited several passages from the Bible that encouraged Bill, some from the Book of Psalms, a couple from Proverbs, and some from New Testament teachings. Harry did not use these passages as justification for his viewpoint, but as references for Bill to ponder and meditate on with Ruth as they formed their final decision. Harry did not use Scripture as a weapon of condemnation as Eve had in an earlier case study.

Bill said he appreciated Harry's input and returned home. One week later, Bill called Harry and requested a coffee meeting. At the meeting, Harry could see through Bill's demeanor that a decision had been made and it was one both Bill and Ruth were comfortable with. Bill eagerly reported his and Ruth's decision and informed Harry that he and Ruth had called Amy to say they were going to be in her town and wanted to spend some time with her. At their meeting, Bill and Ruth let Amy bring up the topic of the impending wedding, knowing how important it was to her.

In response to her desire for both parents to be at the wedding, and for Bill to give her away as in traditional heterosexual weddings, Bill and Ruth calmly yet clearly declined to participate. They said they loved her with all their hearts, but they simply couldn't go against God's principle concerning homosexuality. They assured Amy they wanted a relationship with her and would not condemn her for her decision to marry another woman, but that their participation would be condoning such a relationship that God did not deem normal, and it violated their conscience.

They said that if Amy were to wed her lesbian partner, the two of them would be welcome in Bill and Ruth's home and would be shown God's love but there would be no acceptance of this union. Should Amy and her partner marry and visit Bill and Ruth, the two would have to abide by the rules of Bill and Ruth's home by not sleeping together, and refrain from all manifestations and affections associated with heterosexual marriage.

Bill and Ruth also said that should they visit Amy and her partner, they would stay in a motel and should Amy and her partner indulge in signs of affection associated with heterosexual marriage while in a social environment with Bill and Ruth, then Bill and Ruth would immediately leave. They further said they would not use Scripture as a weapon of condemnation against Amy and her partner at any time the four of them were together.

Bill also told Harry that Amy was not shocked at the decision her parents made concerning the impending marriage. She appeared irritated and disappointed, yet relieved she wasn't preached to about her desire for a lesbian union. Amy also revealed to her parents that she had received a response to the invitation sent to Harry that paralleled what Bill and Ruth stated. Her response was somewhat angry, stating the people she loved needed to be more tolerant and accepting, like society was, to homosexuality. Finally, Bill told Harry that Amy, after telling them of Harry's response, fought back tears, and said she felt conspired against by both her parents and Harry.

On the ensuing trip back, Bill and Ruth prayed together, giving God praise and glory for His guidance and assistance in directing them in this situation. They thanked God for His Holy Spirit's counsel, strength, and protection during their meeting with Amy. Their final prayer was thanksgiving, asking that their words and actions would have impact on Amy that she would hear God's voice of admonishment.

Harry did not interrupt Bill at any time during Bill's summary of the meeting with Amy and their decision. Once Bill had finished, Harry thanked him for informing him of what happened and then asked Bill how he and Ruth now felt after informing Amy of their decision. Bill said they had a sense of peace and calm about their decision and their emotions were free from anxiety, doubt, and anger. They believed God's will had been done. At the end of their time together, both men prayed with thanksgiving to God and went their separate ways.

Amy fulfilled her desire to wed her lesbian partner without the approval or the attendance of either her parents or Harry and his wife. Six months after their union, the two lesbians visited Bill and Ruth and did abide by the ground rules established earlier by Bill. After their visit, Amy's lesbian partner indicated she liked and respected Amy's parents and Harry and his wife. This came as a relief to Amy who wanted to reconnect with her parents. Three years later, Amy called her parents and tearfully informed them she and her lesbian partner had separated because the partner had found another woman she wanted more than Amy.

Bill and Ruth welcomed Amy into their home and comforted her over this break-up. They addressed Amy's emotions. They did not attempt to instruct, preach, or otherwise say or imply a "We-told-you-so" attitude. Amy spent the weekend with her parents; then feeling comforted, returned to her home and resumed work and life on her own. Amy often called or visited her parents and there were times Bill and Ruth visited Amy. They never referenced the lesbian break-up, but were observant of Amy, her words, attitude, and body language. Bill and Ruth would meet with Harry and his wife and thank God through prayer for His continued intervention and brokenness in Amy.

On a visit with her parents two years after her break-up, Amy declared to Bill and Ruth that she was no longer a lesbian. She had found a group of women who were former lesbians and who had established a support group for others coming out of this lifestyle. Bill and Ruth were ecstatic over this development and pledged their support to Amy in whatever way they could and however Amy wanted. Buoyed by their support, Amy relayed to her parents how the support group worked and that she had a sponsor, a woman from this support group, who was her mentor in her recovery from lesbianism. Bill and Ruth were pleased to learn that Amy's sponsor met with her on a regular basis and they had conversations about shared emotions and freedom from the bondage of homosexuality. A series of telephone calls, emails, and personal visits took place, and Bill and Ruth witnessed God's healing, grace, and growth in Amy. This process was enlightening to Bill and Ruth. They realized early on that Amy was right where God wanted her and that they should not interfere or impede God's work.

Amy's association with the support group led to her becoming a sponsor. She also began attending a different church than where the support group met and established a branch of the support group that aligned with the women's ministries of the church. While attending this church, Amy met a man who was recovering from drug abuse, anger, and co-dependency. They began talking, then had casual dates together. Over time they realized their love for one another was deep and decided to get married.

This wedding was attended by Bill and Ruth, with Bill giving Amy away in marriage. Harry and his wife not only attended but directed the reception for the newly married couple. The only created being not pleased with this union was the devil who gnashed his teeth.

What were the mentoring dynamics in this case?

Bill sought the advice of his mentor/friend Harry because of his trust and confidence that Harry would provide him sound, godly advice.

The relationship factor that developed between Bill and Harry was a key factor in Bill's decision making.

Harry did not preach to Bill nor did he become offended that Bill had not disclosed Amy's lesbianism to him earlier. Often in mentoring situations the mentee withholds pertinent information or incidents to the mentor until developments crest to the point that external help is needed.

Harry listened to Bill before making any reply. This is important to mentoring. Listening becomes a very important tool in assessing an issue, offering understanding how the issue is impacting the mentee, and allowing the mentor to obtain necessary information so that he can ask questions and make a determination of what the true, bigger picture is. Mentees will focus on those aspects of the issue that impact them the most emotionally and may not include other vital details the mentor may need in order to assist the mentee. The mentor must ask specific questions that will reveal the hidden aspects.

Harry manifested the fruit of the Spirit to Bill through his relationship with Christ and by living his life as a follower and servant to Christ. Harry was kind, empathetic, compassionate, and loving to Bill.

Harry, Bill, and Ruth did not hide their emotions, but they controlled their emotions created by this issue. By controlling their emotions they were able to confront the issue and not have it explode into a conflict. This was especially important when Bill and Ruth stated their refusal to attend Amy's lesbian wedding. Controlled emotions allowed Amy to see Christ through her parents, and they were able to remain steadfast in their principle of obeying God's command.

Bill, Ruth, and Harry prayerfully went to God, seeking His direction, demonstrating their total dependence on God.

Bill and Ruth were under a spiritual attack of fear by not disclosing Amy's lesbianism to Harry. This spiritual warfare included the influence of the worldly culture, evident even in their church environment. Many of their Christian friends were under the deception of the devil in their ungodly attitudes towards homosexuals.

Harry did not preach or scold Bill for not disclosing Amy's lesbianism. He did not allow his emotions to influence the advice he gave to Bill. Harry's wisdom and listening to the direction of the Holy Spirit resulted in his addressing the core of the issue--Bill and Ruth's emotions and thoughts. His simple question went to the heart of the matter that led to the solution. Harry's question took self (the source of all pride, arrogance and control) out of the matter.

Harry's simple question requesting Bill's thoughts on the issue resulted in Bill's revealing the various components of their struggle and how much their emotions were impeding and influencing their decision. A mentor does not have to be a trained psychologist to determine sources of conflict. The simple questions of who, what, when, where, why, and how are keys to unlocking doors that will expose the spiritual warfare. Taking time to consider sources that perpetrate deception, confusion, fear and undecidedness is time well spent. Although it's not necessary to be a trained psychologist, professional counselor, or pastor in battling spiritual warfare, it's vital to have a dynamic relationship with God. A relationship based on humility, obedience, and surrendering to His will results in being blessed with wisdom, discernment, and power to let God work through you, the mentor.

Bill's answers to Harry's question revealed his and Ruth's spiritual mindset that led Harry to the proper godly solution. Harry gave Bill a suggestion and did not impose any demand based on an emotional reaction to the issue.

Had Bill been more emotional, without any thought of seeking God's help, or had he indicated anger towards God for allowing this to happen, then Harry would have made a different suggestion.

Bill and Ruth remained firm to their *principle* of obeying God's command concerning homosexuality and manifesting love. They did not succumb to the temptation of *preference* when Amy tearfully reacted to their decision. This is also an example of resisting the blurring that sometimes occurs in mentoring and parenting. Their parental involvement with Amy did not go beyond the boundaries God states in His Word about being parents. Proverbs and Galatians have examples of this.

ৡৡৡৡ

ANALYSIS: CASE STUDY #5, MARK AND MARSHA GET RIPPED

Following the court proceedings, Mark, Marsha, and the children began the process of coping, living, and adjusting to the major change that always occurs as a result of divorce. Mark was able to spend time with his biological son, but the courts sided with Marsha in preventing Mark from having visitation time with his step-children. Losing total contact with Mark was devastating to the step-children who considered Mark to be their dad. This loss, plus the fact that Marsha refused to give them a bona fide reason for preventing them from having any contact or gifts, resulted in deep emotional problems for the children.

Shortly after the divorce was granted by the court, Marsha began seeing another man who was married. The two had met through a co-worker and began dating. Within two months, the man filed for divorce from his wife and married Marsha. This soon began to have a negative impact on Mark's relationship with his son. Marsha's new husband began to influence her, restricting Mark's visitation time with his son, and attempting to interfere with Mark's business. This resulted in several court appearances and caused hostilities between Mark and the new husband.

Mark experienced a lot of harassment and spiritual warfare during this time, and his friends Jim and Dan were very supportive and helpful. Ray was the opposite. Ray's approach was dictatorial, based on his limited lay counseling experience. Mark began spending less time with Ray. Five years after the divorce, Mark's friend Jim died and Dan was transferred to another state. Dan remained in contact with Mark via telephone and e-mails, and once a year he would visit Mark. Their friendship grew deeper, but when Mark would make overtures for Dan to accept Christ's salvation, Dan would refuse. Mark realized any further attempts to convince Dan to accept Christ as Lord and Savior would only weaken or end their friendship.

Twelve years after their divorce, Mark remarried. It also was the same year of his son's high school graduation. Dan attended the graduation and was Mark's best man at the wedding. Marsha made repeated attempts to influence the son not to have contact with Mark, but the son elected to move in with friends and curtailed contact with his mother.

God used Jim as a minister and mentor to Mark. Jim's divorce experience included his reliance and dependence on God. This paved the way for God to use Jim to mentor Mark. Ray, on the other hand, had no personal experience with divorce, and despite his previous lay counseling experience could not be an effective godly mentor to meet Mark's needs and situation.

In the Old Testament, God used a donkey to speak to a rebellious prophet. This answers the question of Mark seeking and listening to Dan's advice. God will use anyone or anything to accomplish His plan and purpose. If people say they believe in Him, but prove to be hindrances in allowing His plan and purpose to take place, He will remove them.

The Christian lay counselors did not have a positive influence or impact on Mark and Marsha's marital difficulties because they sought to follow the guidelines of the secular world. They were licensed by the state, which meant they had to take secular higher educational classes in counseling. These counselors chose to follow and to blend the secular with godly principles. This proved disastrous in their efforts to counsel Mark and Marsha.

Marsha's salvation indeed is questionable, considering her actions during the time she was married to Mark. Just because someone says they believe in God or say they know that Jesus died on the cross for their sins does not mean that person has accepted Christ into their heart. If a person doesn't accept Christ into their heart, they cannot receive the indwelling of the Holy Spirit whose role and purpose is to be counselor, guide, and teacher, just as Christ told His disciples prior to His ascension into heaven. In mentoring, it is important to establish the issue of salvation at the beginning of the mentoring process with the mentee. The simple question, "Who is Jesus to you?" addresses this issue. The prospective mentee's answer should be, "Jesus is Lord of my life and my personal Savior. His death on the cross and resurrection gives me eternal life with Him and His Holy Spirit dwells forever in my heart." Anything that simulates this answer reflects a person's acceptance of Christ as Savior. Should the person say, "I believe Jesus died on the cross and rose on the third day and is the Son of God and is preparing to someday return to earth." This does not state that Jesus is Christ, Lord and Savior to *him*. It is merely stating a fact. Remember, the devil spent time with the Godhead and acknowledges that Jesus is the Son of God, did die on the cross, was resurrected by the Holy Spirit, and knows He will return in glory to earth.

Mark and Marsha continued to experience marital problems after Mark accepted Christ's salvation. Spiritual warfare was directed toward them in the form of financial difficulties. This is one way the devil works. Mark was immature in Christ, and Marsha probably wasn't saved; so the two essentially were unequally yoked, making it easier for the devil to operate. The struggle and accompanying emotions allowed the devil to use the ways of the world to influence their decision making. The couple chose to follow a secular path to find solutions to their financial situation, rather than go directly to Christ and seek His help through the guidance, instruction, and direction of the Holy Spirit. They did not receive the spiritual solution because they leaned on their own understandings, and their emotional impatience became a barrier to hearing the Holy Spirit's voice.

Many Christian churches are unprepared to handle the spiritual warfare of divorce. Some denominations treat a divorced person as if they had the plague. In one particular denomination, an ex-con, convicted murderer can become a deacon or elder, but a divorced person cannot. Should a deacon, elder, or pastor experience divorce, that person must resign from his position and pressure is applied to leave the church and denomination. Many churches do not allow people who have experienced divorce to become lay counselors or ministers. Nor do they offer support group sessions for people going through this spiritual battle. Classes devoted to marriage offered through these churches exclude the issue of divorce and instructors do not have personal experience with it.

So, where was God in this situation? Good news. Where He always is—waiting to be humbly asked to intervene and save their marriage. Too often the simple solution, based on spiritual truth, is overlooked and not sought. Fear is the emotional tool of deception used in these situations to keep the afflicted from seeking God and His sovereign power to overcome the difficulty. Some vital points concerning divorce, and its associated spiritual battles, need to be stated at this juncture for those either entering the ministry of mentoring or already in mentoring.

There are at least eight fundamental points to remember when mentoring a mentee who is experiencing the spiritual battles of divorce.

1. **Contagious fallout.** When children are involved, divorce becomes a never-ending story. Despite the divorce, both parents have roles to execute in the developing and the raising of children. Often the emotional issues causing war between the parents carries over to the children who end up being the victims. Children are torn by divorce and when a parent attempts to use them against the ex-spouse, this makes matters worse. Even after the children are adults, warring between the parents can continue in blatant or subtle forms with the children stuck in the middle. The ongoing anger between the parents becomes an infectious disease to the children.

2. **Emotional victimization.** Divorce doesn't end in the courtroom. Even if there are no children involved in the divorce, the personal pain resulting from the break-up of the marriage continues and can even escalate. There is *always* a victim in divorce. The one who either doesn't want the divorce or is surprised when the spouse announces their intent to divorce is usually the victim. This person's emotions are similar to a rumbling volcano that ultimately erupts. The eruption can take the form of depression, loss of confidence, not trusting others or oneself, second-guessing one's decisions, inability to establish relationships, involvement with addictive behavior (alcohol, drugs, co-dependent relationships or promiscuity) and loss of faith and trust in God. In our case study, Marsha remarried much sooner than Mark who manifested several of these emotional reactions common to victims.

3. **Wrong assumptions.** In the United States, 99% of divorce cases result in the mother becoming the custodial (primary) parent, and the court makes generous allowances to the mother. Many states have civil statutes that curtail the father's visitation, parenting time, and financial status. The secular courts have labeled "deadbeat dad" and have made this assumption without regard to the individual circumstances of a particular divorce case brought before them. Some readers may take exception to this statement, nonetheless it's often true and another way the devil deceives to get his end result. A famous attorney, F. Lee Bailey, once was quoted as saying, "In the American civil court system, the only time a mother isn't granted primary parental custodial rights is if she dies, becomes incarcerated, is officially declared incompetent, or officially gives up her primary custodial rights. No other factors are taken into consideration and the father is made to look unfavorable as a parent. This is why I refuse to get involved in divorce cases." This is

stated here to alert mentors to some misunderstood aspects in divorce cases.

4. **Lost relationships.** There's a paradigm shift in relationships. Friends and family always end up taking sides in a divorce. Usually the friends made prior to a marriage remain such after divorce. Friends and acquaintances made during the marriage split allegiances and go with the person they feel more comfortable with. In some cases some friends and acquaintances end contact with both parties of the divorce. The same occurs with family members. Rarely will one person's family side with the other person of divorce. In our case study, Marsha's parents were receptive to continuing relationship and contact with Mark, but chose not to do so out of concern of offending Marsha. Mark's father did not support Mark for reasons besides the divorce.

5. **Insufficient understanding.** The courts are busy and often seem blind to justice. The current American justice system makes available a simple no-hassle form of divorce; unfortunately, this option isn't used that often and isn't allowed when children are involved in the divorce. The result is costly involvement with attorneys and court filings, with heavy monetary involvement for both parties. The court system doesn't care about one's personal feelings, it's treated like a business and the court has the ultimate power and control. The court makes some attempts at considering the impact on children, but often adds to the problem rather than making it easier, due to generalized rulings, insufficient time and lack of understanding the true picture.

6. **Financial crunches.** Money is always a stumbling block and a frequent issue. This issue is powered by one's emotions, with emotional fuels like anger, bitterness, envy, hatred, arrogance, fear, resentment, and retribution. Many times the warring parties can't agree on who gets what "stuff" so they allow the courts to make the final decision. Part of the complication involves joint accounts, credit cards, timeshares, debts, savings, investments and other assets that came about before or after the marriage. With children in this mix, there is child support, which often results in the father paying more than what it actually takes to raise the child. Attorneys refer to their version of "creative financing," whereby the mother's financial statements have more leverage than the father's, and the formula used to calculate the child support is based on the number of over-night visitations allowed the father. As an example of this, an attorney for the mother may become adamant about limiting the overnight visits to the father to 92 visits or less in a year. In some states,

151

93 or more overnight visits causes the child support amount to drop dramatically in favor of the father.

7. **Desperation for control.** Control is an ugly and powerful factor present in negative emotions. Anger and fear combine to lead one or both of the divorcees in attempts to influence or control the personal aspects of their ex-spouse. When infidelity is involved, the ex-spouse victimized by the cheating too often wants revenge, sometimes at any cost. Another control issue often related to money. After the divorce decree, should one ex-spouse begin to acquire more money or seem to have the better life, the other ex-spouse feels offended, cheated, robbed and often wants to take measures to get "their fair share." Attorneys are quick to return to the courts for adjustments. The real winners are the attorneys and the courts in the fees charged to the warring parties. The building emotional pressure for all parties comes closer to erupting.

8. **But God has the answers.** The Phoenix cometh. Divorce has many dark days of pain and suffering, but out of the ashes of this destruction sprouts new life. Time is not the healer of deep emotional wounds resulting from divorce. People may get involved in other pursuits and personal relationships, but the emotional impact from divorce often becomes baggage that influences who they get involved with and what activities, organizations, churches or occupations a person chooses for personal rebuilding. God is the only true Healer and all a person has to do is submit his or her will, emotions, and mindset to His, and He will restore, renew, and create a better life. God wants to do this, but it requires obedience, humility, and realization of one's total dependence on God. Pride, control and fear are the enemies. They stand in the way of God becoming involved. Pride in believing you can go it alone, control in doing it your way only, and fear of unknown possibilities, rejection or failure. God is willing, but our strong-willed self can be an obstacle to receiving God's blessing.

This case study of Mark and Marsha shows what happens when a person who isn't qualified gets too deeply involved in the dynamics of divorce and attempts to be the problem solver. This is a disaster in the making, and regardless of the mentor's intentions, it is still disobedience to God to begin, however confidently, without praying for His guidance and approval of your involvement.

One of the key components in ministering to people going through divorce is the mentor's personal experience factor. Experience becomes the foundation for understanding, and God chooses who He wants to minister to His special one who is enduring the pain and suffering of that particular form of spiritual warfare. Remember the cliché, "The road to hell is paved with good intentions." The Biblical counterpart to this is that God considers partial obedience to be serious and complete disobedience, and our final accountability to God will be the one that counts.

කරන්නකරන්න

ANALYSIS: CASE STUDY #6, PHIL AND SUSAN DOUBLE THEIR BET

This particular case study depicts the entwining of several stand-alone spiritual inflictions in both Susan and Phil and their impact on Jan and Wayne. The details of this case study also reveal the devil's subtle deception and tactics that combine multiple weapons of spiritual attack to confuse, weaken, and ultimately destroy the selected target.

When a couple marries, usually part of their intention is to produce children in the marriage. Not only is this part of the culture, but the love shared by the couple leads them to want children. Phil wanted children with Susan; after discovering he was physically unable to produce children, he became depressed. The spiritual warfare tactic was to attack his sense of manhood, worth, and to instill fear of failure and possible rejection from Susan. Added to this was the announcement by Jan and Wayne that they were to become parents. Phil did not feel normal. He felt like an outsider who didn't fit in.

Phil's background and involvement with athletics became his consolation. The memory of his second year as head football coach, when the team finished second in the state finals, was confirmation to him of his coaching ability and his manhood. However, the spiritual battle tactic was to attack this again with the fear of failure. The team, the student body of the high school, the administration, and the community had high expectations for him, and this created undue pressure on Phil to succeed. These combined elements led Phil into gambling.

Involvement with gambling became a bitter-sweet experience for Phil. It contributed to his depression and sense of failure. Phil believed he was knowledgeable about the sport of football and as such could accurately predict potential winners. He had done this either alone or with friends who shared the same passion for the sport. When Phil began betting money on the outcome of games, the dynamic changed and the spiritual battle began. With every success in predicting the winner of a game came more losses. Phil was negatively impacted by the loss of the money bet on different games. As the losses exceeded the wins, Phil doubted his manhood, his abilities, and self-confidence, all of which became fiery arrows that impacted Phil's emotions and attitudes.

At first, Phil believed he could regain control of the gambling, which would allow him to regain control of his life. However, his repeated losses proved otherwise, and he felt relief when Susan confronted him about their depleted checking account. Phil's solution of transferring money from his personal savings account was a dual message he wanted to convey to Susan. First, that he had accepted responsibility for the actions he was able to admit to her. Second, it was a cry for help in a subtle way which pride and fear prevented him from openly saying. Unfortunately, his subtle cry was not received by Susan who naturally focused on the top layer of the iceberg—money and trust. Phil's bondage to gambling led to a second confrontation, but this time, his non-contrite attitude delivered a message to Susan, scolding her for not helping him the first time he revealed his problem. Again, the message was subtle, but with an edge indicating Phil really wanted to get help, but couldn't or didn't know how to approach Susan.

Phil sent a third message to Susan when he informed her of the $2,000 gambling loss. This message was louder, but when Susan added the stipulations before giving Phil the needed money, her message to him was she was the one taking control. Phil was relieved to get the money. But his relief was overshadowed by Susan's control, which he felt as another blow to his manhood. Susan misinterpreted Phil's agreement to her solution and believed he would follow through with her demand that he get counseling for his gambling.

The unplanned intervention by Jan, Wayne, and Susan and how they approached the subject of Phil's gambling problem resulted in Phil giving them a believable diversion that covered his deep anger. Phil's fear of failure, the unknown of what his wife and friends would do, and the fear of exposure motivated his diversionary explanation.

Phil's third confrontation with Susan based on the escalated loan default with their bankers was his loudest appeal for help. This time, Susan heard the cry, but she realized she could not help Phil. Susan came to the realization she was in over her head and sought the assistance of Wayne. It was Phil's broken spirit that allowed him to take the first step in recovery from his addiction. It's significant to note that Phil's brokenness opened the door to escape the bondage of gambling and the Holy Spirit responded by leading Phil to the support group.

Included in this case study is the co-dependent relationship that was a negative force and accelerated Phil's problem. Co-dependency can become a positive or a negative in a relationship. When two people have

155

a shared goal and use their respective talents, gifts and experiences to achieve that goal, co-dependency is positive. Both parties are aware of each other's attributes and they communicate with understanding during the developments involved with attaining the goal. Co-dependency becomes negative and a weapon in spiritual warfare when two parties cling to each other in unhealthy behavior patterns to compensate for the fears of failure, rejection, or uncertainty. One's emotions become very strong and lead to overlooking or not accepting the truth of the situation.

Susan was initially co-dependent with Phil during her college work on her Master's Degree. Phil's involvement during this time was appreciated by Susan. Spiritual warfare turned this into an unhealthy co-dependency when Susan struggled early with Phil's gambling. Reflecting on how much she had benefited from Phil's help during her college period made her reluctant to confront his gambling problem. Essentially, Susan's actions were also a message to Phil that she would allow his dysfunctional behavior if it meant they remained together. Further, this message was meant to convey her love for Phil and her willingness to stand by him in a way she felt would help him as he had earlier helped her.

As Phil continued his addiction to gambling, Susan realized his bondage was beyond her control and she sought the help of their close friends whom they loved and trusted. The unannounced intervention by Jan, Wayne, and Susan had elements of being positive, but to Phil it had more negative connotations. Wayne missed the opportunity to confront Phil and to help him when Phil asked him for money a second time to cover his gambling debts. It's possible that had Wayne been more aware of the bondage that gambling has on a person, he could have been a proactive vessel in assisting Phil down the road to recovery.

Susan's breaking point following the revelation by the bankers led to an emotional confrontation with Phil. Her sternness and body language showed Phil she was embarrassed by his actions and felt hurt, even betrayed, by his continued gambling and by his hiding it from her. Playing the divorce card to Phil drew a line in the sand, and reflected her frustrations and anger. The divorce statement was a release of the anger that had built up over the three years she had learned and dealt with Phil's gambling addiction.

Had Phil not reached that point of brokenness in his spirit, Susan's comment about seeking divorce would have caused an entirely different reaction from him. He might have become defiant and drawn his own line in the sand by saying, "OK, go for it." The devil hoped for this type of conflict, but did not count on God's Holy Spirit intervening with protection over both Susan and Phil at this point in their shared struggle. The key to the Holy Spirit's help was their individual brokenness and receptivity to listening to God's Spirit.

Phil joined a support group at a different church than the one he and Susan attended. This was not by chance; he was led there by the Holy Spirit because that church used its facilities as a refuge for the sick, the struggling, and those in pain. That church exhibited the love Christ talks about in the Gospels and is reiterated in the Apostle Paul's writings. The church allowed lay ministers to use their gifts, experiences, and ministry callings from God. The church delegated the authority, and monitored the methods, but did not interfere by attempting to get involved in matters the pastor or the staff were not qualified or authorized by God to do. The same could not be said of Phil's and Susan's home church.

Phil's addiction to gambling strained his relationship with God just as it did with his relationship with Susan. The gambling bondage weakened relationship with God and led them to rely on their own understanding to deal with a spiritual warfare problem. Jan and Wayne missed seeing this spiritual warfare tactic and did not approach it from a spiritual basis. Fortunately, despite being strained, the couple's relationship with God did not break. Each exercised freedom of choice throughout this struggle, and both Phil and Susan followed the conviction of the Holy Spirit reminding them of their sin of idolatry, putting themselves ahead of God, and not relying on His wisdom and power to solve the problem.

It's important for mentors to realize the extent and the subtle nature of spiritual warfare and also the simple steps that have been given us to combat the devil's deceptive tactics of destruction. It's impossible to battle spiritual warfare and spiritual principalities without God-given wisdom, methods, and faith. Humans have distinct limitations in battling the devil. God does not. The details of this case study reveal how much Phil and Susan needed individual mentoring early in this battle. Friends, relatives, co-workers, and anyone in relationship with others who experience similar symptoms to Phil and Susan, or Jan and Wayne should pray to God about this, seeking His counsel and direction regarding their potential involvement. Alertness to the subtle nature of evil is the first step in recognizing spiritual warfare.

As in other mentoring scenarios, there are other factors and aspects that may be apparent to you. Any of your additional questions and thoughts not answered by this analysis should be taken to God in humble prayer, seeking His face and His answers. He will give you further insight and wisdom.

ஒஒஒஒஒ

ANALYSIS: CASE STUDY #7, YVETTE'S INFERNO

Death is a difficult situation with the majority of humans. The Old Testament has examples of the impact death had on the people involved. Nothing has changed since those early days. Death is inevitable, but the real issue is how a person deals with this issue. It becomes extremely difficult when an infant or young child is "taken before their time." The death of a child is more devastating than that of an old person and more difficult to reconcile. Unfortunately, the secular world is quick to pounce on emotionalism via media outlets. At times, the media outlets exploit and inflame the issue, creating more turmoil and more fodder for the devil to use in his spiritual warfare tactics.

Such was the case for Yvette and Dan as well as the immediate family and close friends. The devil played on their heightened emotions to influence as many people as possible. The intent was to use anger as a tool to destroy their personal relationship with God. When the media became purveyors of this demonic weapon, people who did not even know the family were impacted by Alisha's early earthly departure. It's extremely easy for any parent, grandparent, or single person to fantasize about the passing of a child. Quickly their emotions become ignited, and they wonder and think about their own children, grandchildren, friends' children. Often, anger towards God ensues. It is important to remember this is spiritual warfare and demonic.

When one is involved in this type of situation it is imperative to immediately turn it over to the Godhead to thwart the devil. Christ's disciple, Paul, instructs the church to "take every thought captive" and this type of situation is a prime example of what Christ's servant implores. So how are we to do this? The answer is to prayerfully ask God for His discernment, wisdom, and discerning spirits for controlling our emotions. The second move is to rebuke the devil and his hounds from hell by stating, "In the name and the blood of Christ Jesus, I rebuke these emotions and thoughts and I command all demons of deception and harassment to flee." Jesus was not the only one to rebuke demons. Read the New Testament to learn how Peter and Paul emphatically urge and instruct believers in Christ to do this. Both of Christ's servants were experienced with demonic warfare and knew how to handle it effectively.

The third move is to immerse the mind in the words of truth that God gives us in His Word about His love, His wisdom, and His comfort. Truth is the strongest antidote for lies and deception.

Too often, believers in Christ don't do this, mainly due to ignorance or fear of the unknown. Sadly, very few churches adequately teach that this is the Biblical way to deal with demonic harassment. The result is the believer in Christ loses an opportunity for God to bless him or her with wisdom and discerning spirits and in the process draw closer to Him.

Insights for the questions posed at the end of the case study:

God does not promise physical healing in every instance here on earth. Both the Old and the New Testament have examples of God's healing miracles, but since He is the sovereign creator and giver of life, He also has a specified time He calls His children home regardless of age, gender, or anything else. Yvette's thinking was really based on an expectation of God doing things her way. This is idolatry. We are to be His servants and not vice-versa. In Isaiah 55:8-11, God is very clear about not only who He is but how He operates. Read this passage and meditate on it.

The support group took Bible verses out of context and attempted to use them for their own desires in dealing with the inevitable issue of death.

Praying can be a waste of time if prayers are based on emotions, presumption, attempted manipulation, or ungodly speculation and thinking. Prayers based on the leading of the Holy Spirit are never a waste of time. At times when we don't know how or what to pray, we can rely on the Holy Spirit to communicate our heart's anguish, needs, and requests to God (Rom. 8:26-27).

In addition to providing physical needs, Sarah was there as a spiritual counselor and mentor. When Sarah heard Yvette's reasons for her anger towards God, Sarah knew her own limitations. The action she took was to first pray with Yvette for God's guidance for the both of them, that He would comfort them and bless them with His protection, and finally give them His strength to continue dealing with this issue. Sarah then sought the advice of her mentor who later assisted Sarah by counseling both Yvette and Sarah. This mentor had experienced the death of a child and was skilled and understanding in grief counseling. Sarah did not go ahead of God, but listened to the Holy Spirit and followed God's counsel and direction.

ɶɶɶɶ

ANALYSIS: CASE STUDY #8, HENRY'S CALL TO DUTY

This particular case study reveals several key aspects of mentoring when an issue, a personal struggle, is not properly confronted and results in conflict.

After Jake walked out of the restaurant, he walked away from Henry and the church they attended with Henry and Joan. Jake, in a calm but stern tone, told Pam she was not to discuss any of their private matters with anyone, and if she were to do so, he would file for divorce. Jake also stated that his personal beliefs were his, and that he could handle any of life's problems himself and didn't need any hypocrite Christian—who didn't have a clue as to who he was—meddling in his life. Jake said that Pam should be content with their life together, that after all he was providing a good home for her and their children, was working hard to secure their future, and was not harming anyone in any way.

He asked how she believed that what they did to enhance their sex life could be considered a sin; after all, she told him she enjoyed their sex life together. He went on to say that what they did in the privacy of their bedroom was between them, and if he really had a pornography problem he would be having affairs, which he wasn't, because he loved her. He stated what they were doing wasn't breaking any laws, they weren't harming themselves, their children, or anyone else; and therefore, the problem was in Pam's head and the beliefs of hypocritical Christians. He emphatically informed Pam he would not be attending their church again or any church for that matter, but if she wanted to associate with a bunch of losers that was her problem. He emphasized that he felt religion was a thing of the past for weaklings who weren't strong enough to handle life's problems.

Jake also told Pam he would not associate with either Joan or Henry and they were not welcome in his home under any circumstances, but if she wanted to continue being friends with Joan that was her decision. He wouldn't interfere so long as their friendship did not cause problems between Jake and Pam in their marriage.

Pam continued to meet periodically with Joan for a short time, but the friendship dissolved after six months. She remained married to Jake, and worked at making amends with him for disclosing to Joan their private life. Jake did not stop his participation in pornography. He had several affairs that Pam became aware of and confronted Jake about. He assured her he would stop, but it's unknown if he actually followed through on his promise to Pam. Jake refused to have any associations with Christians.

The impact of the incident with Jake resulted in Henry leaving the church mentoring program and the men's breakfast Bible study group which he led. He continued as director of the vacation Bible school and as leader of the ushers and communion distributors, and he became more involved in the church's financial matters. At the conclusion of two years' participation, the church ended their affiliation with the national men's mentoring organization, citing financial costs plus lack of church members stepping forward to become mentors.

Henry resumed contact with Terry and eventually disclosed the details of the situation with Jake, asking for his input and advice. Terry willingly walked Henry through each phase of the situation, explaining and teaching what he had learned from his years of involvement with mentoring. Henry listened intently, often asking probing questions. Three months after seeking advice and counsel from Terry, Henry received closure on the issue involving Jake. What Henry learned is that walking with the Lord in the Spirit is not the accumulation of facts or involvement in "church" activities and programs per se, but following Christ and the prompting, guidance, counsel, and the direction of the Holy Spirit. Walking with the Lord meant the Spirit's manifestation in his character, developed through obedience to God.

Henry realized that God had not called him to the mentoring ministry because that was not where his talents and gifts were pertinent to fulfilling God's plan and purpose for his life. Henry realized and admitted his participation in the mentoring program of the church had been based on his emotional reaction to statements by the senior pastor. He wanted the approval and position that would come if he took on the task the pastor asked him to do. Henry also learned that mentoring is not the same as establishing a friendship with someone.

Humbling to Henry were the events following the devastating meeting with Jake which resulted in the loss of Jake and Pam's friendship. He saw that his actions, chosen because they satisfied his desire for approval, had impeded the work of God. Through Terry's counsel, Henry also realized the nature of spiritual warfare, how it had been involved in this situation, and he recognized the necessity of going to God first before getting involved in any ministry.

Joan should have first asked Pam why she was telling Joan these intimate details of her marriage with Jake. Joan also should have asked Pam what she wanted concerning this matter. Clearly, Pam was distressed and under the conviction of the Holy Spirit about her willing participation in Jake's pornography. By listening more and asking questions, Joan would have had a better idea of the issue and insight how to proceed.

Likewise, if Joan had more detailed information about Pam's distress and her permission to consult with Henry, he would have been in a better position to take the next step. Joan and Henry should have prayed to God, turning the issue over to Him and allowing Him, through His Holy Spirit, to guide and direct their actions. It's entirely possible that God wanted them to just listen to Pam before taking any action. Had Henry waited on the Lord, he would have received instruction about going to the senior pastor or the mentoring director with this issue. God may have shown them to avoid both the mentoring director and the senior pastor because their motives were to advance their church membership numbers more than to be servants of God. This is found in all four Gospels, telling how Christ dealt with the Pharisees.

Involvement with the national men's mentoring organization in this case was wrong because of the wrong motives and ultimate goals of the organization. Mentoring has structure and form and definite guidelines, and those things are good, but the sole purpose should be to make disciples, and carry out The Great Commission, not to grow membership lists. *"Whatever you do, do heartily as to the Lord and not as unto men, knowing that from the Lord you shall receive the reward of the inheritance, for you serve the Lord Christ."* (Colossians 3:23-24) Neither should the national mentoring organization have limited participation only to men. Making disciples is not gender specific.

Henry wasn't a real mentor to Jake because Henry's spiritual immaturity and focus was on conducting a Bible study and adhering to the program's dictates. Henry did not attempt to find out where Jake was emotionally, mentally, or spiritually. At the very beginning, Henry should have asked Jake who Jesus was to him. This simple question would have given Henry insight as to where to begin. Henry should have asked Jake why he believed the things he did about Christ. The core reason for Jake's refusal to turn his life over to Christ remains a mystery because he was not asked a very simple question. Before evangelizing, Henry needed to explore in depth to find out Jake's pain, struggle, and fear of accepting Christ into his life. Evangelizing was first needed, followed by mentoring. This is an essential prerequisite to mentoring, and Henry blew it big time. Henry's background did not lend itself to mentoring because his focus was not on dealing with pain, suffering, or struggles. Henry wasn't skilled in dealing with people, or with confronting spiritual forces fired by the devil. He did not have the spiritual maturity or the authorization from God's calling to become a mentor, yet he volunteered based on his emotions while overlooking who he was in Christ.

The only way Henry should have become involved with Jake's issues was if Jake had asked him to become involved. It is one thing to observe and discern a person's struggles and pain, but it's another to become involved based solely on observations. Jake's real struggle was with God, and his defiant spirit was rejecting God's conviction from the Holy Spirit. Jake did not have ears to hear or eyes to see God's attempts to establish a relationship with Him. He was not open to help or spiritual mentoring.

The simple fact of the matter is that a person has to be broken free from his flesh and bondage to worldly culture before he or she will accept Christ as Savior. The cliché of leading a horse to water but his refusal to drink is an apt analogy in evangelizing, mentoring, or any other bona fide ministry established by God.

Our spiritual war is not fought by conventional methods and it's not based on our three dimensional experience here on earth; it is fought against spirits and principalities in the spirit world.

> *"For we wrestle not against flesh and blood, but against principalities, against powers, against the rulers of the darkness of this world, against spiritual wickedness in high places. Wherefore, take unto you the whole armor of God so that you may be able to withstand in the evil day..."*

Jake's imperious command to Pam clearly indicated he was in bondage to the devil and that previous evangelizing attempts by people whom Jake encountered were a turn-off. These encounters had a negative and lasting impact on Jake. He equated accepting Christ's salvation to having a religion (a common erroneous assumption), rather than understanding it is about having an eternal relationship with God. It's also evident that Jake's church attendance and the so-called mentoring sessions with Henry were a ruse. Jake used his participation to fortify his worldly beliefs. Forcing Pam to participate in his sin further convinced him that he was right about Christians and all religion. It strengthened his resolve to continue his life as a passenger on that hell-bound train. Pam's participation was an indication to him that her faith was not strong, and no better than his own beliefs and lifestyle. This was a co-dependent marriage that Pam willingly accepted.

In mentoring or any other ministry, confidentiality is core and the glue for sustainability. There will *always* be those moments and issues that rock a mentor's boat, stunning them, and taking them into uncharted waters. A person's spiritual maturity and gifts, personal experience, and the comfort and guidance of the Holy Spirit provide the stability to handle these often disturbing issues. How firmly persons are grounded determines what steps they take when they learn of the nature and details of another person's struggles and pain. There should be no surprise at life's issues, because the depravity of the struggle is a demonstration of how deviously the devil operates. The sins of the flesh and the world have been around since the fall of Adam and Eve and are clearly exemplified throughout the Bible. What makes them suddenly seem more real is when one becomes personally involved. Confidentiality is vital in mentoring, because it is relationship-based. Non-confidentiality is a betrayal to someone who may have had great difficulty in disclosing intimate, personal information yet took the risk. The fear of failure, rejection, and the unknown can be at extreme levels within the person making the revelation. Any sign of betrayal will cause long lasting harm, possibly even eternal damnation for the devastated victim who was denied a message of salvation and hope due to ungodly decisions and behavior of an unwise mentor. This is what the devil hopes for from those who engage in ministry when they are not called, or authorized (given spiritual power) by God.

The church mentoring director should not have become personally involved with Jake. This was an example of betrayal against Jake and meddling from someone who knew very little about the details. This is why Jake called them hypocrites, because they were. Getting personally involved also reflected how little the mentoring director really knew about mentoring. His actions were based on a cerebral decision and not spiritual discernment or wisdom from the Holy Spirit. Confronting Jake in a public environment didn't reflect common sense. It impressed Jake that both the mentoring director and Henry were men of low character, not to be trusted, and that he should be defensive in reacting to them. Both Henry and the church mentoring director's actions showed how little they knew of human nature and the psychological factors involved. They had little discernment or wisdom as to how the sins of the flesh and the worldly culture are tools of the devil used against followers of Christ or those who are being drawn to Christ through His ambassadors.

Significant to this particular case study were the series of events that followed the incident with Jake. The church ended affiliation with the national men's mentoring organization and all mentoring efforts. The hand of the Lord was evident in that no other men from that church stepped forward to become mentors and no new men sought mentoring from that church. Apart from the local church's failing, the national men's mentoring organization disbanded, only to have several of the founding members begin another so-called mentoring ministry involving men. At the time of this writing, several have disbanded and according to reports, the others soon will disband. The hearts of these men are not right with God and do not honor Him. He is removing them just as He eliminated the Pharisees centuries ago.

The conviction of the Holy Spirit was strong in Henry, so that he followed the prompting of the Spirit to seek counsel from Terry. Henry knew spiritually that Terry was God's vessel assigned to him. God spoke to Henry through Terry and the Holy Spirit, and Henry and Joan successfully fought and received victory over the deception of the devil. Their relationship with God was restored. Neither Joan nor Henry had any future contact with Pam and Jake, who moved from the community. The wisdom learned from this incident continues with them today.

Within several months, Henry and Joan stopped attending the church where the deception began. They remained churchless for nearly six months before the Holy Spirit led them to another church. One year after being led to the new church, Henry heard God's call and became involved with a ministry other than mentoring. He does not participate in any other church programs. Joan is involved with a women's ministry. They continue to be harassed with deception, as all of Christ's children are, but the power of the Holy Spirit and their willingness to listen and follow His guidance make it possible for them to avoid the trap that previously ensnared them. Henry and Joan often reflect on their experience with Pam and Jake and sometimes use different aspects of this experience in their respective ministries. The couple says the blessings received from God as a result of their experience with Pam and Jake are wisdom, awareness of spiritual deception, and a closer marital relationship. They feel drawn closer to the Godhead.

ﾍﾞﾍﾞﾍﾞﾍﾞ

ANALYSIS: CASE STUDY #9, TWO MAGPIES HARMONIZE

There are several important dynamics involved in this particular case study. Like other dynamics, these may not enter into every mentoring relationship. The main purpose is to identify them and illustrate how mentoring can go beyond the original perception. HIV probably has not been a regular topic in the majority of mentoring relationships; however the probability factor of this topic becoming a mentoring issue is increasing every year. Teenage rebellion is common, but there are some topics that are best resolved by neutral mentors. One's individual testimony must be used selectively in mentoring. As in some of the other case studies, here the time element of mentoring is worthy of note. Let's begin.

It was not coincidence that brought Chloe to Denise. The hand of the Lord began when Janet and her husband selected that particular counseling agency. At some point after the counseling/mentoring sessions between Chloe and Denise, the four participants realized the hand of God was involved. This is a common experience in God-ordained mentoring and in other aspects of a Christian's life journey. It's unknown which of the four participants was the first to realize how God was working in this situation. Ultimately, all four shared their thoughts that God was involved from the very beginning. Denise could see God's involvement in her first meeting with Chloe and prayed to God, acknowledging this discernment and asking that the Holy Spirit would guide her throughout this mission. Janet and her husband saw God's involvement as Chloe began to understand, receive spiritual discernment, and obey the counsel and guidance of the Holy Spirit. Chloe's emotions and lack of emotional and spiritual maturity were at first barriers to understanding God's hand of grace. Her early focus was to get the counseling sessions over, her punishment would be satisfied, and she could resume her normal lifestyle.

Janet and her husband made a major decision to seek assistance from an outside source regarding the pre-marital sex issue that many parents deal with during their children's teenage years. Research indicates that teenage sexual involvement has steadily risen the past several decades. More teens are electing to engage in sexual activity as early as age 13. Research has found that many of these sexually active teens are successful in keeping this activity unknown by their parents.

Many parents believe it is their sole responsibility to inform their children about sexual matters and in dealing with this issue. Other parents are so embarrassed in discussing the topic with their children that they avoid it altogether and rely on schools, churches, or their child's common sense to deal with the issue.

In Janet's and her husband's case, they saw Chloe's stubborn resistance to listening to them about pre-marital sexual activity. Janet's difficulty in communicating with Chloe was not conducive to getting Chloe to understand the spiritual disobedience and the physical danger of such activity. Janet's husband had the discernment to know someone else needed to intervene on their behalf. It's important to note that Chloe's father did not argue with her. He obtained necessary information for understanding the basis to make the right decision. He and Janet could have proceeded to handle this situation, but the emotions of all three of them would have escalated into arguments with demonic barriers to a godly resolution.

In today's culture, there are times and certain topic areas that teenagers believe their parents are not current enough in their understanding of the issue or how it pertains to them. Their reasoning is indicative of the ways of the world and stems from demonic influence. In society, cultural influence is such that many teenagers become rebellious for a variety of reasons and make choices that are harmful to themselves spiritually and physically. It is important to remember that culture, society, and its manifestations can be tools of the devil.

Janet and her husband realized that Chloe was disregarding their earlier teachings on the subject of sex, and also whatever their church had taught during their youth activities. As parents, they did not want spiritual or physical harm for Chloe, and knew intervention was needed.

Obtaining assistance from an outside source was a decision Janet and her husband did not hesitate to make. They wanted someone who was reputable and relied on the guidance of the Holy Spirit. The couple chose an agency that specialized in teen sex, had counselors with personal experience, and who could easily connect with teenagers, and was not a front for an abortion clinic or Planned Parenthood propaganda endorsing pre-marital sexual activity. They chose the counseling clinic because it dealt with sexual issues in a practical manner and did not preach or condemn. This particular clinic was not opposed to ministering tough love when needed. The counselors' experience was factored into knowing when and how to minister this type of help.

Denise was placed in a position by God that was not an everyday experience. She was confronted with mentoring a troubled teen who happened to also be a friend and the daughter of her best friend. The very beginning of her involvement with Chloe as a mentor was critical and required spiritual discernment on Denise's part in using part of her personal testimony as a tool to overcome the fear that Chloe felt. Another element Denise did not expect or plan for was how to balance her mentoring with Chloe and her relationship with Janet. Denise did realize this pairing was based on the invisible hand of God.

These potential problems and pitfalls became resolved with Denise's revelation of her HIV. Chloe's friendship with Denise was good, yet there were boundaries that both observed to maintain their amiability. This changed when Chloe walked through the door for counseling on a subject that she had not divulged earlier to Denise. This was an important element in Denise's sharing a very personal and private part of her life that neither Chloe nor her mother knew about Denise. In essence, the friendship between Chloe and Denise became one of two adults, rather than one adult and one daughter-like teen. Denise's testimony became a foundation for this new relationship and Chloe interpreted it as showing her respect and consideration. Chloe was expecting an overbearing, dictatorial adult intent on lecturing and preaching to her. What Chloe received from Denise went far beyond her expectations.

Another important aspect to the beginning of their new relationship was that Denise did not demand that Chloe continue the counseling with her. She allowed Chloe to make that choice after hearing her personal revelation. It is vital to allow the potential mentee to make the decision to enter into a mentoring relationship with you. Forcing the issue and requiring the person to become your mentee does not work. At some point, that person will stop the mentoring relationship. It is always in the back of their mind that they were forced to participate and the first available excuse becomes their opportunity to end the relationship. The mentee locks this experience into their memory banks and it impedes future mentoring possibilities.

Denise did not use the HIV part of her testimony as a weapon to convince Chloe the two of them were of the same mindset. Her HIV experience was truthful, used to convey to Chloe she would not preach or lecture power points as Chloe expected, but it also let Chloe know she was a real person with real problems. Chloe discerned that Denise was authentic, and their counseling time would be practical without demanding that Chloe must take a predetermined course of action.

God's Holy Spirit moved through Chloe when Denise brought Janet into the proceedings. Denise maintained that Chloe was free to choose another counselor or another agency if they felt uncomfortable with Denise's involvement in the situation. Chloe's verbal request to continue with Denise sent a clear and important message to Denise. At that moment, Chloe took another step into adulthood.

Once the initial counseling sessions began, Denise was able to change them into mentoring sessions. She began each session in prayer with Chloe (despite the agency's formal stand against prayer), and asked Chloe about her thoughts, emotions, and reasons for engaging in pre-marital sex. This is important to the sustainability of any mentoring relationship. The mentee must feel recognized, valued, and not that they are merely being lectured or preached to.

Denise showed genuine concern and interest in Chloe and the struggle she was going through not only with her boyfriend and her parents, but also with the conviction that she felt from the Holy Spirit that her sexual activity was disobedient to God. Mentees often are under the conviction of the Holy Spirit and a mentor's wise approach can open doors for mentees to express themselves and identify the deception and temptation affecting their activity. Denise knew from her own personal experience how important it is to always be genuine with them, showing them respect and honesty.

At any given moment, the mentoring relationship can end should the mentor become prideful, arrogant or controlling. Denise did not get flustered when she first encountered Chloe in the counseling room. She also did comply with the clinic's requirement of keeping her name a secret from Janet. There were many emotions involved at that particular time, but Denise controlled hers and trusted in God. Her previous counseling/mentoring experience, discernment, and wisdom became her foundation for counseling Chloe. Through prayer and supplication to God, Denise later obtained permission from Chloe and revealed to Janet that she was Chloe's counselor. This prevented demonic deception from gaining a foothold in God's purpose and plan for Chloe, Denise, and Janet. Denise much later, in God's perfect timing, revealed to the clinic director her personal involvement with both Chloe and Janet.

171

The decision to reveal a very private part of her life was huge for Denise, because she was wise to know that revealing her HIV disease to anybody and everybody is not how God wants His special creation to use the grace and mercy He provides. But she discerned that part of her personal testimony was necessary to cut through the barrier of fear of the unknown, and the fear of rejection that Chloe was experiencing. Mentors must exercise discernment and caution in making public those aspects of their testimony because the recipient of the testimony may not be prepared spiritually or emotionally to understand why or how this revelation pertains to them.

Individuals can become turned off to certain aspects of one's testimony to the point of ceasing all involvement with the person giving the testimony. An important aspect of personal testimony is that it's a reflection of your personal relationship with the Godhead. If your testimony is limited to only how you came to accept Christ's salvation and the sins you committed prior to accepting life with Christ, this reveals your relationship with Christ is mainly in the past, not the present. This also suggests that one's current relationship with Christ really isn't a vibrant one.

A person's life journey is a process with progress. God works in and through you for His grace and your progress to be made known, and so that you do not remain stuck in the past. The past is dead and should be categorized as a learning experience and a springboard for God's mighty work to be done in you today and tomorrow.

Mentors can and should take past life experiences as reference points for discerning the struggles of the mentee and as sources for guiding the mentoring relationship. Denise did exactly this. The story of her HIV disease was used to make a connection with Chloe. It also served as a practical teaching tool that Chloe understood and accepted so that her counseling relationship with Denise could continue. Denise's genuine concern for Chloe, showing her adult respect during each of their counseling sessions, became substance that resulted in Chloe's asking Denise to become her mentor after the required counseling sessions were completed. Their involvement started as counseling, but evolved into mentoring.

Janet and her husband learned first-hand how deception enters into the ranks of any church. The parents of Chloe's boyfriend manifested the carnal rather than the spiritual. They opted to go the way of the world rather than to trust God and let Him resolve the issue in a way that would bring Him glory and honor. Their lack of spiritual maturity became evident in their statement of possibly suing Janet, her husband, and Chloe. Their emotions prevented them from seeing the deception and questioning their son about his sexual involvement with Chloe. This is in contrast to what Janet and her husband did when they confronted Chloe with the issue of pre-marital sex. One set of parents succumbed to worldly ways, while the other surrendered and submitted to God.

The church youth pastor interviewed both Chloe and her boyfriend before making his decision to ban both teenagers from participating in youth activities. He interviewed them separately. This did take a certain amount of courage on his part because of the prominence of the boyfriend's parents within the church. The boyfriend's parents attempted to use their influence with the church senior pastor to override the youth pastor's decision and have the youth pastor fired. This ploy did not work.

An interesting aspect to the youth pastor's recommendation given to Janet to consult with the three Christian-based organizations that specialized in pre-marital sex counseling was his acknowledgement it would be best to seek a female to counsel Chloe and not himself. He realized the seriousness of the situation and used his knowledge of the counseling organizations to benefit Janet and Chloe. The youth pastor knew his limitations and stayed within the talents and gifts that God had given him.

The time Chloe and Denise spent together reflects how the counseling blended and transitioned into mentoring. Denise focused first on learning Chloe's reasoning for engaging in pre-marital sex before instructing her on the dangers, both spiritual and physical, of such activity. Seeking Chloe's viewpoint not only showed respect to Chloe but it sped up the process of determining the core reason for her behavior. Chloe's emotions and feelings were such she readily revealed more of the demonic deception that was impacting her. Their time together was well spent and Denise used her mentoring experience and wisdom to instruct Chloe and bring in God's view.

Denise's action showed how God is very concerned with the carnal, how His Word protects and guides us through the valley of the shadow of death. She made the practical application of God's Word easier for Chloe to accept. Denise's techniques led to Chloe's decision to follow Christ and become His disciple. There was no hell-fire preaching, no condemnation, but guidance in a practical manner just as Christ did during His three years of earthly ministry. By following Christ, Denise allowed the Holy Spirit's to convince Chloe, so that she accepted Christ's eternal salvation.

Denise and Chloe came to the same conclusion at the same time that the period of mentoring was complete. In two short months, Chloe forsook the demonic deception that was controlling her young life. She chose to follow Christ and to obey His commands. Despite the ending of their mentoring period, the two remained friends.

Chloe, Janet, and Eric witnessed Denise's character and it solidified their relationships with her. The four participants all brought honor and glory to God.

ↄↄↄↄↄ

ANALYSIS: CASE STUDY #10, NATE NAVIGATES CHURNING CHURCH WATERS

After leaving the church, Pastor Nate and Buck grabbed some fast food and went to a park to discuss what they were going to do now that they no longer wanted any association with their former church.

Both friends acknowledged how calm they felt with the peace and the joy of the Lord throughout the meeting. In exchanging how they felt emotionally and spiritually, there was relief and comfort that they had made the right decision to leave the church. Buck stated that as the pastor spoke, he felt the presence of the Holy Spirit and could spiritually see the false reasoning given by the pastor as well as the pastor's orders to both him and Nate to not confront any member of the Kansas protestors. In spiritual terms, this was spiritual discernment—seeing the spiritual side.

In between bites of food, Buck thanked Nate for his sound teaching and mentoring that assisted him throughout this event. Buck began to be teary-eyed as he reflected on how he had felt during his time with the deceased soldier's family. He had felt free, strong, and empowered while giving encouragement to the family and explaining to them that God loved them. He had emphasized to the family that God was not condoning the actions of the protestors.

Buck assured them that God's endearing love and compassion was waiting for them and all they had to do was ask Him. He then shared with the family several of his own struggles during his time in Iraq and how God came to him giving him hope, peace, encouragement, and direction. Again, Buck was manifesting spiritual discernment that only the Holy Spirit can provide. (Refer to Acts chapters 2-5.) Spiritual discernment is an important tool for mentors to possess; only God can bless any human with this part of His grace and mercy. Non-saved cannot experience God-given discernment of spirits, and are vulnerable to deception.

Despite their anger towards the actions of the protestors and their church, the family expressed thanks and appreciation for Buck coming forth the way he did. They asked him many questions about his time in Iraq. When their conversation ended, the family stated they still were angry with this situation and not to expect them to immediately forgive the protestors or attend a church anytime soon. Buck told them he understood, and assured them there was nothing wrong with taking time to mourn their loss of their precious son. He left the family's home with a great sense of peace.

After this report, Buck and Nate became silent for a while, but exchanged looks of communication that went beyond speech.

Nate was the first to speak after their meal. He strongly urged Buck to continue evangelizing his unsaved friend, but cautioned Buck not to let his emotions and feelings about the protestors and the particular denomination interfere with doing God's work. Buck nodded his head in agreement and said he felt this incident had motivated him more to speak to his unsaved friend about Christ and His supernatural love.

They exchanged hugs before getting into their cars to leave, and both had watery eyes knowing their friendship had taken another stride forward.

The two remain friends despite Buck's being transferred to another location. They often talk on the telephone and email each other about how God is leading them in their respective ministries. Buck's unsaved friend did accept Christ's eternal salvation and continues to grow in Christ and maintains communication with him.

Nate and Buck do not attend any church, but they are involved with making disciples and have seen how God brings forth those whom He wants Nate and Buck to disciple. Nate is involved with several men in his community who regularly get together on a weekly basis for fellowship, encouraging each other, and stories about how God is providing opportunities for them to use their talents and spiritual gifts.

The false accusers and protestors continue throughout the country creating upheaval wherever they can despite public outcry. The denomination's leader continues to send the protestors money for their expenses in protesting against homosexuality.

The answers to the questions posed at the end of the case study are dependent on several factors. If we are steeped in a denominational doctrine or bias, then our answers to the questions will likely reflect the biases and indoctrination of that particular denomination. Another influencing factor will be our previous experience with true ministry and not just church activity. The third factor will be our level of spiritual maturity.

In discussing the questions, it is imperative not to be condemning. The answers given by your group will reflect each member's level of spiritual maturity and background experiences of each life's journey. Not everyone is at the same spiritual level of maturity at any given point in time.

What is important is having basic understanding of how followers of Christ Jesus project themselves to the world and the unsaved. The questions for each person to answer in any given situation are, "Did I reflect Christ Jesus to the person(s) I just encountered?" "Are they going to go away with a sense and feeling of seeing Christ through me or will they say I'm just another one of those religious zealots who is nothing more than a hypocrite?" "Did I truly exhibit Christ Jesus by following only Him?"

In the secular world of sales and marketing a truism is that when a person has a negative experience with a company or product, that person will tell eleven other people about that experience. Their purpose isn't just to vent, but to sway the decisions of others to not buy that product or deal with that particular company. Businesses are instructed to be very mindful of the image they project and how it can have adverse effects on their sales.

The same is true when we Christians engage the world. In this particular case study, the actions of the particular church sect were seen via television and print in all the major networks and newspapers. Approximately 8,000,000 people learned about the actions of this particular church. Of this number, approximately 6.2 million are unsaved, and the remainder claim to be Christians. The main question is, "What effect did this particular church have on those 6.2 million unsaved people to invite them to bow before the throne of God and accept eternal salvation? Did the actions of those church members really reflect the image of Christ?"

How many felt these church protestors were nothing but hypocrites? Did the protestors' actions reflect the love that Christ Jesus wants to project? Do these church members really have Christ's love within their hearts? Did they show compassion, empathy, and love to the grieving family members of the deceased soldier?

In discussing this case study, read Matthew 13 and the two parables about the soils and the tares. After reading these two parables, and Acts 20:24, apply them to this particular case study.

At the conclusion of your study and discussion, if you don't find this particular case study sobering and even chilling from a spiritual perspective, you may need to reconsider engaging in mentoring, evangelizing, and true ministry.

೬ೊ೬ೊ೬ೊ೬ೊ

ANALYSIS: CASE STUDY #11, THE CASE OF THE DISILLUSIONED DETECTIVE

A tragedy such as the type briefly described in this case study unfortunately happens too often in America and other world cultures. It can be construed as exampling the advancing of the end times as predicted in the Bible. Events such as those depicted in this case study are common story lines in the media, and meant for sensationalism to sell and to gain market share by the media outlet.

When a senseless act of violence takes place, such as these murders, a human reaction is to blame God. Popular opinion is that only truly bad people should die a violent death, all children should grow to adulthood and lead productive lives, and everyone should die in their sleep at an old age. This type of thinking reflects emotional mindsets based on fantasy and an avoidance of real life that has taken place since Adam and Eve were banished from the Garden of Eden.

Followers of Christ must be prepared for events such as these, as well as non-violent ones that impact our belief structure and the illusion that Christians are immune to horrific events. The fact is, some events will take place in our life's journey on earth which will test our faith to its core.

The four gospels at the beginning of the New Testament illustrate this. When Christ suffered and died on the cross, the apostles' faith was so shaken they hid, in fear. These men had walked with Christ, had witnessed Christ's miracles, and had been taught for three years by the Holy Savior; yet, despite their intimate relationship with Christ, they crumbled in this crucial test of faith. In Mark 16:9-14, emphasis is on the disbelief of the apostles. Instead of rejoicing in anticipation of Christ's forthcoming resurrection, they cowered, mourned, wept, and withdrew into themselves for their pity party. Faith and trust were nowhere to be found.

When Christ did fulfill prophecy with His resurrection, the first persons He appeared to were the women, Mary Magdalene, Mary the mother of James, and, as the Bible calls her, "the other Mary." The women believed, and because of their faith, they were blessed to be the bearer of divine news to the disciples. They were instructed to go and tell the mourning disciples about Christ's resurrection. But, the disciples didn't believe the women. When Christ first appeared to them in His resurrected body, He chided them for their unbelief (Mark 16:14). At His rebuke, each apostle knew in his heart he deserved the risen Lord's rebuke.

Chuck had a major encounter with core belief. He had accepted Christ's salvation, he had been baptized, he attended a church, he was involved in church activities. But this activity did not advance his spiritual maturity. He remained disillusioned about horrific acts which he thought weren't supposed to happen to Christians—especially, those involved in his circle of influence. Disillusionment caused him to stumble spiritually. It is noteworthy that as a police detective, Chuck was not only trained, but had previous experience with horrific events. However, when it became personal, he was shaken, and he crumbled. Chuck's statements and actions following the murders of his friends and fellow Christians reflected his spiritual immaturity in the form of a spiritual tantrum. Because he didn't really understand God's ways, he was going to show God. His mistake resulted in his not walking with Him anymore. Yes, he sure was going to show God by saying just like a child, "No, I'm not going to trust You!"

On the other hand, Doug perceived why Chuck was reacting emotionally and did not get sucked into Chuck's self-imposed pity party. As a more mature follower of Christ, Doug knew that Chuck needed to be taken to the desert the same way Christ took Paul. Chuck needed Christ, not Doug.

Had Doug suggested or demanded Chuck continue with mentoring, Chuck would not have heard Christ's still small voice but only the words of a man. In essence, Doug would have been disobedient to Christ by putting himself, his gift of spiritual wisdom, and his personal relationship with Christ into jeopardy. In Matthew 4:5-7 the devil tempted Christ by saying, *"Cast Yourself down and see if God will take care of You."* What the devil really wanted was for Christ to "show off" His deity. If Doug had insisted that Chuck continue with mentoring, Doug would have been "showing off" his faith and be disobedient to Christ by saying, "I can handle this, You just watch." God works in mysterious ways. As we truly study His Word, we find example after example that God wants us to "be still and know that He is God" and to surrender our ways to His ways. It's probable that at some point earlier in his walk with Christ that Doug did that very thing and paid the price for such action. The important thing is he learned from it and similar to David, did not repeat the same offense twice.

Doug knew that Chuck's being angry with Christ was impeding Chuck's relationship with God, but Doug also realized how important it was for Chuck to reconcile his differences personally with the Godhead. The only way this could happen was for Chuck to go to his desert, alone with Christ. Doug's faith and trust plus his own growing personal relationship with Christ offered him assurance that Chuck would reconcile with God.

By turning Chuck over to Christ, Doug was letting Chuck see Christ through him despite Chuck's initial inability of perceiving this. Being truly obedient to God at times requires a person to take action that is vastly different from what the world sees or expects. Doug also let Chuck see Christ through him by maintaining a relationship with him despite his period of spiritual angst. It was a time when friendship became the bond that would lead to renewed fellowship.

Following the young murderer's trial, Doug accepted the governor's request to head the state bureau of investigation. Despite basing out of the state capitol, Doug could easily commute daily to work. He and his wife agreed that Doug would hold this position for five years to get the bureau functioning professionally. Should the process take less time, then Doug would resign and retire. It took Doug the five-year commitment he made to the governor.

During this period of time, Doug interacted with his former boss and learned of Chuck's progress as the new chief of detectives. Based on Doug's recommendation to the chief, midway in the five-year period, Doug had to interact with Chuck. This occasion served as an opening for Chuck to inform Doug that he had reconciled with the Godhead and once again enjoyed personal relationship with Christ, and was experiencing the joy and peace that is a part of this relationship.

After Doug resigned from his position as head of the state bureau of investigation, he and his wife took some time to travel. Once back home, Doug and Chuck maintained their friendship by getting together often. Concerning the mentoring, there were times Doug was able to show Chuck how God's Word could and should be utilized in daily secular life to cope with life's issues. Doug was fulfilling Christ's Great Commission.

The heavens sang psalms of joy and the devil suffered another battle loss.

Concerning the question to identify the spiritual warfare involved, reread the section that deals with this issue. The devil directed this form of spiritual warfare against Chuck, the youth's surviving family, the friend and his family, other police officers, the community in which the murders took place, and in the broader scope against the media which sent out the gory details both regionally and nationally. The devil uses emotions and thoughts to ignite and fuel hatred, anger, and confusion in his quest to rob, kill, and destroy humans from having eternal life with the Godhead. The devil's tactics here are the same ones he used to get Cain to murder his brother Abel, and to get the Pharisees to murder Christ Jesus.

ๅๅๅๅ

ANALYSIS: CASE STUDY #12, TRISHA'S FINAL BATTLE

It's been said that a person doesn't fear death, but fears the process of dying. Everyone knows that death will come; but it is placed on the back burner, pushed to the recesses of the mind, not to be addressed until old age. Not knowing what to expect, the potential pain involved in this process, and for the unsaved permanently leaving behind loved ones are issues that arise when confronted with death. These are examples of unrighteous fears. Unfortunately, these fears can impact both those who have accepted Christ's salvation and the unsaved when the focus is directed on the earthly experience rather than on the eternal.

One of the common questions posed by the unsaved about death is, "Why, God?" Maybe the person is a child struck down by disease or an accident, thereby ending the future and enjoying life; a seemingly good person accomplishing a lot of admirable things in this world killed by a fanatic or a drunk driver; a person wracked with pain, being consumed in a slow process despite advanced medical products. In the case of Trisha, it was a young mother, much too young to leave her family. "Why, God?" is a reflection of emotions and natural feelings. It's also a test of faith accompanied by trials.

People want answers to comfort them and enable them to confront their own upcoming death which they hope will take place when they are old and asleep. We don't always get what we want. It's a very difficult issue for many to accept and to deal with, long after the loved one is deceased. This issue can impact a person's perspective on life, God, and eternity in one of two ways--either they reject God totally, or they accept His saving grace of eternal salvation. There is no middle ground. Some people will initially reject God, even curse Him for His seeming insensitivity, only to ask Him for eternal salvation at some point later in their life. The fact remains—there is no middle ground and no maybes.

This is very important for mentors to realize and to ask God for His help and blessing of discernment, wisdom, and discerning spirits to answer the question of "Why, God?" Many times Christians are asked this question; and too often they provide an inane or poor answer if they elect to answer the question at all. Included in this is their own personal experience with this issue and how it impacts their walk and relationship

183

with Christ Jesus. What happens during a confrontation time with death is either a retreat due to emotions and feelings, or a step forward, viewing it as an opportunity to witness and let others see God working in and through us. A renowned Christian leader was asked how he felt about his own impending death from cancer. His reply was that it's not about the dying, it is about the attitude that is important. Amen!

Trisha's dying process is a perfect example for learning to seize the opportunity for perspective concerning death rather than the woe-is-me, why-God reaction. It was difficult and very emotional for Trisha and Jason to come to grips with her impending death via terminal breast cancer; but they did, by the grace of God and the empowering of His Holy Spirit through their total surrender to God. At these times, realizing our total dependency on God's grace and mercy, and acting accordingly, shows the depth of our spiritual maturity.

Jason's and Trisha's actions are inspirational for us who are yet to face this issue, either personally or with a loved one. After coming to grips with the facts, Jason vowed to support Trisha and do whatever he could to comfort her physically, emotionally, and spiritually as the godly husband he wanted to be. Jason did what God wanted him to do. He prayed for strength, physically, emotionally, and spiritually. He had no previous experience to rely on, but he did have the sovereign power of Almighty God and he used it. Jason did not react in a selfish manner. He stepped back and allowed Trisha to freely interact with both Sheila and the women's support group facing terminal breast cancer. He accepted the role God had for him and acted when the prompting of the Holy Spirit directed. He directed his prayers that God's will would be done and for protection over Trisha and Sheila during their times together.

Sheila's action was somewhat parallel to Jason's in that she listened to God's prompting and let the support group come first with Trisha. Sheila had the shared experience of breast cancer but she did not have the shared experience of hearing it would be terminal. Sheila extended the blessing of God's wisdom to be there for Trisha, to listen and to learn from Trisha's experiences. She continued to mentor Trisha as God's servant through being obedient to His promptings and direction from the Holy Spirit. Sheila realized the value of the support group for Trisha and waited in the wings, so to speak, for Trisha to come to her for input or simply to share what she was experiencing. Another important aspect to Sheila's mentoring was not condemning either the support group or Trisha's decisions.

The support group performed several valuable functions for Trisha. They shared their emotions, feelings, thoughts, and concerns with Trisha; they created a confidential environment for Trisha to vent; and they were real with her, as real people who didn't have answers, but knew about coping and exhibited courage when others might not. In the process, they taught Trisha how to communicate and deal with those in close relationship with her.

Several important points were shared by Trisha to her loved ones. First, that communication is vital for all involved with the issue. Second, don't pity the terminally ill person. Empathize by listening, and doing (making meals, errands, etc.). Third, be willing to accept the fact a terminally ill person may not want to discuss certain aspects of the illness until they are ready. Fourth, cry with the person, laugh with them and be real with them; in other words, simply have relationship with them. Fifth, accept whatever changes take place within that person. Trisha was initially surprised at some of the off-color jokes the other terminally ill women made concerning their breast cancer. She quickly learned they were an attempt to cope with the situation, and not let it take away what life they had left.

Things that Trisha learned about herself included: First, realize your life isn't the same and will never be what you expected. Second, limit attempts to educate others about your condition. Third, don't feel compelled to answer questions from people who mainly are curious and not willing to really be there for you. Fourth, follow God's timing in sharing certain aspects of the illness with others. One of these was the off-color jokes by the women in her support group that were intended for the comfort of each other and ways to cope with the inevitable. Fifth, don't attempt to make excuses or rationalizations for the terminal illness and don't accept excuses or rationalizations from others. One of these insensitivities from others is saying the cause was due to some sin, or some alleged disobedience to God. Sixth, carefully choose whom you have continued relationship with. The fact is, some loved ones simply can't handle the situation and unwittingly become a negative factor. It's okay to love them, but it's not necessary to have them close to you or in your inner circle.

The greatest way Trisha was able to mentor Meg was in the spiritual aspects of terminal breast cancer. Meg was spiritually immature and struggling with her faith during this crucial time. Trisha was able to give a deeper, Holy Spirit-led answer to Meg's question of "Why, God?"

Trisha stepped up to the plate and let God use her. He empowered her physically, emotionally, and spiritually, so that Meg was able to retain relationship with the Godhead, and not fall victim to the deception of the enemy by questioning God or rejecting him. Trisha proved to be God's mentor, just as we all should be.

Compare this analysis to what you may have already experienced in your life and how you handled the issue. These are extremely difficult circumstances. Did you succumb to deception, or did you let God use you for His glory and to further His kingdom? If your answer is not the one you wish it were, it is never too late. Bring it humbly to God in prayer for His gracious involvement, your restoration, and His glory.

CHAPTER 8: CASE STUDIES CONCLUSIONS

LOVE, DISCIPLINE, CAUTION, RESPONSIBILITY

These twelve case studies addressed different types of struggles that have besieged mankind since the great fall of Adam and Eve. They are reflective of the devil's tactics of spiritual warfare, and illustrate the need for godly authorized mentoring (fulfilling the commandment of the Great Commission of making disciples).

These twelve case studies and numerous others have elements in common with the Apostle Paul's first epistle to the church at Corinth in chapters 8-10. In these particular chapters, Paul admonished the Corinthian church for straying from God's Word that was the foundation of their church and of all other churches (the body of Christ).

Paul addressed this epistle to the immature, new believers in the Corinthian church. He was particularly upset about how they had allowed false teachers into the church and how they had succumbed to immorality and were compromising God's Word, blending it with the worldly culture surrounding them. In chapters 8-10, Paul gives the Corinthians four basic principles in making personal decisions about those so-called "questionable" gray areas of Christian life that serve as deceptions. What Paul said to the Corinthians is applicable also to today's mentoring, using four principles:

1. Love must supersede knowledge (1 Cor. 8).
2. Discipline must supersede authority (1 Cor. 9).
3. Caution must supersede experience (1 Cor. 10:1-22).
4. Responsibility must supersede freedom (1 Cor. 10: 23-33).

Paul focused on righteous living as a follower of Christ. He taught the principles to the Corinthians as a way of life that separated them from the worldly culture that was pervasive in Corinth at that time. What Paul wrote to the Corinthians applies to those who have accepted Christ's eternal salvation today. The apostle's teaching turns them from mere believers in Christ into warriors following Christ. They become members of His army (those involved in ministry, not just church activities) fighting the spiritual war against the devil. The four principles aptly apply to any ministry that God makes available to man, his special creation. Let's address each of these principles in greater detail.

Principle #1: Love must supersede knowledge (chapter 8:1-13). Knowledge is neutral and comes from acquiring facts through studying and receiving instruction from someone who already possesses these facts. Knowledge is both worldly and spiritual. Knowledge can either build or destroy. An example is man's discovery of the power of the atom. After the awe of this initial discovery, some men sought to benefit mankind with this new knowledge, while others pursued it as a weapon of warfare to destroy a nation's enemies and presumably shorten or prevent wars. As a weapon for human warfare, knowledge without balance becomes a force of brutality.

The most prominent use of the atom as a weapon is the historical depiction of its usage by the Allied Forces, chiefly the United States, against Japan to hasten the end of World War II by destroying two cities, Hiroshima and Nagasaki. Since that act of devastation and warfare, scientists have turned their study to more peaceful uses of the atom as a source of energy and power.

Knowledge and the pursuit of facts solely to acquire intellectualism, often results in a know-it-all attitude that is a major component of pride and arrogance. When these two forces combine, they lead to control and domination. Desire for control and dominance are attributes of the devil and they caused his fall from grace and eternal damnation. A person who is "puffed-up" by intellectualism cannot build up a person who is ignorant of facts and in need of learning. Sometimes academics fall into this category and description.

In the Christian community, inappropriate intellectualism is rampant. This was manifested in case study #8 in the guise of the senior pastor of the church, the mentoring director of that church, and the national men's mentoring organization. These individuals had plenty of knowledge about the Bible and doctrine, but little appreciation for how God uses His truth. In short, they were spiritual academics and modern day Pharisees.

These people grew in knowledge, but did not grow in grace to become doers of the Word as the Apostle James urges in his epistle (James 4). Those who focus on knowledge alone have limited relationship with the Godhead because they neglect or refuse to follow Christ through the prompting and the leading of His Holy Spirit. If a person can't hear the counsel, guidance, teaching, and direction of the Holy Spirit, that person cannot be a servant of God and will be of no use to the Godhead in carrying out His plan and purpose. This type of person can never be God's mentor, although he may be a particular church's or denomination's mentor. When Christ said, "Follow Me," He was looking for servants willing to forego their personal desires to carry out His plan and purpose. We should surrender to Him totally and not put anyone or anything above Him.

Love is the counterbalance to knowledge. Paul explains this in 1 Cor. 8:1-13. He also states this in Eph. 4:15 about the necessity of speaking the Truth of God in love. In chapter 13 of the first epistle to the Corinthians, Paul refers to love as the greatest gift.

Chapter 13 is the shortest chapter in this epistle, but one of the more powerful. In verses 4-8, Paul defines love for the Corinthians and ends this chapter with a note, *"Now abides faith, hope, and love; but the greatest of these virtues is love."* Faith and hope are the cornerstones of God's powering, and love is the action.

If a person has faith and hope, they are free to love and to understand how God loves. Paul is not referring to the worldly definition of love that is a combined emotion and feeling and subject to change. Paul's definition is *agape*—God's perfect love—and *phileo* love which includes caring, empathy, selflessness, and compassion. The worldly definition and interpretation of love is more often centered on sensual desire, physical attraction, and shared interests. Worldly love is not eternal. Manifesting God's eternal love is essential to being His mentor.

The Corinthians felt they were spiritually mature because of their doctrinal knowledge. They used this much like the Pharisees in establishing themselves as power brokers over new or spiritually immature Christians. Paul strongly admonished them for their actions in chapter 8 and also in Phil. 1:9-11. He informed them that the stronger

Christians were not using their knowledge in love and were tearing down the new or immature Christians.

Paul also pointed out that the new and spiritually immature Christians were prone to judging and criticizing and looking to the security of rules, rituals, and regulations. The same is true today. It is the job of the spiritually mature to teach and guide the spiritually immature to understand their freedom in Christ and how to let God draw them closer to Him in wisdom and relationship. This is the mandate of today's God-chosen mentor--to make spiritually weak believers stronger, leading them to a deeper relationship with Christ that they may be blessed with His wisdom. It is the whole function of God's mentors.

Paul's explanation of love, and its need to supersede knowledge, takes into account that the spiritually mature Christian must exercise patience, understanding, compassion, and self-control over their emotions and feelings when teaching, instructing, and counseling. Paul illustrated that admonishment is part of the growth process for all believers.

Paul also emphasizes that a spiritually mature Christian cannot force-feed immature Christians, hoping to transform them into spiritual maturity. The young Christian still has freedom of choice in accepting the efforts of the spiritually mature Christian or rejecting any or all that is offered them.

Should the new Christian or the young believer in Christ (the mentee) repeatedly reject the teaching, counseling, and instructing of a mentor, then he should be admonished. If the mentee rejects the admonishment, all mentoring arrangements ought to stop. Continuation is a waste of time and energy, and as stated in the Bible, we are warned not to cast pearls before swine.

Coinciding with knowledge and love is conscience. Paul refers to this in 1 Cor. 8:7-13 concerning the consumption of meat offered to idols. Conscience is a person's conformity to their inner sense of right or wrong. Because of spiritual immaturity, the spiritually weaker Christian is more easily defiled, wounded, and offended. This is lack of spiritual understanding.

The wise Christian will take this into account when mentoring. Spiritually weaker Christians do not know how to separate themselves from the culture and the sins of the flesh. They are in need of sound advice. This is why Paul was severely admonishing the church in

Corinth; they were allowing false teachers to blend worldly culture with God's truth, and the weaker Christians were suffering.

This is very important for anyone involved in mentoring to be aware of. They must apply only God's Word and Truth and not their opinion, denominational doctrine or rituals, or anything associated with religiosity. God's Word is intended to build faith in Him and must be the focus in making disciples.

Principle #2: Discipline must supersede authority. This principle is explained in 1 Cor. 9 and the Apostle Paul uses himself as an example. Our focus for mentoring purposes is on God-given authority—not man's—to engage in the ministry and properly exercise this authority with a mentee, God's way. It is all about God-given authority.

The Corinthians questioned Paul's God-given authority mainly as an excuse to not abide by God's Word, but blend it with the worldly culture, thereby puffing them up before weaker Christians in need of solid teaching.

Paul correctly reminds the Corinthians that he was chosen by Christ. Prior to his conversion, he had been chosen by man's standards to become a Pharisee. Christ changed that with the Damascus road conversion when Christ made Paul His disciple. This reminds us of God's superiority over any man's organizations, clubs, or structures.

The second reason Paul gave for his authority was his experience of following Christ whole-heartedly. After his authorization by Christ, Paul's entire life was devoted to establishing churches, nurturing them, and encouraging them to expand their churches throughout the often pagan strongholds where God wanted his church established. During his efforts, Paul never once established a church to puff himself up before man. This is sound advice for mentors and ministers today. It must be remembered that when Paul references the Church, it is the body of Christ—those who are saved—not a building, edifice, denomination, or any religion for that matter.

Paul's third defense statement was centered on the fact he did not take financial support from the Corinthians. When he established God's churches, he supported himself through utilizing his God-given skill in tent making. What Paul wanted to stress to the Corinthians is also found in Matthew 6:33 about seeking the Kingdom of God first, then God will provide all the necessities needed to support life and the ministry.

Paul intended the Corinthians to realize that when their focus is on seeking God first and obeying His plan and purpose, God's Word prospers, goes forth, and does not return to Him void. In mentoring, or any ministry, if a person puts their self-interest ahead of God's, His Word cannot prosper or expand as the Great Commission commands— to preach and teach the gospel to all nations. The third defense statement by Paul included three clear issues the Corinthians were to remember when dealing with the weaker Christians:

- *For the Gospel's sake, not their own.* In 1 Cor. 9:16, Paul says, "Necessity is laid upon me; yea, woe unto me if I preach not the gospel!" Earlier in 1 Cor. 4:2 Paul also stated, "It is required in stewards that a man be found faithful." Combined, these verses emphasized the Corinthians must not blend or otherwise change God's Word in any way to draw attention to them and away from God's Word. Too many times in today's world, denominations and organizations change God's Word to meet their agenda and to glorify themselves, just like Pharisees of the first century did.

- *For the weaker Christian's sake.* Weaker Christians come from various backgrounds, with a variety of pain, struggles, and opinions that influence their thinking and their actions. In 1 Cor. 9:19-23, Paul informed the Corinthians they should take into account who the weaker Christian really is, and adapt their teaching and mentoring style so that person will understand God's Word without being offended, insulted, or belittled.

Paul imitated Christ's evangelical and teaching style by being flexible and adaptable, establishing where the person was emotionally, physically, and spiritually when giving them God's Word. Christ did not speak to Nicodemus the same way He spoke to the woman at the well. In short, there is no set formula or rigid rules that must be adhered to; rather a disciple must follow the counsel, guidance, and direction of the Holy Spirit.

- *To receive God's reward.* Paul used the Corinthians' athletic interests to drive home this point. At that time, the Corinthians established their Isthmian Games patterned after the Greek Olympic Games and these events were quite popular. The winner of each event received a reward, a laurel worn on the head in public, plus recognition and stature among the Corinthians and, at times, financial privilege.

Paul wanted the Corinthians to realize that similar to the laurel for manly effort, there is a heavenly reward bestowed by God for obedient, faithful service. Unlike the Isthmian game reward given to only one person per event, God's champions are numerous—faithful followers of Christ who carry out His plan and purpose. Paul illustrates this by honing in on discipline.

A champion athlete learns early on that being a champion is earned through discipline—hard work, dedication, perseverance, training, denying of unhealthy pursuits, and obeying the rules of competition. Adhering to these championship component parts is accomplished only through discipline. Another way of expressing the choices involved is, "Just because I can, doesn't mean I should." The ancient athlete fully understood that breaking the rules of competition meant being disqualified (Greek word is *castaway*).

Paul was saying that if the Corinthians continued breaking God's rules in ministering, they would be disqualified, cast away, and there would be no reward in heaven. Paul also stated this in another way when he said followers of Christ must die to the self (the flesh), and discipline themselves for the sake of serving Christ.

Serving Christ is the perquisite for mentoring or any ministry. To emulate Christ and to become more Christ-like, it's important to understand that Christ stated He came not to be served, but to serve. This is the role all his ministers must take to be His servants, His true followers.

Principle #3: Caution supersedes experience (1 Cor. 10: 1-22). The first 22 verses in this chapter deal with spiritual warfare tactics being employed against the spiritually stronger Christian, especially one who is involved in mentoring or other ministry pursuits. These first verses also contain three important warnings Paul issued to the Corinthians:

1. *Privilege does not guarantee success.* Paul used the saga of the Israelites' escape from Egypt as an example of his statement. The Israelites had God's gifts of food (manna, birds), clothing, and protection (the cloud and the pillar of fire); yet they fell into sin first by complaining; second, by making the idol of the calf; and third, by sending spies into the Promised Land.

The result was that an entire generation died in the wilderness. The ancient Israelites felt entitled, became overconfident that God would protect them no matter what, and became disobedient to His commands. The price they paid was very heavy.

In mentoring, God opens the door, allowing a person to engage in this ministry. It is the mentor's duty to always obey God's Word and Truth only; otherwise, there will be utter failure and dire consequences. This is exemplified in case study #8.

2. *Good beginnings do not guarantee good endings.* Paul stays with the ancient Israelites' escape from Egypt and journey to the Promised Land as an example for this warning. These ancient sojourners began their journey praising God, giving thanks, and making vows always to obey Him. Within a short period of time, the deception and temptation of the devil led them into immorality, idolatry, complaining against God, and seeking to overthrow God's chosen leader. In essence, these Israelites were tempting God and daring Him to take action. Not a wise frame of mind to have.

God takes this sin very seriously and acts on it accordingly, and soon. It must be noted and stressed that this sin in the church today is no less serious than during the time of the ancient Israelites, because now the church has the Bible with examples to learn from. The church today also has the empowering of the Holy Spirit as Christ's delegated counselor, teacher, guide and comforter as our personal trainer. We are to rely on Him during those times of deception and temptation. In short, we have no excuses.

Mentors who take God for granted and dare Him to take action when they don't teach, encourage, and provide an example for the weaker Christian to mature in Christ have a very heavy price to pay for their disobedience. This happened in case study #8. When the national men's mentoring organization folded, the church that opted to incorporate that organization's methods could not get the desired result promised by the organization, and no men came forward seeking to become mentors.

All these things plus others were the result of the Godhead saying "No, it's not going to happen!" Unfortunately, the senior pastor and the mentoring director of the church did not have the spiritual maturity to discern God's hand. Neither did the leaders of the men's organization that folded. Paul put it succinctly in 1 Cor. 10:12, *"Therefore let him who thinks he stands take heed lest he fall."* Paul is clearly talking about the pitfalls of pride in this statement.

3. *God empowers those to overcome temptation if they obey His Word* (vv. 13-22). When a person steps forward similar to the prophet Isaiah and says to God, *"It is I, send me,"* in response to God's beckoning to serve Him, the devil will try to interfere, using deception, temptation, and other forms of spiritual warfare.

The only real safeguard for God's appointed minister is to rely on God's sovereignty, and trust that He is in control. During any ministry, the minister will be tested and experience moments of pain, anguish, doubt, and concern. When these emotions and feelings occur, a spiritually strong and mature minister knows that God always provides a means of escape, and does not lose hope.

All that is required on the part of the minister is to have faith, trust, and the discernment that escape will happen in God's perfect timing. These times are referred to as defining moments, moments during which a minister remains steadfast on the Word of God and his personal relationship with Christ and the Sovereign Truth.

This minister is able to confront (face the issue head-on) and not get into conflict with the Godhead. Confrontation not only is facing an issue, acknowledging its reality, but also having the wisdom to know the power and source behind the issue. Confrontation is also remaining in control of one's emotions and feelings, thereby preventing the issue from escalating. In case study #12, Trisha, Jason, and Sheila learned this.

Conflict arises when emotions and feelings escalate to a boiling point and prevent clear thinking. People coming to that point often fall back to rely on familiar patterns and practices rather than on God. It may provide immediate relief, but the result is likely to be without amiable long term solutions that honor God. Conflict allows the devil to gain control. Caution may also be stated, "Beware that you can be aware."

Those involved in mentoring or other ministries become targets of the devil who will employ any and all spiritual warfare tactics to attempt to disrupt, hinder, and ultimately destroy not only the ministry but the minister. The Apostle Peter spoke about this in his epistle, (1 Peter 5:8-11), referring to the devil (the enemy) as a roaring lion searching to and fro, seeking to devour.

Mentors and other ministers must always be cognizant that the devil wants to take them out. Therefore, one must always "be aware" of this in order to "beware" of the spiritual warfare tactics, and not succumb to any of them.

Principle #4: Responsibility must supersede freedom (1 Cor. 10: 23-33). This particular passage can be summed up in the following short statement: *"Just because I can doesn't mean I should."* Paul was stressing to the church at Corinth that they needed to realize who they were as servants of Christ; that as spiritually mature believers they were personally accountable for the spiritual welfare and well-being of the weaker converts from Judaism to Christianity. Today, Paul's message is the standard for the dictionary definition of the word responsibility: *legally or ethically accountable for the welfare or care of another person; being a source or cause.*

Paul was admonishing the Corinthians to understand their particular responsibility to be role models for the weaker Christians and to build up the weaker brothers in their faith. This is repeated by Paul in his letter to the Philippians (2:1-4) and was a major exhortation that Paul gave to all the churches he established during his mission trips.

The mature Christians had forgotten the basic premise that goes with mentoring, that as a person grows in spiritual maturity and receives discernment and wisdom, he also learns how to handle the freedom given by Christ through the Holy Spirit. Proper use of this spiritual freedom is to teach, instruct, and mentor the weaker Christian so that they also learn, receive discernment, and apply wisdom in order to realize the spiritual freedom given by Christ. This is a fundamental cornerstone of making disciples and therefore fulfilling the Great Commission.

Weaker Christians simply cannot be mentors, and aren't ready to be called by God to perform this particular ministry for all these reasons. Sadly, many churches, denominations, and organizations sometimes recruit spiritually immature believers to be mentors. The result might be emotionally satisfying, and might fulfill man's mantra, but the reality is that it isn't what the mentor needs to grow spiritually. It is vital to understand that mentoring carries a heavy responsibility that God establishes, and He is the One who selects His servants to carry out His ministry.

Mentoring is *not* dictated by any denomination, independent church, senior pastor, or associate pastor assigned to church ministries. A particular church can offer mentoring and be a vehicle for the Godhead, but it cannot usurp God's authority in being the final source of approval for who does or who doesn't become a mentor.

This fact is evident in case study #8 and the decline never would have happened had the senior pastor or the national mentoring organization stayed obedient within the guidelines God establishes through His Word—in this case, 1 Cor. 10:1-33. God's displeasure was carried out in the disbandment of the national organization and the church. The lack of attention to God's direction resulted in no men coming forward either as mentors or mentees. God's intentions were for the church and the national organization to follow His guidelines, not just carry out man's ideas. If it had been God's idea, they both would be thriving today.

Paul's authority to admonish the Corinthians over their disobedience in dealing with weaker Christians came from Christ, probably when Paul was in the desert shortly after his conversion. Undoubtedly, Christ mentored Paul, and tested him through various experiences for Paul to truly understand His teachings. This combination of mentoring and experiences became etched in Paul's heart so that he had the wisdom and insight to realize the Corinthian's were disobeying Christ's purpose. Paul's own obedience to Christ gave him credibility.

During his personal mentoring time with Christ, Paul experienced Christ's love first-hand. So powerful and overwhelming is Christ's Holy Love, those who experience it are changed. This Holy Love drives home the point of properly relating to those who come across our path in need of spiritual training. Paul experienced this and wanted those he taught to realize that how they use their spiritual freedom is an indication of their spiritual maturity in Christ.

The stronger, more spiritually mature Christian and the weaker Christian must be bonded by Christ's love in their dealings together. If Christ's love isn't one of the cornerstones in a mentoring relationship, it is doomed for failure. Sheila in case study #12 understood this and submitted her will and emotions to Christ.

CHAPTER 9: FACTORS INFLUENCING MENTORING

At this juncture, attention should be given to eight influencing factors which affect mentoring. They shall be discussed in limited detail. Additional influencing factors may arise once a mentor and mentee begin their relationship. Bear in mind the emphasis of making disciples is always on the spiritual aspects and not concentrated on the worldly culture. The eight chosen influencing factors include: *time/timing, H.A.L.T., habits, rituals, routines, choice, outside sources, and health.*

TIME AND TIMING, factor #1. *Time* essentially is a continuum in which events occur in irreversible succession. This continuum creates a past and a present but never a future. Continuum is measured by very, very brief interludes (nanoseconds) or longer periods ranging from minutes to years to decades and beyond. Time is also used to designate seasons, systems, rate of speed, work/activity allotment, structure, and defining lifespan. Essentially, time is finite and beset with limitations.

Timing is different than *time.* Timing is an analytical tool to measure success or failure. Timing is based on coordination of people, things, or a combination of the two to achieve a desired result. In the secular world, an example of timing is when a quarterback connects with a wide receiver for a long pass completion. In the business sector, timing can be the introduction of a new or improved product or service to match economic conditions.

God's perfect timing often is revealed after a chain of events occur. This is exemplified in the Book of Acts, chapters 3-5. Only after Christ ascended back to heaven did the Holy Spirit indwell the Apostles to empower them to go forth and make disciples. Peter's imploring speech on Pentecost is an example. Peter's words came from the Holy Spirit and resulted in 3,000 lost souls becoming eternally saved.

In the spiritual world, too, time and timing have entirely different meanings. In the spirit world, there is no past, only the present. Mankind's finiteness (mortality) simply cannot calculate or fully understand how the Godhead is always in the present. This is because mortal man can only perceive with the three-dimensioned earthly perspective and not the infinite spiritual realm until after earthly death takes place. Since the spirit realm is always in the present tense, there is no need for the concept of time or finiteness. But God's timing is part of His plan and purpose for His man to carry out His will and to further His kingdom.

Another way of perceiving this is to envision pieces of a puzzle floating around in space. God sees these various pieces and selects those that connect to each other and places them on the continuum board. Prior to God's involvement, the various pieces had no idea they were connectable and possibly didn't know each other existed. God establishes timing to bring these pieces together.

Once the connection is made, understanding comes, or one of those "Aha" moments humans often get. It must be noted that the various pieces of this super-sized puzzle were created by God and placed on the continuum until such time He decides to bring them together into the greater whole to make His puzzle more detectable. It is God's puzzle and He puts the pieces together in His timing.

A fact about God is that He is never late. Man imposes a time element on God, based on his expectations that are influenced by emotions, feelings, and desires. Man may see events unfold that evoke emotions and create an air of urgency requiring immediate action. Sometimes the result is a panic prayer that implores God to do something now before things get worse. Other prayers may reflect man's petition that God will protect family, relatives, or friends during travel, an upcoming event such as an operation, a court appearance, a job interview, etc., that are tied to future projections or schedules. Again, man communicates his desires to God via prayer, based on the worldly constraint of time, which is man's reference point.

God's timing is perfect because He is the Creator of all the heavens and the earth. As such, He controls time and timing based on His perfect will, plan and purpose. Often His will is not what man envisions, and therein lies a potential problem because man foolishly attempts to manipulate God to meet his earthly desires that are often based on time and worldly pleasures.

Biblical theologians agree that God's will is to have relationship with man, His special creation. God's purpose is to have His man accept His salvation. This is where the Great Commission and making disciples enters the picture. God's plan is utilizing those pieces of the puzzle that make His purpose attainable. Following God's will, plan, and purpose becomes the focal point for mentors. The pieces of the puzzle (in our case, chosen mentors) are those who surrender their will to God and freely choose to follow Christ in securing lost souls for the Godhead. Those who are unwilling and choose not to make disciples are eventually removed and replaced by one who is willing to follow Christ only in making disciples.

In His Great Commission, Christ commands His followers to go forth and make disciples—period. Nowhere does the Bible state that making disciples includes making them members of a denomination, converts to any religion, or part of any regional or national organization. Nor does this mean incorporating any form of politics into mentoring. A mentee should not be judged by any affiliation or non-affiliation with any political party. Political parties are of man and the world which lures and detracts from truly serving God.

Realizing this command and following the guidance of the Holy Spirit, the mentor transforms from thinking in the worldly realm of time to thinking with the spiritual concept of timing, God's timing. God's mentor realizes that God through the Holy Spirit will bring the mentee to the mentor in His perfect timing. You don't have to recruit, solicit, or advertise for mentees; God will do this for you and all He requires is for you to be ready and willing to act in His timing.

God isn't obligated to explain His actions, desires, or reasoning to man. God wants our obedience first and foremost without our demanding question, "Why, God?" When a mentor is obedient to God and follows the teaching, guidance, and direction of the Holy Spirit to his mentee, God will communicate His approval by means of confirmation and affirmation. God's timing is sovereign. He alone controls it. Case study #12 is an example of this.

The obedience God seeks is not from obligation or manipulation ("if I do this, then You will give me what I desire") but from a willing heart. This is best exemplified by the prophet Isaiah's statement to God,

"Here I am, it is I, send me." Another sign of a willing heart is, *"God, I really don't see the purpose of this; but not my will, Your will be done."* God loves to hear a willing heart!

H.A.L.T., factor #2, used as an acronym, represents Hungry, Angry, Lonely, and Tired. Anytime any one or combination of these acronym letters comes into play, mentoring becomes less effective. These letters indicate how man's finite humanness impacts what he does and the results of his actions.

Hungry. Should either the mentor or the mentee meet and one or both be hungry prior and during the mentoring session, hunger will not allow for full focus and concentration. The hunger issue is such that many mentoring sessions occur over lunch; thereby ensuring both mentor and mentee are physically satisfied prior to the mentoring session's focus on spiritual food and satisfaction.

Angry. Mentoring sessions involve confrontation (facing an issue). Confrontation may include a disagreement between the mentor and the mentee, or a dispute the mentee has with another person such as a parole officer, a boss, a spouse, etc. The mentee is upset and clearly in need of the counsel of the mentor. The mentor must not allow the mentee's anger to influence or become part of the mentoring session. This will lead to conflict (hostility by not reaching agreement). An example is the mentee makes a statement to the mentor who replies the mentee shouldn't have said or done what they did and they clearly are wrong. This can cause the entire mentoring relationship to end because the mentee perceives it as being condemning. The mentor must always choose his words carefully. Disagreements will happen, but inappropriate words can result in confrontations escalating into conflicts.

Should the mentor be involved in some personal issue that results in him being angry, it may be best not to conduct the mentoring session, especially if the issue is such the mentor has difficulty controlling his emotions and feelings. Anger is a common weapon of spiritual warfare and one the devil enjoys using. Far too many mentoring relationships end prematurely because of anger issues that erupted into irreconcilable conflicts.

Lonely. This feeling can be caused by a relationship break-up, divorce, death of a loved one, remembering a tragic event, depression, stopping a medication, side effects of medication, and personal health issues. The devil will use loneliness as a deceptive tool that whispers to the person he or she is not valued by God, and that He has rejected them. This particular list is not complete, and other reasons for feeling lonely may occur during a mentoring session or relationship. It's advisable for the mentor to pray for discernment when the mentee exhibits traits of loneliness.

Any one or combination of items on this list may be felt by either the mentor or the mentee. When this feeling occurs in the mentor, he must take control, first by going to the Lord in prayer about the issue. If the mentee is the one with this feeling, the mentor needs to address it and attempt to get to the cause by having the mentee talk it out. It is vitally important that the mentor simply listen, ask questions, and exhibit love to the mentee.

Don't attempt to be an amateur psychologist, because it won't work and may even lead to more difficulties with the mentee. The mentee can become angry very quickly and the confrontation can erupt into conflict. Should the mentor experience this feeling and it prevents the mentor from discipling the mentee, the mentor should end the session and reschedule for another time.

Tired. Tiredness is either physical, psychological or a combination of the two. Physical fatigue can be coming from overwork, over-involvement, or sleep deprivation. It is not recommended for a mentor or mentee to engage in moderate to extreme physical activity prior to a mentoring session. Physical fatigue impacts mental sharpness. Psychological fatigue can result from stress, work, a relationship issue, study assignments, or in some way be associated with loneliness. Again this can be experienced by the mentor or the mentee and in either case the mentoring session must be rescheduled.

These brief descriptions of H.A.L.T. should be enough to illustrate how the devil hopes he can use them to disrupt or destroy a mentoring relationship. Should this take place, then those pieces of God's spiritual puzzle become disconnected, possibly damaged or broken. Other pieces must replace the damaged ones, so that the puzzle can retain both shape and purpose. Fortunately, these are some of the more manageable aspects of mentoring. The mentor guards the work God has begun when he guards against these.

HABITS, factor #3—an activity or action done without thinking. There isn't a person living on earth who doesn't have at least five different habits. People are not born with habits and do not inherit them;

they are acquired through frequent repetition and often are the result of mental reaction to an emotion or feeling. A person may get excited when speaking about a certain topic and gesture with their hands. Hand gesturing then is a habit.

Another example of a habit is a person who repeatedly interrupts people they talk to, sometimes by not letting them finish what they were saying. Some people are known to make facial expressions while talking. Some people will stutter when talking about something stressful.

Habits often are unconscious immediate reactions to a stimulus or catalyst. The initial emotion or feeling elicits a response, sending a message to the brain to do that same response the next time that emotion or feeling takes place. The response is interpreted by the brain as being comforting or protective, therefore worthy of repetition.

There can be a habit for anything and everything—negative or positive—depending on the mindset of the individual. Some habits are learned such as saying please and thank you. A parent may do an activity a certain way that their offspring emulate the same action and therefore learn by observing, then doing the same. Some habits are passed down by cultural dictates of acceptance and conformity. Removing one's hat and placing the right hand over the heart during the playing of the national anthem are cultural habits. Not doing this is perceived as being disrespectful, or disloyal and unpatriotic, and the result is cultural disapproval.

Habits can lead to addictions. Any activity that results in a person receiving comfort or protection can become addictive. The resulting comfort or protection can be physical, psychological, or both. It can begin with the physical then center on the psychological. This is how the brain operates in conjunction with the body.

For decades people took up the habit of smoking because it was socially acceptable and also gave a person a false sense of sophistication. Print, radio, movie, and television ads reinforced this habit. The chemical properties within the cigarette eventually caused a physical dependency that effectually replaced the cultural aspects of smoking.

Once the physical addiction took hold, the smoker would light up based on physical reactions being sent to the brain and not any cultural motivation. Much the same is the case in alcoholism. Many alcoholics state they are only social drinkers. The problem is everything is social to them.

In the case of alcoholism or drug abuse, continuation of the addiction is in response to emotions and feelings. Stress, anxiety, and worry are often contributors that cause a person to drink or get high. Cigarette addiction often accompanies alcohol or drug addictions. The physical addiction is reinforced and fueled by the emotions and feelings.

A person may become free of the bondage of one addiction but not another. There are alcoholics who have remained sober for decades yet they are one or more pack per day cigarette smokers. Other addictions include food, pornography, sex, or anything the brain interprets as being pleasurable or protective.

In each of our case studies, habits are big contributors to the problems of each of the participants. Phil's gambling habit stemmed from fear which factored into Susan's habit of co-dependency. Case study #8 has Jake deeply involved with pornography that led to the involvement and participation by his wife Pam. One person's habits can not only heavily influence another person but also lead to their addiction as well. People often are defined by their habits even if they conquer bad habits and replace them with good habits. The habits acquired and acted out during elementary or high school often are strongly associated with that person years later, especially if little or no contact was made during the elapsed period of time.

Habits can be formed in as little as three days and can remain with an individual for life. There are instances where a person realizes they have a peculiar habit and develops another habit in an attempt to quit the one habit, but ends up with both. The majority of habits can be difficult to break or exchanged for other habits.

Breaking habits is difficult because of how the brain retains association with the habit. In the case of addictions, the physical aspects of the dependency nature of the addiction must be addressed in conjunction with the mental cause. There is no medication that is always effective for everyone to overcome their habits. Medications utilized in cigarette or drug usage can become new dependencies while intending to eliminate an original, potentially deadly, habit.

Habits can and will infiltrate mentoring relationships. It is vital to realize habits will occur and to pray to the Holy Spirit for counsel and discernment about them; that the bad ones will be eliminated and the good ones retained. Examples of bad mentoring habits would be when the mentor doesn't really listen to the mentee or wants to make every mentoring session a forum for preaching and pontificating his opinions.

Raising one's voice or interrupting in order to make a point can be a bad habit. Making excuses for repeatedly being late can be a bad habit.

Being legalistic and requiring the mentee to do things the mentor's way is a very bad habit. Listening to the mentee without interruption is a good habit. Retaining eye contact with the mentee when they are speaking is also a good habit. Asking questions and getting the mentee to relay their emotions and feelings about different topics is a good habit. Encouraging rather than dictating to the mentee in problem resolution is a good habit. Habits impact all relationships and will either foster growth or contribute to ruination of the relationship.

ROUTINES, factor #4. A routine is defined as *a detailed course of action followed regularly.* A characteristic of a routine is that it is repeated to the extent it becomes formulaic, mechanical, and becomes standard operating procedure in certain circumstances. Routines are found in every aspect of life. In business, beginning the work day at the same time every day, and the same number of hours worked per week are routines. In the military, doing physical activities prior to doing assigned duties is a routine. In sports, warming up muscles and stretching before playing the game is a routine. Routines can usually dull one's senses throughout the involvement. An example is driving a familiar route, and suddenly realizing you don't remember passing a very familiar landmark.

Some people use routines to influence or obtain favor that provides them comfort or protection. This begins as an infant and continues until death. Parents are familiar with the routine tantrums of toddlers who create this routine when wanting something or not wanting to do something the parent requests.

Routines become a major part of co-dependent relationships. In co-dependency, person "A" exhibits mannerisms and verbiage that impact the emotions and feelings of person "B" who provides "A" their desired comfort or protection. Person "B" is often a willing participant, falsely believing that their actions and acceptance will inspire person "A" to change. This is common where alcohol, drugs, pornography, and abuse take place regularly. This happened in case study #6 when Susan allowed herself to be controlled by Phil's gambling and financial mismanagement. In case study #8, Pam also exhibited codependency in her marriage relationship. She became a reluctant part of Jake's pornography addiction by allowing him to be in control, because she didn't want to upset or displease him. Her acquiescence had become routine in their relationship, and so it evaded her awareness of it.

In unhealthy routines, the sick person knows what to do, say, and act on a regular basis to get their relationship partner to supply whatever will allow them to continue their unhealthy and often addictive behavior.

This type of routine can develop in a mentoring relationship. The mentee will explore and test the mentor to determine what boundaries exist between acceptable and unacceptable behavior. Sometimes this is intentional while other times it's not. Some mentees engage in this behavior pattern without actually realizing what they are doing. This is true for both secular and spiritual mentoring. A mentor can employ routines to gain their desired goal as well.

Regardless of the core reason for this behavior, the mentor must take control and not allow it to become part of the routine with the mentee. Every relationship, including mentoring, will have at least one routine. It is the responsibility of the mentor to make sure whatever routines are involved with the mentee they remain healthy and are conducive for spiritual growth of the mentee, making a disciples.

Routines sometimes develop as a result of one or more habits. When unhealthy habits spur an unhealthy routine this can result in a *phobia,* which is *a persistent, illogical, and abnormal fear of a specific thing or situation.* Phobias are difficult to overcome and are examples of spiritual warfare and demonic bondage. They are illogical and irrational and the victim often knows this, yet is powerless to change due to their bondage.

Breaking this bondage becomes easier when the habit and the negative routine are identified and turned over to the Godhead for healing. The secular world of psychologists and psychiatrists refuse to acknowledge or accept the spiritual warfare aspect of phobias and attempt to "treat" this illness with enabling methods that too often result in the patient becoming worse instead of better.

The New Testament Book of James states, *"You have not because you ask not."* Christ also implores His followers to take up His yoke and to bring all our concerns to Him. This is an invitation saying, "Look, I know you can't do this in your humanness, so give it over to Me." The Godhead is sovereign and is waiting for the opportunity to heal and break the chains of demonic bondage and will do it!

Breaking the chains of demonic bondage is not the same as healing a physical abnormality or disability. God is fully capable of doing this and often does do physical healings that man refers to as miracles, and indeed they are. God's plan and purpose may not be to heal the physical disability, affliction, or pain a person experiences. Paul acknowledges this in his writings as a thorn in his side that God refused to remove. Paul accepted this. This constant reminder helped Paul remain humble and totally dependent on God's grace and mercy, thereby strengthening him to continue being God's servant. (2 Corinthians 12:7-10)

Aside from phobias, demonic bondages include addictions, co-dependent relationships, pride, and negative emotions of all kinds, to name a few. There isn't a single one that God isn't capable or willing to intervene on behalf of His special creation, YOU! Simply give Him the opportunity to turn things around. It may not be easy, may take some time, but He will break the chain of demonic bondage. In counseling women involved in abusive relationships there is an adage: *"If he hits you once, you are a victim. If he hits you twice, you are a willing participant!"*

Don't be a willing participant to demonic bondage. As a mentor, it is your responsibility to ask God to identify these demonic bondages and help the mentee break free of their hold. This identification comes from God's blessing of wisdom and discerning spirits that all followers of Christ should pray to receive. This is part of making disciples and why reducing a mentoring relationship to a mere Bible study time is not what God wants. Remember, God wants relationship with His people, and He can't have that when demonic bondages have a stranglehold on the victim.

Failure to be God's mentor is manifested in several of the case studies cited in this study. In case study #8 when the ministry director of the church, the national men's organization, and Henry did not use their mentoring opportunities according to God's plan and purpose, God in essence said, "Do it My way or it's the highway." Unfortunately for the disobedient individuals involved in this case study, it was the highway, and God took away an opportunity to serve Him. In addition to being removed of their ministry, each person involved will have to answer to God for their disobedience.

RITUALS, factor #5: A ritual is a prescribed sequence and order for conducting a religious or fraternal organization's solemn ceremony. Rituals may include a lot of pomp, even theatrical components, intended to impress and to evoke an emotional reaction for allegiance and control by the organization or the religion.

In four of the five Old Testament books written by Moses, God-instituted rituals are clearly evident. Many of the rituals during that particular time were to change the Jews from observance of pagan rituals that impacted their mindsets. God's rituals were meant for the Jews to honor, praise, and focus their attention on Him. Some rituals were meant as ways for the Jews to keep themselves separated from pagan influences. Some rituals were imposed by God as specific ways He wanted the Jews to have relationship with Him. Disobedience to some of God's rituals resulted in death.

God's requirement for rituals came to an end the moment Christ died on the cross. It is stated in Matthew 27: 51-52: *"Then behold, the veil of the temple was torn in two from top to bottom; and the earth quaked and the rocks were split, and the graves were opened; and many bodies of the saints who had fallen asleep were raised."* The veil separated the Holy Place from the Most Holy Place where only the high priest could enter. Christ's sacrificial death symbolized that the barrier between God and humanity was removed. God's replacement for rituals is the indwelling of His Holy Spirit, whereby those who are saved become a part of Him, making rituals unnecessary. Some religions and denominations are steeped in rituals. But the indwelling Holy Spirit does not require any intercessor to perform a ritual to have relationship with Him.

Christ imposed only one ritual prior to His death on the cross, the partaking of communion in remembrance of His bodily sacrifice and His shed blood that cleanses us of sin and empowers us against demonic forces.

The early church did participate to a degree in certain festivals such as Passover but the emphasis for new followers of Christ was establishing a relationship with Christ. When Gentiles accepted Christ's salvation, they no longer engaged in Jewish rituals. It's odd that today many Christian churches and denominations require participation in observance of their rituals that clearly are not recommended, stated, or demanded in the New Testament. Every pagan religion since the fall of Adam and Eve has had rituals as foundations of their beliefs and worshiping of false gods.

In mentoring there is *never* any reason to impose rituals between the mentor and the mentee. There will become plenty of occasions for celebrating milestones such as healings, blessings, marriage, births, etc. but these observances should not include meaningless rituals. Rituals, devised by man to glorify his mind, invite demonic deception and often open the door for demonic entrance into a church, an organization and then into the heart of the observer. Rituals in spiritual mentoring are merely a control device on the part of the mentor.

The question arises about the observance of baptism. Is this a ritual? Many Christian churches do turn this observance into a ritual but nowhere in the New Testament is it stated that baptism must be a ritual with pomp, elaborate costumes, chants or whatever else may have become part of a modern day observance. In fact, when the Apostles and Paul and their disciples made disciples of newly converted followers of Christ, they immediately went to the nearest river for full body emersion. The important aspect of baptism to remember is that one method honors God while the ritualistic method honors man.

There are recorded times when a new convert to relationship with Christ baptized themselves. There was no fanfare because the indwelling of the Holy Spirit was so powerful, filling their hearts with joy and peace; and any ritual was meaningless. Baptism always has been and will remain part of that special bonding to Christ. It is not a requirement of salvation and it should not be a requirement to belong to any Christian organization or church. There also is no routine associated with baptism because baptism needs to take place but one time. A new convert to Christ Jesus only has to immerse his whole body into water and thank Christ for his salvation and the new creation he has now become. That's it, in a nutshell. The essence of baptism is acknowledging the surrendering of the old self to being a new creation in Christ.

One final thought on habits, routines, and rituals is for you to take a closer look at your church, or another church, and observe the different routines and rituals that take place on a given Sunday. Write down these observations then go to the New Testament and compare them to what the Bible says the church should do.

You will find this exercise both interesting and revealing. Finally, write down how these church habits, routines and rituals affect you and impact your relationship with Christ. Again, compare your emotions and feelings to what the New Testament says about relationship with Christ. Should you be a mentor, take note and list any and all of these church habits, routines, and rituals that are part of your mentoring. If there's one that reflects only religion, denomination, or organization, it is time to change and start mentoring Christ's way.

CHOICE, factor #6. This section deals with decisions, decision making and the resulting consequences of our decisions. These consequences, good or bad, are merely a matter of inches--six inches, the space between one's ears. This short measurement can result in great happiness and satisfaction and carry an individual to a high emotional summit. Conversely, this same small distance can plunge an individual into a deep, dark, emotional abyss weighed down by pain, confusion, turmoil, regret, despair, and loss of hope. Just six inches can create a chasm and potentially eternal separation from life with the Godhead.

It was a mere six inches that resulted in the fall of Adam and Eve; six inches caused an entire generation of people to wander in the wilderness until they died; six inches put Christ on the cross. This same six inches had Moses agreeing to be God's leader to an oppressed people; a small youth to conquer a giant when grown men cowered in fear; admission by the wisest man that everything is vanity except obeying and honoring the sovereign God; for twelve diverse men to forsake their life for a new career that led to execution and thousands becoming followers of Christ; a former hater of Christ to become His great servant and write epistles that instruct, guide and change lives over 2,000 years after being penned. A mere six inches, the width of one's brain.

This all comes under the category of *choice: the liberty of making a selection from various available options.* God gave mankind the liberty of choice at the time He created Adam and Eve; and despite the horrendous consequences of this liberty, choice remains intact to every person born into this three dimensional world and also remains in the spiritual realm. The devil manifested choice when he elected to disobey God, and because of his choice he was cast away from relationship with the Godhead.

Ever mindful of the consequences of one's decision, the devil attempts to influence the choices and ultimate decision-making of God's special human creation. The devil relies on deception as the main tool to confuse, distort, incite, and inflame to the point of disobedient decision-making.

The Apostles were taught this by Christ and the Holy Spirit. It is why Paul in his writings heavily cautions individuals to *"take captive every thought,"* and to *"work out your own salvation."* Peter in his first epistle cautions, *"Beware; the enemy is like a roaring lion, searching to and fro seeking to destroy."* The experiences incurred by the Apostles become reference points for the understanding, discernment, and wisdom in evaluating one's choices now and for our future. Today, followers of Christ have the luxury of the Bible and the indwelling of the Holy Spirit to assist in the making of godly choices that are obedient to God's plan and purpose and to bring Him glory and honor. Hallelujah!

In mentoring, mentors must be ever cognizant that their words, actions, and demeanor have great impact and will influence the mentee's choice of decisions. Whatever the choice, it will either honor God or honor the devil; there is no middle ground. The sad reality in many choices is that there are no do-overs, absolutely none. But as Joseph emotionally declared to his brothers in Genesis 50:20, *"What you intended for evil, God meant for good."* God can take a mistake and use it to get the person back on course with Him, or bring about a surprising result that displays His sovereign power and goodness. Or He will use another person to do what the first person did not do. As depicted in the story of Joseph, turning evil into a good outcome is done by God in His perfect timing to accomplish His plan and purpose and not man's. That is comfort, but it is God's work in spite of us, not because of us.

At some time in a person's life an action takes place they regret and would like to do over. Too many times when a person attempts a do-over the results are just as bad as the initial action. The reason being the do-over is attempted in the flesh and not from the heart. In such a case, the reason for the attempted do-over is more likely to be self-serving, and guilt-driven, but not true repentance.

Adam and Eve did not get a do-over, but Christ's sacrifice on the cross makes it possible for all their descendants to have eternal relationship with Him. The wandering Jews in the desert did not get a do-over by refusing to enter the Promised Land, but their heirs did. Saul did not get a do-over in allowing David to kill Goliath, and he abdicated his responsibility as king. The Apostle Paul did not get a do-over in his persecution and execution of followers of Christ.

Parents today do not get do-overs when they belittle or abuse their children; employers do not get do-overs when they abuse their authority that results in harm to employees, customers, and the environment. Pastors do not get do-overs when they lead their flock into false belief. And denominations do not get do-overs when they espouse their man-made dogma over the truth of God's Word. The alcoholic, drug abuser, child molester, pornographer, and abuser do not get do-overs. In today's vernacular, "It is what it is."

Not having do-overs does not mean that all is lost. Christ's sacrifice and His position at the right hand of the Heavenly Father in full power and authority make for redeeming, reclaiming, and rescuing offenders by changing their behavior, state-of-mind, and future actions. This is what Christ did on the cross and when a person acknowledges and believes this with all his heart. Through confession, forgiveness, and repentance God's grace overpowers earlier bad choices. This is what took place that fateful day when Saul was travelling to Damascus and had his first encounter with Christ and His confrontation of his sinful actions. Faced with the realization of the impact and consequences of these decisions, Paul's next choice was to admit his sin and surrender his life to Christ. Surrendering to Christ is the central theme of Paul's writings. In the case of the two epistles to the Corinthians, he warns of the consequences when choices are disobedient to God.

Mentors, teachers, pastors, and leaders must always be mindful of the consequences their influence has on those they are involved with in any capacity. When placed in a position of authority and influence, we become God's steward or influencer over another person's affairs. Accepting responsibility with anointing answers Cain's arrogant challenge to the Lord, "Am I my brother's keeper?" (Genesis 4:9)

Stated in another context, being a mentor, teacher, pastor, or leader is heavy-duty stuff and whatever the position, it should not be taken lightly or become a platform for one's selfish expressions. Again, there is no middle ground in stewardship. When placed in such a position of authority, we cannot ride the fence at any time, in any capacity. This is exhibited in the various case studies used in this guidebook. This is why God requires spiritual maturity when He chooses His mentors. Mentors must diligently guard against the power of our pride and natural self.

In the Book of Psalms, David authors repeated instructions to wait on the Lord, and this is especially true for the mentor. The worst thing to do in moments of confrontation is to immediately react out of fear (fear of failure, rejection, or the unknown). David's counsel (wisdom from the Holy Spirit) is to wait, let the emotions subside, and follow the guidance and instruction of the Holy Spirit. Don't let the sensory elements or the culture dictate your course of action.

In case study #2, Eve's emotions resulted in a lost opportunity to mentor/minister to Stacy. In case study #5, Marsha's fears ended up in divorce; and in case study #6, Phil's fear led to his gambling addiction and to Susan's enabling, co-dependent behavior. In case study #8, Henry, his pastor, the ministry director, and the national men's organization fell into the deception of pride and control. It had a huge negative result in the lives of Pam and Jake.

Conversely, in case study #4, Bill and Harry responded to the deception of lesbianism in a God-honoring way that allowed Amy to hear and accept the admonishment of the Holy Spirit that led to her redemption. Both men remained steadfast as stewards, waited on God's direction, and were God-honoring in their obedient actions. Much the same can be said about Terry in case study #8 when he did not jump ahead of God despite knowing that Henry was going down the wrong path. It's one thing to know and to see the deception, but another to take action when and how God wants.

These case studies and the Biblical references illustrate the liberty of choice that God has graced man with; and when our six inch space between our ears is used properly, our choices will be obedience, storing up our personal treasures in heaven. Obedient choices and stewardship cause the angels and saints in Heaven to loudly rejoice and the devil and his hounds from hell gnash their teeth in anguish. What's your choice?

OUTSIDE SOURCES, factor #7. This first aspect will be referred to as "The God Card", and will be divided into two segments; prayer versus man's resources.

Envision yourself socializing with friends playing a game of cards. The rules of the game are that every player, in a predetermined order, lays down a card. Each card has to be in that particular suit such as diamonds. Should a player not have diamonds, another suit can be played such as clubs. Points are awarded for having the number 10 or any face card also worth 10 points.

Numbers ranging from 9 down to the number 2 aren't worth any points. Aces are worth 15 points each. One particular suit is declared trump, let's say hearts. Any time a player lays down a heart, it trumps the highest played card laid down during that turn; and the player who laid that heart down, wins the hand and all the points from the other cards played. If one player lays down a ten of hearts but another player lays down the queen of hearts, the queen wins that hand. The ace of hearts is the highest and most valuable card.

This description of the card game becomes an analogy for our mentoring study in that God is always the ace of hearts, the highest trump card that can be played in the game. In mentoring, there is always something that impacts the relationship between the mentor and the mentee. These items can include something that ignites irritation or anger; something that causes confusion and doubt; something that causes fear and timidity, or something that causes emotional pain to the extent it may threaten continuation of the relationship.

In addition to the flesh, these "somethings" can also be associated with the culture; what currently is in vogue or isn't; what one's peers believe is acceptable or unacceptable, and what man's changing laws may deem to be true and just.

All these items/factors are point cards in our analogy game of spiritual mentoring. The mentor and the mentee lay down their cards and the devil lays down a higher card in the same suit (deception/temptation) thereby gaining possession of that played by the mentor and the mentee. The devil is about to pick up the cards, but then God says, "Excuse me, it's My turn to play." He lays down a trump card that supersedes what the devil played and God wins the hand. The devil loses, God wins. The next hand is played and God trumps what the devil plays and wins again. This continues until the game ends, the points are added up and God is declared the winner. This is life and will continue until such time as Christ returns to reclaim His kingdom.

For the mentor and the mentee, it's important to use this analogy from the perspective that the devil will attempt to derail their relationship, but God is waiting His turn to trump the devil's hand. There will be times when the mentor makes mistakes in his leadership with the mentee; and conversely there will be times when the mentee stumbles and encounters a setback. Rather than get into an emotional anxiety or worrisome state of mind, the mentor and the mentee simply have to "play" the "God card" of letting Him trump whatever caused the problem.

"Playing the God card" in this analogy refers to humbly going before the throne of the Almighty Sovereign Godhead in total submission and asking God's grace, mercy, counsel, guidance, and direction to overcome whatever the issue may be. Doing this is manifesting one's total dependency on God, which is what He wants us to realize and do. When either the mentor or the mentee, or both, neglect going to God for resolution of the issue it's the same as playing our card game and having the devil use a higher card to derail our efforts.

If God isn't allowed to participate (our choice) in the resolution, He cannot trump the devil who then wins the hand. The mentor and the mentee lose, and their relationship with the Godhead suffers and is weakened.

Case study #4 illustrates how God triumphs by trumping the devil. Both Bill and Harry played the God card by seeking God's advice, will, and direction in resolving the issue with Amy's proposed lesbian wedding. They knew that the devil was using higher cards in the suit involving cultural acceptance of the homosexual sin via social acceptance and legal allowances.

Undeterred, the two men humbly prayed from their hearts for God's resolution. God willingly entered the hand, laid down his higher trump card (the Holy Spirit) and won the hand. Bill and Harry received discernment, wisdom, joy, and peace. Amy was freed from the bondage of her sin, and God was honored and glorified by the simple act of Bill and Harry manifesting their total dependency on God by means of prayerful petition.

Prayer is a very powerful weapon in this "card game" that is actually very serious spiritual warfare. Prayer can literally turn the tide of the battle, if the participants choose to use it the way God intends. Christ Jesus knew how powerful prayer, with humility, brings about life-changing results. His life was a life characterized by going to His heavenly Father daily for guidance, direction, comfort, and communion. This is found throughout the four gospels, Matthew, Mark, Luke, and John.

Christ used parables to illustrate important spiritual truths; such is the case in Luke 18:9-14, Christ's parable of two men who went to the temple to pray. Take a few minutes and read this passage in the New Testament and meditate how this section of Luke affects mentoring.

In this parable, Christ is exposing and debunking false teaching, and illustrating how important it is to follow Him and obey His truths. The Pharisee went to the temple more for show, to make an appearance whereby he would receive the compliments of men and instill in the minds of men that he was superior to them and had a special relationship with God other lesser men could not have.

This Pharisee stood before God and prayed about himself, boasting how good and righteous he was. The Pharisee's prayer revealed his inner feelings and beliefs about other people; his words show how he actually

215

despised others. His prayer indicates a spirit of condemnation and elitism, all reflective of pride and arrogance. There was nothing God-honoring in the Pharisee's prayer.

The tax collector was entirely different. At that time, tax collectors were not warmly received by their fellow Jews because they took money from their own people for the gain and the benefit of the Roman conquerors. They were considered traitors to their own people. For the tax collector to even go to the temple was a big sign of faith and trust because the people there could have inflicted physical harm on him and prevented his entering the temple. What the Pharisee and the other people in the temple witnessed was a manifestation of honest humility and response to the conviction of the Holy Spirit.

The tax collector knew who he was in the sight of Almighty God, knew the severity of his sin, and was willing to risk his physical life for God's forgiveness. The tax collector revered God so much he could not stand or even look towards heaven because of the heaviness his sin had on his heart. This man's prayer was short and to the point, verbally stated for others to hear his confession of being a grave sinner and asking God for mercy. In contrast, the Pharisee really did not pray, merely boasted, and made no private or public confession of being a sinner.

The tax collector exhibited his dependence on God, while the Pharisee insisted on being accepted by God for his outward signs of fasting, tithing, and comparison statement of not being an extortionist like the tax collector. The Pharisee also boasted of not being an adulterer or being unjust. The Pharisee's public prayer was meant to glorify himself, and demean not only the tax collector but anyone who likened themselves with the tax collector.

When the tax collector openly petitioned God for mercy because he was a sinner, he accepted the spiritual truth that we all fall short of the glory of God and need His grace and mercy to have relationship with Him. Relationship with God is not based on works or an accounting ledger, but on a submissive and surrendering heart.

The people who gathered around Christ and heard this parable included Pharisees, and they were stunned and shocked. No doubt many were speechless and even held their breath, hearing Christ's bold parable. In all probability, many of the common people turned their gaze to the Pharisees, intently looking to see and hear their reaction to Christ's accusation. As stunned as the people were with the parable, they really were rocked by Christ's final statement about His parable, *"I tell you, this man went down to his house justified rather than the other; for everyone who exalts himself will be humbled, and he who humbles himself will be exalted."*

In essence, Christ was stating the spiritual truth to the people that man does not justify himself to God through his own efforts, but by surrendering his spirit and heart to the Sovereign God. Christ also pointed out that while it was good that the Pharisee wasn't an adulterer, an extortionist, or evildoer of other sins, his pride and subsequent arrogance over what he claimed made him a friend of the devil. That leads to eternal ruin. No doubt Christ's final words of this parable cut deeply into the hearts of the people, including the attending Pharisees.

On the one hand, the people who identified with the tax collector went away with hope, guidance, and direction, and learned about the power of praying to the Godhead. The Pharisees went away fuming at being humiliated and exposed by Christ. The people were receptive to Christ's teaching thereby allowing the Holy Spirit to work in them, whereas the Pharisees' hearts became more hardened with hatred.

For mentoring, it is important to learn from this parable two important keys. First, don't be a Pharisee. Second, pray humbly to God and realize that prayer is the key to receiving God's intervention in the spiritual warfare that accompanies mentoring. Mentors should always take some private time in their own quiet place, and pray before their mentoring session for God's guidance, direction, and control over their emotions, feelings, and subsequent words in order to serve Him.

Their mentoring time is a special period that God uses to carry out His plan and purpose. The mentor who prays in submission to God's help and direction is similar to the tax collector in admitting they aren't in control and asking for their words and actions to glorify God and defeat the devil. Mentors must always have the heart of the tax collector and not that of the Pharisee.

During this private time of meditation, the mentor should confess any sins, ask His forgiveness, and let the Holy Spirit assist in his repentance. In essence, he is asking for a clean heart so that he can be God's servant. The mentee should be instructed by the mentor to do the same. This is one of the steps in making disciples. Mentors must remember the mentee may not be spiritually mature or may be facing intense spiritual warfare and needs spiritual truths to lean on for guidance to have a closer relationship with the Godhead.

The mentor should also initiate a closing prayer at the end of the mentoring session, praising God for the time spent with the mentee, and asking the Holy Spirit for His continued guidance and protection during the rest of the week. Any issues discussed during the mentoring session can be included in this final prayer. After the mentoring session, the mentor should humbly go to God in prayer, thanking Him for the opportunity to be His servant to the mentee and petitioning the Holy Spirit for discernment and wisdom in preparing for the next session.

This is especially necessary if any issues brought forth by the mentee require extra guidance from the Godhead to cut through the deception of the devil. This is playing the God "card" the way God wants it "played."

If the mentor goes the route of the Pharisee, pride and arrogance will rule as it does with the devil. The Pharisee way is the way of believing one can manipulate God by good works, rather than truly loving and serving God.

The second aspect of influential outside sources includes pastors, churches, organizations, the culture, and other people. "Other people" may consist of one's spouse, best friend, or one's own mentor. Pastors usually are looked upon as sources of guidance and spiritual wisdom and it's natural to consult one's pastor for answers to questions. Often churches have lay counselors or ministry directors whom the church directs people to seek out for answers to their spiritual questions and concerns. Organizations can be specific to mentoring, such as in case study #8, or they can be locally known and accepted people throughout a Christian community. Another example of organizations are online "colleges" that offer short courses in how to be counselors dealing in a wide range of issues including divorce, homosexuality, evangelizing, and church growth.

The culture is a blend of people and organizations and can be the Christian community or the secular culture. Whatever the outside source, the mentor must use extreme caution and ascertain that these outside sources are based on God's truth and not man's definition or twist of truth. While some of these outside sources may appear righteous, the reality is some are really Pharisees and instruments of the devil. Again, this is illustrated in case study #8 with the national men's mentoring organization whose intent was to glorify the organization, to get referrals by pastors, and to grow monetarily and in status within the Christian community. The senior pastor of the church bought into the mantra of this organization because his real intent was to use any means that would hopefully result in his church growing and getting prominence within its town. Both had a Pharisee's heart.

Both the national men's organization and the church pastor received notice from God that their efforts weren't consistent with God's Word, yet they chose to continue down the path of self-centeredness. Henry became drawn into this self-exalting plan until God played His trump card. God will always play His trump card in His time and timing, but He also will give offenders opportunity to choose to repent, just as Christ demonstrated through the parable of the two praying men.

When outside sources become primary to the mentor, they easily can morph into a golden calf of worship. Outside sources should always take second place after the mentor's primary sources of reading, studying, meditating on God's Word, the Bible, and petitioning God for discernment and wisdom.

HEALTH, factor #8. Common colds, flu, muscle aches, and internal malfunctions of the body can cause physiological changes to the extent that the mentor or the mentee cannot concentrate or focus on the mentoring session or confrontation of issues. Medication taken for physical ailments can influence the mental process. The mentor should be familiar with the side effects of any medication and how they might influence his thinking.

There is also the mental health of both the mentor and the mentee. In case study #2, Eve's emotional, mental rejection of abortion affected her mental health and prevented her from being a mentor to Stacy. Her mental health had a negative impact on her spiritual health, and she went the way of the Pharisee with a hardened heart, incapable of receiving any instruction from God or being His servant.

Addictions affect both the physical and the mental being of a person. Despite progress in gaining victory over addictions, there will be times when triggers fire, preventing further positive advancement. A mentor should be cognizant of this aspect of addictions and not let their emotions and feelings dictate their actions. This is what happened to Eve and to Susan in their case study situations.

The brief explanation of these eight factors that influence mentoring is meant to alert us to the variety of ways the devil will use the flesh, the culture, and other involvements to try to derail us in our progress to fulfill God's desires for man.

CHAPTER 10: MENTORING THE MENTOR

A mentor, like any other believer, is subject to weakness and failings. There may be times when a mentor needs mentoring from another mentor. Mentoring to a mentor may be focused on counseling on a single specific issue. It may be a struggle a mentor has physically or emotionally with a sin. There may even be a specific time when the mentor should seek on-going or periodic wise counseling throughout the duration of the struggle.

A Biblical example of one mentor mentoring another is found in Exodus when Jethro mentored Moses. First, Jethro mentored Moses on relationship with God, and second, he delegated his authority in dealing with the Jews during their trek through the wilderness. Paul mentored Peter on the necessity of overcoming Peter's prejudice against the Gentiles. Paul also mentored the leaders of various churches he established throughout his missionary journeys. Of course, Paul also mentored Timothy after Timothy became head of his own group that engaged in discipling.

Mentoring another mentor may consist of providing counsel and direction on a particular issue or it may involve convincing a mentor his or her actions are not honoring or glorifying God. Several of the case studies exhibit this, and in 2 Corinthians 10, when Paul admonished the Corinthian church leaders about the infiltration of false teaching, tells us how today's mentors should handle this issue.

Paul's admonishment to the Corinthians was centered on three important facets of all ministries that the Corinthians chose not to keep in mind. The three important facets to all ministries, including mentoring are: *how to wage spiritual warfare* (2 Cor.10:1-6*), how to use spiritual authority* (10: 7-11*), and how to measure ministry* (10:12-18). Let's examine these three facets in more detail for mentoring a mentor. These facets also help a mentor to determine when he or she needs mentoring.

HOW TO WAGE SPIRITUAL WARFARE

This topic has been discussed earlier, but now will be approached from a different perspective. After a person accepts Christ's salvation and is born again, becoming a new creation in God's eyes, like any baby, this new Christian grows spiritually according to how he is taught. Should the teaching be dictatorial, the new Christian will become dependent on man's wisdom, and will find it easier to neglect personal study and prayer.

Dictatorial teaching is tied to pride, arrogance, and control by the teacher's attempt, however disguised, to get a new Christian to revere him and put God second. This is what the false teachers were doing to the Corinthians and what the Pharisees did to the Jews. When God is put first, the new Christian learns humility, love, and total dependency on God, and grows spiritually. When God is revered first, an inner environment within the new Christian is created which makes room for the Holy Spirit to be counselor, teacher, and guide. Mentors must always remember this principle and be cognizant that the devil will attempt to derail their ministry through sins of pride. When the devil does make inroads into one's ministry, God will bring forth a messenger to make this deviation known. That messenger may be another mentor because of the wisdom and spiritual strength God has blessed them with to be His servant. Nathan was God's messenger to David concerning his sins of murder and adultery.

What God's mentoring servant encounters with the suffering mentor is how the offender evaluates and gauges his efforts according to the flesh and to the culture rather than according to the counsel of the Holy Spirit. In case study #2, Eve let the flesh and the culture dictate her actions. The flesh and the culture create mental walls of resistance which appear logical, right, and a source of guidance in dealing with life issues. As with Eve, in the case of the Corinthians, the resistance was very deceptive and subtle. This deception took on the form of spiritual intellectualism, a high-minded attitude that these people thought they knew more than what they really did. Paul addresses this attitude in Romans 12:16.

In Ephesians 6:10-20, Paul describes the believer's spiritual armor of Christ that must be worn every day by the servant of Christ. This full armor of God is comprised of the Word of God, His truth, His righteousness, salvation, the gospel, and the shield of faith, following the guidance of the Holy Spirit. These spiritual weapons are guaranteed to guard against and thwart whatever evil the devil throws at a minister. Demonic darts often are so subtle the victim doesn't realize what is happening until another mentor points them out and assists in defeating their evil intent.

Had Eve gone to a mentor and expressed her emotions and feelings about Stacy's revelation concerning abortion, she could have received sound spiritual advice that would have facilitated an entirely different outcome and prevented the negative effects she encountered. It's evident by her actions that Eve let her emotions and feelings interfere with being God's servant.

In all probability, Eve did not pray to the Godhead for counsel and guidance. She did not seek godly counsel from anyone who was close to her such as her husband, close friend, or pastor. Her first mistake was that she didn't recognize the spiritual attack upon her emotions. Her emotions and feelings impacted her to the degree that she wasn't able to confide them to someone close to her. Otherwise, she could have sought counsel from someone she knew or from a ministry organization specific to the matter of abortion. Her second and biggest mistake was not praying to God for His divine intervention and help.

After addressing Eve's emotions and feelings, a mentor could have directed Eve to:

(1) Simply thank Stacy for her confidence in seeking advice from her, but tell Stacy she didn't feel qualified to handle that subject matter.

(2) Listen to Stacy, find out the core of her feelings and then decide whether or not to counsel her.

(3) Listen to Stacy, then ask permission to have another mentor more qualified in dealing with abortion to meet with them and counsel Stacy.

If you were in Eve's position, which option would you choose? Eve's reaction illustrates the impact emotions and feelings have on mentoring and any relationship. In case study #12, Jason, Trisha, and Sheila rebuked the deception of spiritual warfare by surrendering their will, emotions, and feelings to the Godhead and He was pleased. Because of this, Trisha was able to mentor Meg while being mentored by Sheila.

HOW TO USE SPIRITUAL AUTHORITY

In 2 Corinthians 10:7-11, Paul tells the Corinthian leaders how they were wrong and admonishes them to get back on course. Sometimes one mentor needs to do this for another mentor. Mentors should consider four possible scenarios when mentors deal with other mentors who may or may not recognize they need counseling:

(1) When a mentor seeks advice and counseling from another mentor, this does not necessarily mean the seeking mentor is weak, unqualified, or not following God's direction. Accordingly, the counseling mentor should not interpret the seeking mentor's meekness as a sign of weakness or spiritual immaturity.

(2) A person's ministry and his or her personal life must be unified. When there is separation between the two, issues tend to get evaluated from the worldly view rather than the spiritual perspective. Should the counseling mentor proceed from the influence of the worldly perspective, the seeking mentor is deprived of God's wisdom. The seeker is vulnerable and becomes easy prey for the enemy's deception to gain a foothold in his ministry and everyday life.

(3) There should be no contradiction between what a mentor says and what they do. The word *hypocrisy* comes easily to mind concerning this pitfall. Go back through the case studies and find instances when this took place; then reflect on those times when you engaged in hypocrisy.

(4) Respect is at the heart of properly applied spiritual authority. Paul's admonishment pointed out the Corinthian church leadership's improper use of spiritual maturity. The Corinthians *demanded* respect rather than *commanding* respect. The Corinthians demanded respect based on their knowledge (intellectualism), and lorded this over younger believers who lacked sufficient insight or strength to refuse their wrong teaching.

Paul admonished them to earn respect by being doers, thereby showing the less spiritually mature church body what to do. Prideful

223

leaders who demand respect instill fear and are demeaning by repeatedly using the word "you." When an issue arises, the demanding leader says, "You're the cause for the problem because of your inadequacy." However, a spiritually mature leader says, "There's a problem, but *we* can handle it and get it set straight." One approach creates a barrier to learning, while the second approach fosters learning and creates a foundation of trust and cooperation for current and future problem solving. The second approach is encouraging and includes the subordinate in the solution.

When one mentor approaches another for advice, the mentor who is sought out must always be mindful of their role and not let pride or control dictate their course of action. The positive side of this truism is found in case study #4 between Bill and Harry and also in case study #8 between Terry and Henry. In these studies, the acronym A.L.L. or Awareness, Listen, and Love overpowered the deceptive aspects of emotions and feelings. Controlling one's emotions and feelings is not the same as suppressing them. Emotional reactions will sometimes come to the surface. Although emotional reactions are naturally felt, A.L.L. allowed these ministers to control their emotions and feelings, using them for good without allowing them to dictate an outcome.

HOW TO MEASURE MINISTRY

(2 Cor.10: 12-18): The operative word here is *success*. Whatever project, assignment, or endeavor a person engages in, there is a psychological desire to measure the outcome in terms of either failure or success. Obviously, success is the preferred outcome. Success may be either culturally influenced or God determined.

People learn this at an early age from parents, and it is reinforced later by teachers, coaches, employers, and peers. Sometimes awards and special recognition assist in defining success. Criteria are established that serve as a measuring tool to define success that deserves the award or special recognition. These criteria are based on what the culture, the controlling individual, or organization deem most beneficial to them.

Usually criteria include the acquisition of money, control, increased customers, power, or fame. When an individual's efforts result in one or any combination of the criteria, he is usually lauded. A worldly picture that describes this enticement is, "The carrot in front of the horse." The horse focuses on the carrot, and performs the assigned task without consideration of surrounding factors. The carrot satisfies the horse and allows the master to retain control over the horse. This is how worldly culture operates.

Success in ministry is often dictated by culture. Too many times churches measure success by the number in its congregation, the weekly money from tithing, the size of its building, the stature and power within their community and how other churches perceive them. In case study #8 this form of measurement became the basis for the church and the ministry director to implement the national men's mentoring organization.

This organization used worldly criteria of increased attendance, new congregants, and greater involvement in church activities as the carrot to get the church pastor's involvement. The inference being, along with this criteria would come increased money, power, status, pride, and control. Henry's "carrot" was he would become a certified mentoring team leader, which satisfied his personal desire for status, power, to be an equal to his friend Terry, and to garner recognition.

Paul admonished the Corinthians (Cor. 10:7) for using false worldly measurements to determine ministry success. *"Do you look on things according to their outward appearance? If any man trust to himself that he is Christ's, let that man think again..."* The Corinthians were legalists, the same as the Pharisees, and since Paul was a former Pharisee, he knew the pitfalls associated with legalism. Paul's admonishment revealed that the Corinthians had created a closed-in mutual admiration society whose standards and measurements either eliminated people or made it difficult for them to belong. Admission meant success while denial meant failure. It all was based on man's criteria and not God's.

In mentoring the Corinthian mentors, Paul set the record straight on what is true godly measurement of ministry (2 Cor.10:13-18). The criteria for godly measurement can be found in the answers to three simple questions:

1. Am I where God wants me to be (vv. 13-14)?
2. Is God glorified by my ministry (vv. 15-17)?
3. Can God commend my efforts (v. 18)?

In our case studies; Eve, Henry, the senior pastor, the church ministry director, the men's evangelizing ministry, and the national men's mentoring organization do not get a positive answer to these questions. Conversely, Bill and Harry, Terry, received God's commendation.

The positive answer to question #1, "Am I where God wants me to be?" is to know that you are in the assigned territory where God wants you based on His plan and purpose. Being able to use your God-given talents, skills, discernment, and wisdom is confirmation you are where God wants you.

In answer to question #2, "Is God glorified by my ministry?" the fruit that comes forth from your efforts is evidence that God is glorified. In mentoring, the fruit is the spiritual growth as the mentee seeks Christ more each day.

Confidence must be tempered with humility and continual acknowledgement of God's power, grace, and mercy in one's life. Isaiah 42:8 states; *"I am the Lord, that is My name; and My glory I will not give to another, nor My praise to carved images."* God is demanding of this, and when ministerial efforts are done for self-praise, it is idolatry. God reacted to this in case study #8 and allowed the demise of the national men's mentoring organization and the church pastor witnessing the effects of his true, inner motivation.

In answer to question #3, "Can God commend my efforts?" it is common for mentors and others involved in bona fide ministry to receive God's approval through testing. This includes difficulties such as financial, opposition from teachers of false doctrine, attempts to force the mentor to blend the worldly culture with God's Word, and much more. These tests are similar to a ship that encounters rough seas and storms of various magnitudes. The ship has its course set to allow the ship to continue through the storm and ultimately reach its destination.

God's Word is the foundation and the directional finder for mentors. Perseverance and steadfastness result in the mentor becoming spiritually stronger in the fight against the enemy's spiritual warfare tactics. After the storm, the comfort of joy and peace come from knowing one's efforts were righteous and upright. Testing often results in God's affirmation and confirmation that become the mentor's carrot to continue with the ministry.

Another aspect of godly testing is the revealing of character. People can say anything and make it sound convincing (particularly by using intellectualism), but when they are placed in a position of doing, their character speaks very loudly. Character will either confirm or deny. Character brings to the surface what is hidden within the heart. Again, re-read the case studies and determine the character in the people involved. It's been said that character is a window to see who someone really is.

Most of the time a person's character is made known in such a manner that one will know if they should associate with or believe what that person says and does. There are times when events need to take place before true character is revealed. These assist an individual in making decisions and choices. Stacy thought she knew Eve's character enough to confide a plaguing issue to Eve. This event revealed Eve's true character, and Stacy made the decision not to associate with her.

Events happened with Henry that revealed not only the true character of his church leadership, as well as that of the national men's mentoring organization, but Jake's, as well. Henry was also able to rebound and get back on track because he saw Terry's true character. Many times, emotional milestones, such as Trisha's terminal cancer, reveal character. Trisha's character was instrumental in Meg asking her to be her mentor and confidant. This also happened when Trisha earlier chose Sheila to be her mentor and confidant. Character often is used by God as a magnet between those whom He counsels and directs. A mentor's character is a visible beacon to those in need.

Tests are also defining moments. A person may go through special training, or have limited experience in a certain area, or be thrust into a situation that is unfamiliar. From the onset they may feel a certain amount of confusion, disorientation, and fears of rejection, failure, and the unknown. There is the feeling of hesitation of proceeding and continuing through the event.

When these emotions and feelings arise, one of two things takes place. The person succumbs to the fears, doubts, and retreats. The other choice is this person continues on like that ship in the storm. They know there is difficulty and uncertainty, but faith, trust, and hope fuel them to stay the course.

Once the storm passes, people often learn about facets of their character they didn't realize were even there. This is a pleasant surprise that boosts their level of confidence. In the process, they become blessed with discernment, wisdom, and they're stronger against the next storm that is waiting unseen beyond the horizon. The person who cowers and retreats becomes weaker and more susceptible to deception and false teaching, and their relationship with the Godhead suffers.

Paul knew this, which is why he rebuked and admonished the Corinthian church in the manner that he did. Paul knew that if the Corinthians would not rid themselves of the false teachers, their church would weaken until more deception would end it altogether. Paul's rebuke would be scathing; but waiting for God's judgment would be far worse.

Another positive result of testing is the learned ability to make sound judgments. Many times Christians are taught not to judge others. Teachers of this premise cite the Bible and go so far as to admonish other Christians for voicing their thoughts and opinions about others. Unfortunately, this is misunderstood, and the misinterpretation does not make sense for mentoring or other ministries.

Frankly, it is false teaching, because the word *judgment* is taken out of context from what the original Greek intended. *Judgment*, as related in the Greek, is to *assess and to evaluate prior to making a decision.* In this context, the events that reveal a person's true character allow another individual to assess who the other person really is, and what to do next.

Judgment can be part of God's discipline to lead man into repentance. Man needs judgment to avoid condemnation. During His ministry, and part of His teaching, Christ judged--assessed and evaluated--the Pharisees, and exposed them for the hypocrites and false teachers they were. This exposure showed the spiritually immature Jews who the Pharisees really were and what their true character represented.

The misinterpretation of the word *judgment* leads to confusion and false teaching. Christ judged—evaluated—Saul, but did not condemn him. When Christ confronted Saul on the road to Damascus, His words were direct, honest, factual, and succinct. As a result of this judgment, Saul quickly realized his mistake, received Christ into his heart, and became Christ's chief advocate and powerful minister whom we know as the apostle Paul. Christ rebuked Saul's actions in order to teach him the error of his sin and bring him to repentance and salvation. It was not for condemnation. *"For God sent not His Son into the world to condemn the world, but that the world through Him might be saved."* (John 3:17)

Christ judged Peter's statements about never rejecting or denying Him and also rebuked Peter with the words, *"Get behind Me, Satan!"* Christ was teaching the other Apostles about deceptive tactics of spiritual warfare and the necessity to *judge* the source prior to taking any action.

If God does not want man to assess and evaluate others, why is the compilation of Proverbs by Solomon included in the Bible? Solomon, with his God-given wisdom, makes judgments against people who live in ways that are not God-honoring. Proverbs give direction, teaching, and guidance on how to live a godly life in obedience to the Most High Sovereign God. We simply cannot attempt to live an obedient life to

God without judging, making assessments, and evaluations. The book of Proverbs provides a foundation to make godly judgments.

Nowhere in Proverbs does Solomon advocate condemning someone for sin. To the contrary, Solomon instructs and teaches how to recognize sin and ungodly living, and explains how to rectify this problem. It's ironic that many denominations, churches, and pastors decry making judgments, yet teach on Proverbs.

These same institutions and people make judgments every day, ranging from what to do with tithing money, who can be a member of their church, what qualifications are needed to be acceptable within their sphere of influence, and to what ministries, classes, and events their church should offer or participate in doing. Where do you draw the line, and who makes the decision to draw that line?

Mentors must be ever mindful that during the course of their relationship with their mentee, decisions have to be made. What criteria does the mentor use? Should he make the decision or take it to a church or organization and let them make the decision? How do you know the decision that is made is correct?

Some denominations judge that any member who becomes divorced cannot hold any position of leadership within that denomination. Isn't that really condemnation? Should an individual openly state they believe in the gift of speaking in tongues and claim to have this spiritual gift, some denominations immediately thrust this person out of leadership and membership within that denomination. Again, isn't this condemnation? Plain and simple, it's hypocrisy. Denominations have resulted when judgments become condemnation.

Should a mentor exhibit condemnation or any form of hypocrisy, the mentee will recognize it for what it really is and end the relationship. This is the Holy Spirit giving the mentee discernment or discerning of spirits (seeing the spiritual perspective) to end the involvement before the devil gets a foothold in the mind of the mentee. The mentor must be mindful the mentee may possess forms of false teaching, and make that assessment (judgment) followed by the decision to admonish the mentee and teach, instruct, and counsel the mentee, showing why his belief is wrong. This is exactly what Paul did in penning his letters to the Corinthians, and that church was able to eliminate the false teachers. Paul's epistles are the result of his making sound spiritual judgments.

From Genesis to Revelation, the pages contained within various books of the Bible advocate forgiveness. God judged Adam and Eve and cast them out of the Garden of Eden, He judged their sin and condemned it, yet forgave them and their offspring down through time through the death and resurrection of His only begotten Son, Christ Jesus.

In our case studies, Eve condemned Stacy based on man's dictates, not God's. Had Eve assessed and evaluated the situation from God's perspective, the outcome would have been entirely different. Bill and Harry correctly assessed and evaluated the issue with Amy and the outcome was obedience, pleasing to God.

If a mentor has difficulty judging, making assessments, and evaluating issues with a mentee, there will be no godly solution; and the mentee will not grow as a disciple of Christ. The mentor becomes a barrier and hindrance to Christ's Great Commission, His commandment to go forth into all nations teaching, preaching and making disciples. The criteria a mentor must use in making these assessments and evaluations are the Word of God; listening to the Holy Spirit's advice through His counseling, teaching, and guidance; and not allowing the sins of the flesh and the world culture to influence his ministry.

This also means eliminating any and all false teachings espoused by denominations or errant pastors and churches. Henry discovered this in case study #8, and his assessment and evaluation led to spiritual freedom rather than spiritual imprisonment. Henry left the church that strayed and refused to realign with God. He was led by the Holy Spirit to a God-honoring church. Think what would have become of Henry, his family, and those whom he came in contact with had he remained under the influence of false teaching. Henry might also have turned his back on God's desire to use him in any bona fide ministry.

Paul was well aware of this, and two of his epistles were written to correct the Corinthians. As a result, their church gained many converts to Christ and the Godhead said to Paul, "Well done, My good and faithful servant." Another irony is that today some denominations condemn many sins, yet tolerate others, such as homosexuality. They welcome homosexuals as teachers, pastors, and leaders; yet, they also advocate the epistles of Paul which warn against this sin. This is an example of false teaching and the failure of the people who attend these denominations to correctly judge the actions of their chosen leaders.

To the denominations and individual branches that teach principles that counter God's Word or attempt to modify His Truth, they will never hear those words of affirmation and confirmation spoken by the Godhead to Paul, a bondservant to Christ. Mentors who follow false teaching and modify their godly assignment to align with the flesh and the worldly culture likewise will never hear the rewarding words that God wants to personally speak to them.

By now, it should be evident that mentoring and any bona fide ministry is serious business to God. It's His disciples are engaged in the spiritual war being waged in the heavens and on earth. Is it also clear that disobedience to God's assignment (ministry) will incur serious and the most dire consequences? If we do not take ministry seriously and surrender as God's servant, then we are similar to Eve and those other examples in the case studies who disobeyed God in their mentoring opportunities.

When first reading these case studies and the subsequent analysis, your answers to the posed questions as well as to any questions of your own were assessments. Rethink these assessments and determine how they were made. What were the criteria for your assessment? If you are part of a group study, how did the discussion of each case study go? Did anyone openly state there should be no judgment in the discussion? Did you disagree with any of the case study actions based on God's Word and His blessing of discernment and wisdom; or did you rely on the influence of someone else?

Vine's Expository Dictionary of Old and New Testament words is a collection of over 5,700 Biblical words in their original Greek or Hebrew language. This publication is widely used by theologians, pastors, writers of commentaries, and anyone who does a personal in-depth study of God's Word. In this publication, the Greek word *judge,* as a noun, is spelled *Krites* (a judge) and also *Dikastes* (a juryman). In mentoring, or in any true ministry, and as a follower of Christ Jesus, you become a juryman subservient to the Most High God who will make the final judgment.

Also in Vine's Dictionary is the word *judgment* and the Greek spelling is *Krisis.* The English spelling is *crisis* but both have the same meaning: *"a crucial or decisive point or situation, a turning point, a defining moment followed by a separation then a decision." Krisis* is followed by the word *Krima* or the result of the action. The ancient Greeks then used *Gnome* or *Ginosko* as a process or means of knowing and this word is also associated as a subordinate definition of the mind.

Katadike, or sentence, is also associated with judgment and with condemnation.

Depending on the situation, the Greeks would interchange the words *judgment* and *condemnation* because of their understanding between two key words, *Krites* and *Dikastes*. In the minds of the ancient Greeks, they knew there was one main or supreme judge (Krites) who assigned jurymen (Dikastes) capable of rendering decisions (making judgments) as his surrogate. That's what mentors and those involved in bona fide ministry are expected to do—act as Dikastes.

The apostle John wrote about Christ Jesus from the context of being part of the Godhead. John was chosen by the Godhead to pen the Book of Revelation that tells us that Christ Jesus is now seated at the right hand of the Heavenly Father in full power, authority, and glory. As Judge, Krites, He will return to earth to cast final judgment and eternal condemnation on the devil and those who choose to follow him instead of Christ..

It's important to meditate on this fact to truly grasp that Christ is no longer on the cross, yet many false teachers still seem to keep Him there and teach likewise. Many mentors also hold fast to this erroneous concept because that's what they were taught. This simply is wrong and mentors should not make this same mistake. The unsaved should pray for salvation to Christ who reigns in Heaven—not the personage that died on the cross. Jesus, the God-man, fulfilled prophecy while Christ (God returned to Heaven) sits at the right hand of the Father as our advocate. There is a clear and distinct difference between these two pictures, and they should not be confused or erroneously misused. Mentor with what God's Word says. We must separate and discard any false teaching that may have influenced our perceptions.

There have been instances when a mentor has attempted to admonish another mentor about this, only to be rebuked. The mentor who espouses and continues any false teaching is not following Christ Jesus through the Word of God and the guidance and direction of His Holy Spirit who indwells within the saved and acts as teacher and counselor.

When one mentor is called to mentor another mentor there is usually prompting from the Holy Spirit that says, "Help me get realigned with God so that I can be His faithful servant." Periodically, mentors should submit to counsel because of the subtle nature of the devil's deceptive tactics. It is foolhardy to think we can reach a level where we are beyond spiritual input and wise counsel in God's Word. It's important to stay humble and open to correction and instruction. God's Word cautions us, *"The heart is deceitful above all things and desperately wicked; who can know it?"* (Jeremiah 17:9) David the psalmist knew this and prayed, *"Search me, O God, and know my heart. Try me and know my thoughts. See if there be any wicked way in me, and lead me in the way everlasting."* (Psalm 139:23)

This mentor who neglects counsel and instruction from others is delusional. During WWII officers who were assigned front line duty and repeatedly faced the horrors of combat were continuously monitored by superior officers for signs of battle fatigue that influenced their orders. When an officer crossed over the line, he was evaluated (judged) and either re-assigned (sentenced), or given a period of rest and renewed instruction before returning to battle. This need is the same in spiritual mentoring.

CR

CHAPTER 11: FINAL THOUGHTS

This chapter will address a few final thoughts about this God-given ministry of mentoring that enables us to carry out Christ's commandment to make disciples.

There are many passages contained in both the Old and the New Testaments that pertain to mentoring to help an individual experience a deeper relationship with Christ and be able to serve Him better as His disciple, making disciples. This final chapter will take a few of these passages and explore them in more detail.

Luke 9:3; *"And He said to them, 'Take nothing for the journey, neither staffs nor bag nor bread nor money, and do not have two tunics apiece.'"* For mentoring purposes, the key word of this passage is *dependence.* In mentoring, making disciples, Christ wants His chosen mentor to be totally dependent on His grace manifested through the indwelling power of the Holy Spirit. When a mentor relies solely on anything pertaining to the flesh or the worldly culture, including its educational degrees, awards, and positions, the world becomes his provision and power source, instead of Christ first and foremost.

The beginning of the Book of Genesis tells us that mankind is created in God's image and likeness, thereby making man God's special creation. Throughout Genesis to Revelation are examples of God's anointing and consecrating members of His special creation to perform assignments and tasks that are part of God's eternal plan and purpose.

In the Old Testament, these people were anointed first by God as His choice. Then they are affirmed by the priests with holy oil as a symbol to signify the importance of that task or position. Anointing continues today and is very important and pertinent to any ministry. The anointing comes directly from Almighty God and not by man or man-made institutions. It comes via the Holy Spirit.

God's anointing of one for His ministry tells all His creation (including the devil) that this person is divinely qualified for carrying out His assigned task of ministry. In the Old Testament, the assigned minister was publicly anointed with holy oil as a symbol of this godly consecration. Sometimes there was a ritual (special ceremony) involved with the earthly anointing. This ritual was referred to as consecration to set apart and declare as holy. The chosen godly minister today is inwardly anointed by the Holy Spirit's conviction in the heart of the chosen one.

In the Book of Acts, the Apostles were anointed by the indwelling of the Holy Spirit. This was the symbol and divine consecration authorizing the Apostles, and all who they made disciples, to engage in bona fide ministry. Later, Christ anointed and consecrated Paul who in turn anointed and consecrated Timothy; and this domino effect continues today. Paul was used by the Godhead as a vessel in conjunction with the Holy Spirit. Paul always followed the direction, admonition, and the guidance of the Holy Spirit in his ministry. Paul sought the Spirit's power to overcome the flesh and his sinful human nature (Romans 8:2). Paul, while he was still a Pharisee, reveled in Jewish religious ceremonies and rituals. But as Christ's servant, he disdained them and focused on making disciples of the heathen Gentiles. Paul should be every mentor's role model.

When God selects, He anoints and consecrates, thereby making earthly rituals of consecration unnecessary. Religions, denominations, and outreach organizations have their ritual ceremonies in anointing. It becomes wrong when the emphasis is to glorify that church, denomination, or organization over God. It is nothing more than emotional feel-goodism. When the ceremony for authorization leaves out God or forces Him to take second place to the anointing, then the ritual becomes a huge mistake and an unholy ceremony.

Sometimes those whom God has chosen to perform ministry are not allowed to carry out their assigned plan and purpose because they do not meet a particular church's criteria. Many also have been prevented from performing their God-given ministry assignment when they refuse to adhere to the man-made rituals as the prescribed rite of passage.

This is not to say that man should not exercise discernment and caution prior to allowing someone to engage in ministry. The Bible says we are to test the spirits (discerning spirits), go to God in prayer with supplication, and seek the counsel and guidance of the Holy Spirit to determine who is truly chosen by God and who is a carnal, self-appointed minister, walking in deception. This is also judging, using judgment, but in a righteous manner.

Unfortunately in mentoring, being chosen, anointed, and consecrated by God is not often the criteria churches use in determining and selecting mentors. In many cases, the person first must be a member of a particular church or denomination, followed perhaps by an interview with someone who is a ministry leader and then a class on mentoring. Once the criteria are completed, the person receives a certificate of completion, allowing him to be a mentor through that particular church, denomination, or organization. In reality it is works of the flesh hocus-pocus because prayer to God seeking counsel and guidance was not involved.

The criteria of judging who can be a mentor must be in line with God's procedure. He does not require a mentor to be a member of a church or a denomination, so this criterion must be eliminated. Any interview should be conducted by a designated person who is spiritually mature, exercises his gift of discerning spirits, and listens to the Holy Spirit. Such a person's questions will be centered on spiritual issues and not on denominational dictates.

The requirement of completing a specific class on mentoring is not necessarily wrong. In prison mentoring ministry, those who go inside the prison walls must first meet the state Department of Corrections criteria that include a background check and awareness of prison rules and procedures. This is necessary for the protection of the mentor and the prison inmate who becomes the mentee. In other situations, mentoring to parolees also requires adherence to the state Department of Corrections' rules and procedures.

Prison ministry and other agencies controlled by state regulations supersede those of any church or organization, but only in the criminal justice realm. Failure to abide by state rules and procedures results in immediate expulsion. This includes not only the person who directly violated the state mandates but also the organization the mentor is affiliated with. The state operates under the assumption that one bad apple spoils the rest. The state will also believe the organization's head did not properly train the mentors or use oversight in making sure they conducted themselves within state guidelines. Usually the state is correct in this belief.

Interviews by church officials must proceed with extreme caution. The interview session must not include any doctrine or mantra other than God's Word. One of the key questions to ask is, "Who is Christ Jesus to you?" Should the person not include faith that Christ died on the cross for his or her sins, rose on the third day and now sits at the right hand of Father God in full power, honor, and glory, and directs their life, raises questions if they truly are saved. The world has secular mentors, but the criteria for making disciples are entirely different.

God provides guidelines and procedures for His special creation to carry out our given ministry. In Isaiah 55:8-9, the Heavenly Father states that His ways and thoughts are not those of man, so man should look to Him first in all matters. This passage is exemplified in 2 Samuel 5:17-25. David first consulted God before engaging in battle with the Philistines. Of particular note is verse 23 when David consulted God a second time, after just decisively defeating the Philistines. He prayed to God in spite of the opposite recommendations of his close advisors.

David could have acted on his own reasoning and attacked the Philistines quickly using the same method that secured his initial victory, but he made another choice instead. He realized it was God who made the first victory possible, so he surrendered his will to God's. In verses 23-25, God instructs David how to fight the Philistines in an entirely different manner than how the first battle was waged. David's decision to first consult God, and then to follow His instructions, resulted in a sound defeat of the Philistines who retreated to their homeland. There was no loss of life to the Jewish soldiers.

The Philistines were defeated, God was truly honored and obeyed, and David was blessed with more wisdom. It was wisdom and the prompting of the Holy Spirit that caused David to first consult God before rushing into battle a second time against the Jews' hated enemy. David experienced the joy and the peace of the Lord through his obedience.

David didn't consult the Levite priests or anyone else before sending his troops to engage the Philistines. He went straight to God who earlier had divinely authorized, anointed, and consecrated him. David was totally dependent on God's strength, power, and grace to carry out his ministry of being the warrior king of the Jews.

Equally important is that the Levite priests did not interfere with David by forcing him to first go through any of their ceremonies or rituals prior to carrying out God's plan and purpose. The Levite priests surrendered their religious authority to God's divine supremacy. They knew this was a spiritual matter and that they were subject to the authority of Almighty God.

Although David's great example of obedience to God is a model for us, an example later was his disobedience, involving his adultery with Bathsheba and the subsequent murder of her husband Uriah. It was a terrible mistake, one David was cautioned not to make. But he followed his fleshly desires and greatly dishonored the God he chose to serve. Once David was convicted of his gross sin through the prophet Nathan's confrontation, David immediately repented. Words of his repentance are written in Psalm 51. Verses 3-4 reflect David's sorrowful repentance; *"For I acknowledge my transgressions, and my sin is always before me. Against You, You only, have I sinned, and done this evil in Your sight."*

The simple fact is that all Christians will make mistakes. We are saved by the grace of God and our inherited original sin is washed clean by the sacrifice of Christ Jesus through His death on the cross, His burial and resurrection. This ensures our eternal life with the Godhead, but the time spent under the constraints and deception of the devil due to life on earth makes us susceptible to the sins of the flesh and the world culture. David's terrible sin was the result of his flesh, despite being lauded by God as a man after His own heart.

All who engage in mentoring ministry must realize we too are similar to David, capable of great obedience to God, but also susceptible to terrible sins. Sins caused by the flesh, one's emotions and feelings that influence thought and action. Sins caused by the world culture of doing what the world deems to be acceptable, right, and wrong. This world culture permeates churches, as well, because they are governed by men.

Psalm 51 is a good reference for mentors and one that should be read periodically during the course of mentoring. The Psalm becomes a reminder that it's not a question of if you will commit sin; it's a matter of when the sin will occur and to what extent. Any time a mentor does not surrender his will to God, bad things happen. Psalm 51 indicates the path of repentance. A sincere, heart-felt repentance receives God's grace of forgiveness and the strength of the Holy Spirit. David committed adultery and murder, but he never committed them a second time. David learned his lesson, and during times of deception and temptation,

238

he remembered his earlier sins and did not repeat them. Mentors also make mistakes; the key to not repeat those mistakes. The only way not to repeat them is to totally surrender one's will to the will of Christ.

This is important for mentors to understand. We will make mistakes; some will be sins while others will be oversights based on human limitations. The Holy Spirit, if allowed, will make them known to us and we have the choice to repent, like David, or disregard this conviction and commit gross sin. There is no middle ground.

Repentance is more than merely saying one is sorry. There can be false sorrow or regret based on getting caught. This remains prideful because the sinner has no intention of truly seeking change. There is also remorse, a feeling that after a short period of time goes away. Again, there is no intent for a true change of character (repentance). True repentance is the heart's desire to change as a result of the Holy Spirit's conviction (see Acts 26:20 and 20:21). Acts 3 has a very good example of a truly repentant heart. Peter and John healed a beggar at one of the temple gates. This man's heart became so transformed (repentance) that he lived the rest of his life witnessing and praising God.

Mentors will perceive true repentance in the mentee not only by their words, but also by their actions of witnessing and seeking God in a deeper way. When this happens, the mentor can be satisfied the mentee deserves continued mentoring.

David's acts give us another example of how to be God's minister. Despite his heinous sins, David confessed them, sought God's forgiveness, and relied on the Holy Spirit to help him repent. After doing these things, David continued on as God's servant. He never stopped wanting to serve God. He wanted to continue carrying out God's plan and purpose.

David wasn't just committed to doing good; he surrendered his will to Almighty God's. 1 Samuel 12:24-25 tells us through the words of the prophet Samuel how we as mentors should conduct our ministry. *"Only fear the Lord, and serve Him in truth with all your heart; for consider what great things He has done for you. But if you still do wickedly, you shall be swept away, both you and your king."*

Samuel was speaking to the Jewish people, but his words speak to us today, as well. In verse 24, Samuel tells us to take some time to remember and meditate on what good and great things God has done for us, how He has blessed us and protected us in times of confrontation. This period of reflection also serves to strengthen our faith and keep us focused on being God's servants. Verse 25 is as clear as a bell that when we continue to sin willfully through destructive habits, immoral thoughts, retaining resentments, and failing to heed God's direction, we will be destroyed. During these times of wicked behavior, we automatically lose the most precious and valuable possession we could ever have, relationship with the Godhead.

When this happens, we no longer are God's chosen mentor, but may be allowed to remain a mentor in a particular church or organization by adhering to their dictates. Hebrews 2:10 refers to Christ as the author of our faith. This means that when we completely surrender our will to His, He will lead us into new experiences that often amaze us. During this journey, He will also test our faith that it may grow. In Hebrews 6:1 we are admonished to "press on to maturity." The tests serve as steps leading to our spiritual maturity and ultimately having the Godhead say, "Well done, My good and faithful servant."

In the example of the national men's mentoring organization, the church senior pastor and the ministry director chose to follow the path of their self-centeredness, and God took it away. The national mentoring organization ceased to exist, the church shepherded by the self-centered pastor lost attendance and the worldly idol they sought—money. To date, the people involved with the national men's mentoring organization, the church pastor, and the ministry director have not exhibited any remorse for their disobedience to God when they put their will ahead of God's. They may not during the course of their lifetime, but when they are face-to-face with Almighty God, they will be held accountable. It's better to do as David did and the passage tells us to confess our transgressions when we are made aware of them, seek forgiveness, and take the steps of true repentance.

In 1 Samuel 16, God speaks to the prophet Samuel telling him that He has rejected Saul and has chosen another king for the Jews. God's chosen successor to Saul was David. From the time of David's anointing until the time he actually became king over all of Israel (2 Samuel 5: 1-5), a period of approximately twenty years elapsed. During this period of time, David incurred tests, trials, and hardships that served to strengthen him and mature him physically and spiritually. This was David's training period, earning his doctorate from the school of hard knocks. At the time, David wondered why these things had befallen him. He also must have wondered about God's proclamation of anointing him king of the Jews.

God knew that as a teenager, David did not yet possess the physical or the spiritual maturity to carry out His plan and purpose. David needed the combination of time, tests, and trials to season him and prepare him for his eventual reign as king of all Israel. Had David been crowned king without this maturing process, he would never have been the servant God desired and needed.

His seasoning, involving spiritual warfare, strengthened him for the more intense spiritual and physical battles David was to face as king. David and the Jews would have fallen prey to the enemies of God, the Philistines (agents of the devil), because David would not have had the capability of dealing with such intense adversity. It had to be learned.

In mentoring, God's chosen mentors also need a time period of seasoning prior to joining with a mentee. It's not merely having a variety of experiences that makes a person qualified for the mentoring ministry; it's the spiritual discernment and the gift of wisdom from God through His Holy Spirit that puts it all together. The mentor acquires perspective and a foundation for the tests he will encounter during the mentoring relationship. For Moses, the time period was 40 years, for Paul it was 3 years in the desert being mentored by Christ. God determines your time, based on your willingness to surrender to Him.

The third chapter of the Book of Ecclesiastes (verses 1-8) depicts how everything under the sun has a specified time. Mentors have a specific time of godly training before being authorized to begin their assigned ministry. The mentoring relationship also has a specific time allotment. Thus, it is wise for mentors to realize God's Holy Spirit will signal the completion of a mentoring relationship. There may be a hiatus for a period of time, but then the mentor/mentee relationship may resume.

At the beginning of any mentoring relationship, the mentor cannot and should not say to the mentee they will be together for a specific time period. This is an element that is directed by God. A clear example of this is found in Acts 8: 26-39, the relationship between the Apostle Philip and the Ethiopian eunuch.

Philip was engaged in a very strong ministry as God's servant in Samaria. Philip knew he was doing God's work and the results furthered God's kingdom. Nonetheless, an angel of the Lord spoke to Philip instructing him to leave his ministry and proceed along a hot, dusty desert road. Along the way he encountered the Ethiopian eunuch and began to mentor him on God's Word; teaching, advising, counseling, and directing him. Philip indeed was God's servant mentor.

The Bible does not give the exact amount of time that Philip spent with the eunuch, but when the eunuch sufficiently had a solid relationship with Christ Jesus and professed this through his baptism, the Spirit of the Lord immediately transported Philip to another location. Biblical scholars indicate the evidence of Philip's new ministry location was Caesarea where he remained the rest of his natural life. Philip continued evangelizing and mentoring and his two daughters became involved in the same ministry after being anointed by God.

This was not the first mentoring experience to take place, but it is part of the Bible for Christians and followers of Christ Jesus as an example of how God determines the place, the person, and the time for His chosen mentors to perform their ministry. Philip did not say to God, "OK, I've had enough--now it's time for me to move on." Philip did not question, doubt, or hesitate in answering the angel's call to a different duty station.

Philip did not choose to mentor the eunuch, God did. When Philip encountered the Ethiopian, he soon discerned the eunuch's struggle and desire simply by asking him a question. Philip's mentoring remained focused on the Word of God and not on his own worldly knowledge of culture. Philip's mentoring of the eunuch was not limited to Bible study. Philip mentored the eunuch on his personal relationship with Christ Jesus. God ended the mentoring relationship, not Philip, and not the eunuch. Instead, the two became mentors in their separate environments, according to God's new direction and assignments for them.

After reading this material, one could conclude that mentoring is different than what one's previous definition and interpretation was concerning the ministry. Don't be disheartened should any part of this material appear foreign or counter to what you might expect in the process of making disciples of new or immature Christians. When we obey God, trust Him, and follow the counsel and guidance of His Holy Spirit, the steps we take as a mentor will be in line with God's plan and purpose.

Mentoring—making disciples of new Christians—is one of God's ministries. Ministers are protected, but spiritual warfare is not *eliminated*, because the devil is ruthless and persistent. Therefore, God's chosen mentors know the importance of praying to God for protection and asking for His blessing of wisdom and discerning spirits to thwart deception and the devil's attempts to derail the process of helping a person grow in relationship with Christ Jesus. Those whom Christ chooses for this ministry are and will be protected against the ensuing spiritual warfare.

Examples of prayer and discernment are found throughout the New Testament. In Colossians 4:2-3, Paul exhorts disciples to *"continue earnestly in prayer, being vigilant in it with thanksgiving; meanwhile praying also for us, that God would open to us a door for the word, to speak the mystery of Christ."* The mentor part of Paul realized the importance of prayer. The mentor should consistently pray with faithfulness and a joyful heart. Paul is telling mentors and disciples to pray for God's will and direction in every circumstance. The mentor/disciple should base prayer on having watchful awareness for deception and temptation, and give it over to God.

Paul was humble and asked for prayer for himself; not for his health or safety, but for God's will in opening doors for Paul to speak about the mystery of Christ. Other pertinent examples of proper prayer include Phil. 1:9-11; Eph. 1:15-25, 3:14-21; Col. 1:9-12, and 1 Thess. 5:17. A mentor should meditate on these prayers and ask God for His power, grace, and direction in praying with and for the mentee.

In speaking about the mystery of Christ, the mentor realizes this means witnessing how Christ has moved in and through them in their journey with the Savior. The transformations, some dramatic, fostered by the Holy Spirit, freely admitted and properly used in God's timing, become powerful real-life examples to inspire the mentee in his personal relationship with Christ.

God's chosen mentors receive confirmation and affirmation for their efforts to encourage them to continue despite any spiritual warfare that comes their way. Part of God's confirmations and affirmations are the deep resonating feelings of joy, peace, and contentment. These three blessings become spiritual fuel for the mentor to continue his efforts. The obedient mentor will hear, "Well done, My good and faithful servant." The heavens will rejoice in triumph, and the devil will cower in defeat.

ABOUT THE AUTHOR

Tomas W. Schafer asked Jesus Christ into his heart and life at age 47 after living in the ways of the world under the deception of the devil. After a personal encounter with Christ Jesus which he characterizes as similar to Paul's on the road to Damascus, Tomas became a follower of Christ Jesus. The next 20 years of Tom's life journey included events, issues, and experiences that would eventually be used to help others while mentoring--divorce; being a godly single parent to his son; being chosen by God to a prison ministry; and being blessed with the love of his life ("a godly woman beyond any of my expectations"). In 2008, Tom died from Sudden Cardiac Arrest, but received God's grace of breath for a new miracle life, astonishing his doctors and nurses, and deepening his faith. Soon after, he had quintuple bypass surgery, followed by prostate cancer surgery—a mix of experiences with the ever-present and faithful Christ Jesus as his steady foundation.

During his new life in Christ, Tom has been blessed by God's healing, wisdom, and strength, with opportunities to use his spiritual gifts, talents, and experiences to further the kingdom of Heaven through mentoring, counseling, and small business consulting.

The Holy Spirit placed a heavy conviction on Tom's heart to begin writing a mentoring guidebook for Christian ministry. After months of researching, writing, and editing, *Mentoring God's Way* is completed, with the hope and prayer that it will glorify Almighty God who does superabundantly above all we can ask or think. *"It's quite the experience beyond compare when you ride with the King of Kings!"* is Tom's heartfelt exclamation. He urges Christ's followers to respond with obedience to God's call, for whatever ministry He calls them to, regardless of apparent obstacles.

Made in the USA
Lexington, KY
05 December 2016